FOGGY MOUNTAIN TROUBADOUR

MUSIC IN AMERICAN LIFE

A list of books in the series appears at the end of this book.

FOGGY MOUNTAIN TROUBADOUR

The Life and Music of
CURLY SECKLER

PENNY PARSONS

UNIVERSITY OF ILLINOIS PRESS
Urbana, Chicago, and Springfield

Library of Congress Cataloging-in-Publication Data
Names: Parsons, Penny, author.
Title: Foggy Mountain troubadour : the life and music
    of Curly Seckler / Penny Parsons.
Description: Urbana : University of Illinois Press, [2016] |
    ?2016 | Series: Music in American life |
    Includes bibliographical references and index.
Identifiers: LCCN 2016003067 (print) | LCCN 2016005503
    (ebook) | ISBN 9780252040108 (hardcover : alk. paper) |
    ISBN 9780252081590 (pbk. : alk. paper) |
    ISBN 9780252098291 ( )
Subjects: LCSH: Sechler, Curly, 1919– | Bluegrass
    musicians—United States—Biography.
Classification: LCC ML420.S4446 P37 2016 (print) |
    LCC ML420.S4446 (ebook) | DDC 781.642092—dc23
LC record available at http://lccn.loc.gov/2016003067

*To the memory of Bill Vernon (1937–1996),
who would have enthusiastically supported
and participated in this project*

Contents

Foreword

John Ray "Curly" Seckler has long been regarded as one of the premier tenor singers in the history of bluegrass music. Working with the greats of the genre's first generation, he witnessed the music's birth and growth over the course of seventy years. His professional career, which began in 1935, actually predated bluegrass by ten years. When Curly made his radio debut in 1939, he could be heard by listeners who had been alive during the Civil War.

It was a tough existence at best for a musician during the latter half of the Great Depression and through the World War II era. Curly managed to get by, but none of the numerous bands in which he played had it easy. Curly stated for years what others of his generation witnessed: "Back then, that's when a dollar *was* a dollar."

Lester Flatt and Earl Scruggs had been partners for barely a year when Curly Seckler joined their Foggy Mountain Boys in March 1949. Immediately, the sound of their group changed. Curly's percussive mandolin rhythm gave even more of a bounce to the band's already exciting music. Seckler's full-volume, open-throated tenor harmony gave the group a cutting-edge sound that became its gold standard. When Flatt and Scruggs recorded their first session for Columbia Records in November 1950, producer Don Law, referring to Seckler, asked Flatt, "Where in the *world* did you find *that* guy?" Flatt explained that Seckler had been around for a number of years and had worked with Charlie Monroe and some others. Law exclaimed, "Whatever *you* do, don't let *him* get away!"

Lester Flatt and Curly Seckler had a divinely ordered duet; it was a sound that was meant to be. In the late 1940s and early 1950s, when Flatt and Scruggs were doing live early morning radio programs in the five o'clock hour, Curly would often take a Dr. Pepper soft drink, heat it on the stove in a saucepan until it was warm, and then drink it. He claimed this helped "open [him] up" so he could sing better—often with just a couple of hours' sleep. On recordings and surviving radio air checks, and in video footage, Curly appears never to have had a bad day.

Lester Flatt, Earl Scruggs, and the Foggy Mountain Boys are widely considered to have been the greatest bluegrass band of all time. In their day, they were what every other act wanted to be. They had it all—*Grand Ole Opry* membership, radio and syndicated television programs, a major label recording contract, corporate sponsorship, and strategic management, not to mention a great commercial sound and stage show that was uniquely their own. For almost a dozen years in three separate stints, Seckler was a major ingredient in the Foggy Mountain sound. He looked the part, too. Earl Scruggs told me on several occasions, "Curly Seckler could wear a white shirt better than any man I ever worked with."

Without question, Curly Seckler is best known for his landmark work with Flatt and Scruggs. There was a lot more to Seckler's seventy-seven-year musical career, however, than his time with the Foggy Mountain Boys. In 1981 he told me quite frankly, "I started back in 1935 with nothing. I worked all those years for nothing. And I've still got nothing. But it's okay. The Good Lord and me got together back in '78, and everything changed. I'm ready to go whenever He wants me." He paused for a brief moment, looked upward holding his right hand in the air, and concluded with a smile, "But I'm in no hurry."

Though Seckler lacked in monetary terms after his decades of labor, we gained abundantly through his voice and musical ability. The textbook works he committed to record are an instructional clinic for the ages.

Intrigued and wanting the world to know more about this largely underappreciated entertainer, Penny Parsons set out to learn about Seckler. After her first visit with him, she discovered not only that there was a book's worth of material but that musically speaking, he still had a lot to offer. Certain things are meant to happen, and Penny Parsons's crossing Curly Seckler's path was one of them. He could not have found a bigger fan, better person, or more tireless supporter to champion his work. The result of eleven years of painstaking research, her seemingly inexhaustible labor of love will allow readers to understand the man behind the voice and what he experienced.

The forty-two hours of taped conversations between Parsons and Seckler in thirty-three interviews yielded five hundred pages of transcribed questions and answers. Parsons also conducted forty-eight additional interviews with Seckler's friends, family members, and former co-workers, amassing a treasure trove of material. Parsons traveled extensively to gather the information she needed. She made approximately thirty trips to Nashville, a thousand-mile round trip from her home in Durham, North Carolina. There were investigative pilgrimages to libraries in eleven other cities, in some cases involving multiple return trips. Her exhaustive research is borne out in this book's extensive documentation.

Once Parsons began acting as Seckler's manager and booking agent in 2005, she started to travel with him to about 80 percent of his public appearances. Through the years, Penny became like family to Curly and his wife Eloise. He would readily admit to anyone that in the twenty-first century his life was greatly enriched by his association with Parsons. Her way of telling Seckler's story is fact-filled but at the same time very compelling. As you read about Seckler's life and career, you'll experience vicariously the times of a musical statesman. He was an enduring trouper who faced personal as well as professional triumph and tragedy. You will see determination through adversity, humor through the toughest of times, love and loss, kindness and generosity. Seckler also provides numerous stories from the era before interstate highways were built—from practical jokes to poker games, accidents, fires, and even brushes with the law.

Because of Parsons's unstinting efforts, and with Seckler's full cooperation, we're blessed to have a book that is both educational and entertaining and will serve as a reference for future students of the music and authors alike. For fans of the Foggy Mountain Boys, a substantial wealth of previously undocumented history has been gathered in this book. Well-known historical facts have been enhanced by further details, and numerous inaccuracies—some of which have been in print or verbal circulation for more than fifty years—were appropriately corrected where necessary.

As a fan and as his friend, I thank Curly for every song he sang and played, for every mile he rode, and for every meal he did without. Along the way, he left an indelible imprint on some of the greatest music that will ever be made. His documented God-given talents will continue to bless all who are privileged to hear him.

The door to the era in which Curly was such a vital participant is quickly closing. As a member of country music's greatest generation, Curly Seckler has made a long journey from a small China Grove farm in the Tar Heel State to the International Bluegrass Music Hall of Fame. This book does justice to his amazing legacy.

Eddie Stubbs
WSM *Grand Ole Opry* Announcer
Nashville, Tennessee
June 1, 2015

Preface

The year 1955 was career-changing for Lester Flatt, Earl Scruggs, and the Foggy Mountain Boys. They finally settled in Nashville after years of wandering from one radio station base to another. They realized their dream of becoming members of the prestigious *Grand Ole Opry*. In February 1955 they began appearing regularly on television, the medium that over time would introduce them to millions of households and propel them to superstardom in the country music world.

I was born days after the debut of the *Flatt & Scruggs Show*. It would be another decade before the music of Flatt and Scruggs came to my attention, but once it did, I was hooked. I discovered them sometime in the mid-1960s while flipping the dial on my family's old black-and-white television set in Greensboro, North Carolina. At that time, we could pick up three or four local channels, and on a clear day, we might tune in the two stations in Roanoke, Virginia, one hundred miles away.

One Saturday afternoon I turned to channel 10 (WSLS-TV) in Roanoke, and there was a group of men in cowboy hats playing a lively kind of string music I'd never heard before. I edged up close to the television to better see the individuals in the grainy picture. They bobbed and wove around the microphones when they played the fast tunes and somberly removed their hats when they sang of heaven and Mother. The lead singer had a friendly manner and an infectious laugh, and I liked the song he sang about finding a girl named Nellie walking in the snow ("Footprints in the Snow"). I learned that the bandleaders had the odd names of Flatt and Scruggs and that their jovial announcer was T. Tommy. I enjoyed the antics of the two men they called Uncle Josh and Cousin Jake and the bouncing fiddler with the baby-faced grin, Paul Warren. Though I saw the show only a handful of times, the experience was etched in my mind forever.

Several years later, as I was beginning my freshman year at Guilford College in Greensboro, I heard that Lester Flatt and the Nashville Grass would be appearing there the following week. Realizing that this was the singer I had seen on television, I eagerly made plans to attend the concert. On Saturday, September 16, 1972, I sat mesmerized by the music I was hearing and enthralled by Lester's introductions of the songs and the band members. The audience, made up mostly of students, was exhilarated by the performance, and by the end of the show the aisles were full of dancing teenagers. I didn't dance, but I enthusiastically soaked up every minute of the concert, especially Lester's rendition of my favorite, "Footprints in the Snow."

My life changed that night. I began buying bluegrass records and learning to play the songs on my guitar. I found like-minded friends, and we went to see Flatt whenever we heard that he was coming to our area. We discovered his annual Mount Pilot Bluegrass Festival near Pinnacle, North Carolina, and were introduced to a whole new world of music and personalities.

I soon noticed that a new singer named Curly Seckler had joined the Nashville Grass and that he and Flatt seemed to have a special rapport. As I studied the music, I discovered that Seckler had been an important member of the Foggy Mountain Boys years earlier, and that his was the distinctive tenor voice to which I gravitated on all of my favorite records.

I never mustered the courage to approach Flatt, but on one occasion I ventured over to shake Curly's hand at a festival. He was cordial, and after that I began to make a point of speaking to him at shows. After Lester passed away, I continued to follow Curly Seckler and the Nashville Grass, and was excited to hear the new singer, Willis Spears, who sounded remarkably like Flatt.

By this time I had immersed myself in bluegrass music. I was working for a record company and writing articles for *Bluegrass Unlimited* magazine. I learned about the history of the music and became acquainted with many of the artists. I soon realized that, among aficionados, the Foggy Mountain Boys were regarded as bluegrass royalty.

Curly Seckler retired from touring in 1994, and I rarely saw him after that. Then, at a music party in 2002, I encountered banjo and guitar player Larry Perkins, who had worked with Curly in the final years of the Nashville Grass. We struck up a conversation, and I asked him about Curly. Larry replied that Curly was doing well and that he still played music on occasion. Then Perkins said, "You ought to go and visit him."

That struck me as an odd suggestion, since I had never known Curly well, but the more I thought about it, the more I was intrigued. Always on the lookout for subjects to write about, I realized that to interview Curly Seckler would be a dream come true. After getting the go-ahead from *Bluegrass Unlimited* to write an article, I contacted Curly to arrange a visit.

On the morning of April 29, 2003, I arrived at the home of Curly and Eloise Seckler. Curly welcomed me at the door and took me upstairs to his "office," where we sat for a couple of hours while I quizzed him about his musical experiences. I found him to have an amazingly sharp memory and to be articulate, charming, and funny. Here was a man who had participated in the entire history of bluegrass music and had a treasure trove of memories and memorabilia.

Driving home after our encounter, I knew I had been to the well. I realized that there was not simply an article but a book in his story. I approached Curly, he agreed, and a few months later we met in his hometown of China Grove, North Carolina, for the first of more than forty hours' worth of interviews. He freely shared his time and his memories, and as I got to know him I found him to be a loyal, caring, unpretentious, and generous friend.

In addition, it soon became clear that, even in his eighties, Curly was still a very vital, engaging, and relevant entertainer. During the next several years I had the privilege of working with him in ways that I never could have anticipated and watching the final chapter of this book unfold before me.

Curly was never in the limelight to the extent that Flatt and Scruggs were, but his story is just as compelling. His talent lifted him out of a life of physical labor, but as a hillbilly entertainer he faced a different set of challenges including the less-than-glamorous rigors of road travel before the advent of tour buses and interstate highways. Although he was a sideman for much of his career, he was an essential part of every band in which he performed. His one-of-a-kind, instantly recognizable voice helped set the standard for generations of tenor singers in bluegrass music. His charm and humor, both on stage and off, won him a legion of fans wherever he went.

With a career that spanned more than seventy-five years, hundreds of recordings, and thousands of personal appearances, Curly Seckler's story is that of a consummate first-generation bluegrass entertainer who helped pave the way for all who would follow.

Acknowledgments

My greatest appreciation goes to Curly and Eloise Seckler for opening their home and their hearts to me and being patient through the many hours of questions. Special thanks also to the late Judy McColloh and to Laurie Matheson of the University of Illinois Press for their encouragement, advice, and feedback, to my good friends and fellow writers Eddie Stubbs and Gary Reid for their invaluable support and help with research, and to bluegrass historian Charley Pennell for generously preparing the index.

Thanks to all of the musicians and family members I interviewed, for their time and memories. Additional thanks for their assistance and support to Jay Orr, John Rumble, and Michael Gray at the Country Music Hall of Fame and Museum, Jim Sherraden at Hatch Show Print, Marty Stuart, Dave and Mark Freeman, Randall Franks, Jim Sauceman, Alice Gerrard, Kathy World, Les Leverett, Frank and Marty Godbey, Lee Michael Demsey, Gary Scruggs, Tom Ewing, Doug Hutchens, Harold Mitchell, Jim Mills, Walt Saunders, Dick Spottswood, Larry Perkins, Chris Gowin, Jerry Stuart, Eli Riveire Warner, Tim White, Dan Loftin, Gerald McCormick, and Don Rhodes.

CHAPTER 1

Down in Caroline

1919–1939

In the spring of 2001, after the funeral of fiddler Benny Martin at Forest Lawn cemetery near Nashville, a fan approached eighty-one-year-old Curly Seckler. "Mister Seckler," he said, "you have done so much. You started with the great Charlie Monroe, and then came to Nashville and helped create the Foggy Mountain sound. You've been just like a trademark in country music. There's nothing you haven't seen, nothing you haven't done. You continue to innovate, write new songs, make new records. What is your next career move?"[1]

With a twinkle in his eye and a quiver of his lip, Curly replied, "Well, I guess Forest Lawn."

Though Seckler was joking, as he was prone to do, he had no idea how wrong he would turn out to be. For this pioneering bluegrass entertainer, who began his career a decade before the first note of bluegrass music was ever played, there was much still to come.

John Ray Sechler was born on a farm near China Grove, North Carolina, on Christmas Day in 1919. His baby pictures show that he was born bald, but once his hair finally began to grow in, his family just called him "Curly."

The name John is a derivative of the Hebrew name Yohanan, which means "Graced by God."[2] Though he would rarely be known by his given name, John Sechler would indeed experience grace many times through his long and often challenging life. Curly Seckler, as he preferred to call himself, was a survivor.

Curly was proud of his rural heritage, and he never "got above his raising," although he would become a legendary figure in the music world. He enjoyed being affectionately known to bluegrass music fans as the Old Trapper from China Grove while readily admitting he knew virtually nothing about trapping. The dry, self-deprecating sense of humor that led him to accept and embrace that moniker, bestowed on him by Lester Flatt, would serve Seckler throughout his life, captivating a legion of family, friends, and fans. Seckler would reinvent himself many times during his eight-decade career, but he always stayed true to his roots and, as he would say, "kept it down to earth."

Curly's roots were planted deep in the fertile soil of Rowan County, in the heart of the North Carolina foothills. At Rowan's center, about halfway between the cities of Charlotte and Greensboro, lies the town of Salisbury. Established as the seat of Rowan County in 1755, Salisbury was the economic and political center of western North Carolina by the time Curly's ancestors arrived. In the mid-1800s it became a hub on the newly built North Carolina Railroad line, which extended from Goldsboro to Charlotte. The railroad brought workers and visitors to the area and enabled local farmers and manufacturers to transport their goods to new markets, further boosting Salisbury's economy. By 1900 about 20 percent of the residents of Rowan County lived in Salisbury.[3] The rest, many of whom were farmers like Curly's father, lived in small towns and hamlets that dotted the lush, rolling hills of this predominantly agrarian county.

Just eleven miles south of Salisbury, at the next train stop, sits the tiny town of China Grove. Named for the cluster of chinaberry trees that grew next to the depot, China Grove was incorporated in 1889.[4] About that time it underwent a growth spurt, and businesses began to spring up. Among the first were a sawmill, a cotton gin, a chair factory, and the China Grove Roller Mill. One of the most successful was Patterson Manufacturing Company, a textile mill, which opened in 1893 on Main Street.[5] In 1928 this facility became Plant #8 of the Cannon Mills textile empire, which employed thousands until its final demise in 2003.[6]

Though cotton is no longer king in the southern United States, during the first half of the twentieth century it was the most important cash crop for farmers in Rowan County. Many of the farmers' sons and daughters of Curly's generation saw the cotton mills as their ticket out of the fields. By the late 1920s the North Carolina Piedmont was the world's foremost cotton textile manufacturing area, with over six hundred mills within a hundred-mile radius of Charlotte.[7]

The other important sources of income for Rowan County farmers were grains such as wheat, oats, and corn, food crops like tomatoes and melons, and dairy cows. Most farm families like Curly's were essentially self-sufficient, since they could raise most of their own food and could trade for staples such as sugar and salt. Farmers tended to have large families, which meant a ready-made workforce. Workdays were long, and there was little time for socializing. The only regular gathering place for hard-working families in a tight-knit community such as China Grove was the church. For the Sechlers, it was Mount Zion, the church that had served them for five generations.

According to the Sechler family genealogy, the original John (Johannes) Sechler and his wife Anna Maria immigrated to Pennsylvania in about 1730, most likely coming from the part of Europe now known as Germany. They attended the German Reformed Church at New Goshenhoppen, near East Greenville. John and Anna Maria's son Frederic, born in 1743, married Mary Magdalena Fischer and, in 1767, their first son, Rudolph, was born.

In 1786 Frederic and Mary packed up their family and moved south. The Sechlers were part of a mass migration from Pennsylvania to the Southeast along what became known as the Great Philadelphia Wagon Road. This path, which was originally created by the Iroquois Indians for hunting and trading, was traversed by vast numbers of English, Scots-Irish, and Germanic settlers. It ran through central Pennsylvania, western Maryland, the Shenandoah Valley of Virginia, and the Piedmont region of North and South Carolina to the Georgia coast.

The Sechlers settled in North Carolina along with many other Germanic colonists from the Moravian, Lutheran, and Reformed churches. In the early 1750s a group of Moravians had established the community of Wachovia in what is now Forsyth County, and a Lutheran congregation had settled in Salisbury. Soon there were three German Reformed congregations in Rowan County. A focal point of the early settlement that became China Grove was the Savits Meeting House, which served immigrants of Lutheran and Reformed faiths. Near the site of the old Savits church and cemetery, the Reformed congregation built Mount Zion Reformed Church in 1844.[8]

Most of the early Germanic immigrants were farmers. They were thrifty, resourceful, and hard-working, and they thrived in the temperate climate of North Carolina. Many of them were skilled craftsmen as well, so they tended to be autonomous and for the most part remained sequestered within their own rural communities. They usually married within their own church group, so certain last names recurred often. Records showed that the last names of many German colonists were corrupted by the British clerks of the day, who spelled them phonetically. Thus Karriker became Corriher, Friess became Freeze, Bieber became Beaver, Nantz became Nance, and so on. In various records the Sechler name was spelled Segler, Sickler, Seckeler, Seekler, and Seeclear.[9]

It is likely that Frederic Sechler decided to make the move to North Carolina after hearing reports from other successful settlers. Whatever the reason, he and Mary made the journey south and bought 256 acres of land on Grant's Creek in Rowan County. By 1790 their son Rudolph was married, and in 1792 he and his wife Barbara welcomed their first child, John, who was Curly Seckler's great-grandfather. In 1819 John Sechler married Tenny Correll. They had two daughters and one son, Curly's grandfather Enos.

Enos Sechler married Mary Ann Corriher in 1858. In August 1862 he enlisted in the Confederate Army. He was captured at Spotsylvania Court House, Virginia, in May 1864 and confined at Point Lookout, Maryland, until June 1865. Following Enos's return home, his family grew to include eight children. When Enos Sechler died in 1911, three of his sons and one daughter were still living in China Grove. His obituary in the *Reformed Church Standard* stated that he had been a lifelong member of Mount Zion and that he "was an old Confederate veteran and a splendid citizen."[10] The Sechler family in general seems to have been civic-minded. Enos's cousin General Andrew Jackson Sechler (his given name) was China Grove's first mayor and its second postmaster.

The youngest of Enos and Mary Ann Sechler's six sons was Curly's father, Calvin Burgess Sechler, born in 1877. He married Mary Beaver on December 28, 1904. They had three daughters, Myrtle, Ethel, and Clara, and one son,

Roy Lee, who was born in March 1912. According to Curly's sister Mary, the doctor who delivered Roy Lee was prone to drinking on the job and was careless about sterilizing his instruments. On April 8, 1912, Mary Beaver Sechler died, apparently of an infection she contracted during childbirth.

Calvin soon found a new mother for his children in Carrie Melissa Fleming. They married on March 15, 1914. She was pregnant with their first child when three-year-old Roy Lee contracted diphtheria and died in July 1915.

Calvin and Carrie Sechler had eight children. The first, Marvin Richard, was born on October 2, 1915. Then came Emma Ruth on August 17, 1917, George Enos on October 5, 1918, and John Ray (Curly) on December 25, 1919. Mary May was born on February 21, 1921, followed by Floyd Lee on August 22, 1922, Duard Calvin on April 1, 1925, and Hugh Franklin on September 13, 1928.

The Sechlers lived several miles northwest of China Grove on 150 acres of land that Calvin had purchased after his first marriage. Like his Germanic ancestors, Calvin was a farmer with many skills. He cut timber from the land to build a two-story, nine-room house, a barn, and various outbuildings on the farm. He also provided timber to rebuild nearby Mount Zion Church after it burned in 1918. He grew cotton, wheat, corn, oats, barley, hay, and sweet potatoes and raised cows, hogs, and chickens. Calvin's older brother Jim, who never married, lived with the family and helped manage the farm.

Curly and his sister Mary, who was just fourteen months younger, had colorful memories of family life in the 1920s and 1930s. The Sechlers had no electricity or running water, so their cooking was done on a wood stove and the food was kept in an icebox on the back porch. They carried buckets of well water and heated it over a fire for bathing. Mary and her sisters washed clothes by hand with homemade soap made from lye, wood ashes, and hog fat. Later the family had a gas-powered washing machine, but Curly and his brothers still had to haul water, heat it in large pots over a fire, and then pour it into the washing machine.

There was always plenty to eat. "Myrtle baked pies all day on Saturday, and we'd eat them on Sunday," Mary said. She recalled that Curly would take an entire egg custard pie, fold it in half, sit on the porch steps, and eat it in one sitting. "And now I don't care for them!" Curly laughed. "Our mom cooked a big pan of biscuits every day," he added, "and she bought peanut butter in gallon buckets. We had two gardens. We always raised about three hogs every year, to kill along about Christmas so we'd have plenty of meat and lard." Mary recalled, "Sometimes my daddy would go and get a big mackerel on Saturday, and we would have it Sunday morning and go to church smelling like fish!"[11]

Calvin needed two cars to transport his growing family. "He bought the second car, a T-model Ford, to get us all to church," Curly said. "All of us kids ran out to see that new car. I'll never forget, he said, 'Look, but don't touch!' And then he burst out laughing."

The Sechler children received what formal education they had at the two-room Deaton School, about a mile from the farm. Curly was always self-conscious about his sixth-grade education, but in those days his opportunities for learning were severely limited. In the 1920s Rowan County was divided into eighty school districts, each with one school comprising grades one through seven. Most of the schools were in rural farming communities, and often families within the community donated the land and materials to build the schools. The name of the school was the surname of the owner of the property on which the school was built.[12] The teachers were frequently recruited from the community, and their qualifications were minimal.

"I just didn't learn nothing down there in that schoolhouse," Curly stated. Mary added, "It wasn't none of us kids' fault, it was the teachers." She recalled one lovesick teacher who "sat there and cried all day long," and another who told their brother Marvin "not to come back because he knew more than she did. We kept telling them that we wasn't learning nothing. We got all A's, but we wasn't learning nothing!"[13]

As it turned out, Curly actually learned one of the most important lessons of his life at Deaton School. "That's the first time I did any singing at all, was in that school," he said. "They always had plays at the end of the school year, and they got us up singing. I was singing some regular stuff, and decided I'd go up and hit a couple of high notes, and I said, 'Good Lord!' I didn't know I could do that!"

Curly was only nine years old when his father Calvin passed away on June 15, 1929. For several years Calvin Sechler had suffered with kidney problems, and he was being treated for Bright's disease. When Marvin Sechler had hurt his leg playing baseball in 1924, his father had taken him to Dr. Levi Gibson, a respected African American doctor in nearby Landis. The doctor had referred Marvin to a specialist, then had taken one look at Calvin and diagnosed kidney stones. Sure enough, when Calvin had gone for x-rays, they had shown large stones in both kidneys.[14] Mary recalled that Calvin suffered terribly for the next five years. "He had spells of it, and he passed a lot of them, but this [last] one was too big, and he couldn't pass it. I wasn't very big, but I remember that day very well. I remember them coming and getting him. He was blue when he left our house, and they took him over to Winston, and they never did bring him back, until they called and told us that he'd passed away."[15]

Calvin Sechler was only fifty-one years old. He left behind a wife and ten children at home (Curly's half-sister Ethel was married by this time), the youngest of whom was nine months old. Though Carrie encouraged Calvin's brother Jim to stay on with the family, he felt that it would be inappropriate to do so and moved to Miss Beaver's boarding house in Landis, five miles away. Luckily the farm was paid for. Curly's half-sisters, Myrtle and Clara, were in their twenties and could help with the cooking and other home chores. The older boys were responsible for supplying most of the family's meat. "In the evening my mom would say, 'Well, son, you'd better get your gun and see if you can get up a squirrel or two,'" Curly said. "And every chance we'd get, we'd go rabbit hunting. We had two beagle hounds, Spot and Brownie. You come out with that shotgun, boy, they was ready to go! We had the icebox plumb full of rabbit meat. My mom could make the best fried rabbit you ever eat."

Curly and his brothers were not yet old enough to manage the farm chores, so Carrie enlisted the help of some African American neighbors. "My mother would call Jim Pinkston," Curly said. "He had two sons, Robert and Thelma. She would get them to come and clean out the stables and shock the corn. They were just as nice as they could be to us kids. We had rows of peach trees, and we would take peaches to them and let them take a break so we could hear them sing. They'd sing some of them old songs. They'd say, 'Do you know what one bird would say to the other one? Bob White. Is your wheat ripe? Not quite, not quite.' And us kids would just eat that stuff up."

When it came time to pick cotton the whole family would help. "We'd raise about twenty acres of cotton, and you'd get about a bale and a half to the acre," Curly recalled. "We'd pick a bale or so in a day, with all of us in the cotton patch. My mom was the best cotton picker of the whole bunch. She picked with gloves on, and she'd have the fingers [cut] out of them. She'd get way up the row and she'd look back and see which young 'un was so far behind, and she'd go over and help him catch up."

Once they had picked enough for a five-hundred-pound bale, the boys would hitch the mules to the wagon and make the five-mile trip over unpaved roads to the cotton gin in Landis. They would get up at 2:00 A.M. in order to get to Landis by daybreak. "And then you'd get there," Curly said, "and there'd be fifteen or twenty wagons ahead of you, and you'd be there all day getting that thing ginned, for twenty-eight dollars. Then you took that money to buy fertilizer to put in the ground to get your twenty-eight dollars the next year."

Curly did his part when it came to farm chores, but he suffered from bronchial asthma and was always scrawny as a teen. Many years later he realized that his asthma was likely caused by the straw-stuffed mattresses that the family slept on, but at the time all he knew was that, when he lay down at night to sleep, he would begin to wheeze so badly that he was forced to leave the bedroom. "Through the day I was all right," he explained, "but when I went upstairs to go to bed I was stopped up. I had to come downstairs. Mom would holler, 'Young 'un, come on down here.' And I'd sleep in a big rocking chair. But back then they didn't have no medicine for bronchial asthma, and she kept mustard plasters on me, and all that. Just kept me burnt up, but, bless her heart, she didn't know nothing else to do."

Though they worked long hours to keep the farm going, the Sechler boys still had some time for play, and they found creative ways to enjoy their leisure time. "We had an old mule named Beck," Curly said, "and we took him down in the cow pasture and took a shovel and dug us out a pond, where we could go swimming. There's a spring that ran down through there and filled it up."

The family mules were once again called into service when the boys decided to build a baseball field. "We took mules down there and dug the grass out of there and smoothed us out a place in the old cow pasture and made us a ball field. If you knocked it up in the woods, you had a home run. We had a pretty good little team, back then. We played different schools. [Our neighbor] Murray Belk's daddy always made home brew. Before we went on the ball field one day, he slipped some of his daddy's home brew out, and we drunk that. I got out in center field, where I was playing, and somebody hit a ball out there and I went to catch it, and it landed in my right eye! And I never did drink no more home brew and try to play baseball!

"And [there's] something else we used to do, along about Christmas time," Curly continued. "We had a shed down below the house and we took an old drum and cut the top out of it, and put a pot down in there. We'd go out and hunt rabbits all day, and bring them in and boil them [over a fire], and then we'd have a rabbit stew. We had lanterns [for light], and we had nail kegs that we'd turn upside down and sit on them. Then we'd play music after we'd eat."

Music was always present in the Sechler home. Carrie Sechler played the guitar and the organ, and Calvin played the autoharp. Mary remembered her mother singing old songs such as "Down in the Valley." Curly recalled that Carrie had an unusual style of playing: she rested her little finger on the top of the guitar and plucked the strings with the other three fingers. As they became interested, Carrie showed her sons some basic chords on the guitar, but Calvin discouraged them from pursuing music seriously. "He didn't go too much for music, because he was afraid we'd get off into some place we wasn't supposed to go," Curly explained. "But then, after he passed away, we put together a band."

In the late 1920s and early 1930s, radio was the new medium for entertainment and news, as revolutionary in its time as the Internet was in the 1990s. Radio connected rural folks for the first time to the world outside their hometown and enabled them to hear music that they otherwise might never have heard.

The Sechlers had a battery-operated radio, which they kept tuned to WBT in Charlotte and WIS in Columbia, South Carolina. North Carolina's first radio station, WBT went on the air in 1922. It was purchased by CBS in 1929 and became a powerhouse at 25,000 watts. In 1933 its power increased to 50,000 watts, and it could be heard throughout the Southeast.

In the earliest days of radio, most of the entertainment was presented live, since recording technology was in its infancy. A network affiliation allowed for the presentation of some nationally known artists, but in order to please their local audiences and sponsors, radio stations relied on locally based bands for the majority of their programming. Many of the stations in rural areas would copy the formats of the powerful stations in such cities as Chicago and Nashville.

The Chicago station WLS, which was started by Sears, Roebuck and Company in order to target the lucrative farming market, first went on the air in April 1924 with the slogan "Bringing the World to the Farm." One of the station's first programs was the *National Barn Dance*, a weekly Saturday night show featuring string band music, comedy, and "down-home" entertainment. The master of ceremonies was twenty-nine-year-old George D. Hay, who also played a character called the Solemn Old Judge on the popular program *WLS Unlimited*. This program took listeners on a transcontinental train trip, with Hay blowing a train whistle and proclaiming stops along the way. Both the whistle and the title Solemn Old Judge would remain with Hay for the rest of his career.

About a year and a half after the debut of WLS, the National Life and Accident Insurance Company in Nashville launched WSM in Nashville. At the opening ceremonies on October 5, 1925, the company invited some of the country's most popular radio announcers to perform. Among them was Hay, who had recently been named World's Best Radio Announcer by *Radio Digest*. Within a few weeks after his performance, Hay was hired as WSM's first program director. He immediately set out to create a Saturday night variety show for the station, and in December 1925 the *WSM Barn Dance* made its debut. Its audience soon outgrew the small studio in the National Life building, and the *Barn Dance* was moved to a larger theater. By 1927 WSM had increased its power from 1,000 watts to 5,000 watts and Hay had changed the name of the program to the *Grand Ole Opry*. A 1932 power hike, this time to 50,000 watts, made WSM a clear-channel nation-spanning giant and brought the *Grand Ole Opry* into millions of households each week. Curly recalled hearing it for the first time on a radio with a horn speaker at a neighbor's house when he was about twelve years old.

Stations such as WBT in Charlotte soon followed suit and started barn dance programs of their own. Sponsors also began to capitalize on the potential of radio to greatly expand their customer base, just as Sears and National Life had done. Hillbilly musicians took notice and saw an opportunity to reach a much larger audience to promote their concerts. According to country music historian John Rumble,

> Charlotte's country music scene expanded during the 1930s despite a nationwide economic depression. As falling prices let more and more families buy radio sets, radio stations proliferated. . . . Just as important, demographics were right for country music broadcasting. Most southerners—and a great many northerners—still lived on farms or in rural villages where Saturday night hoedowns were a part of everyday life. For sponsors marketing products to such down-to-earth audiences, country music was a natural advertising medium.[16]

Announcer Charles H. Crutchfield joined the WBT staff in 1933. In 1934 he organized a band called the Briarhoppers, and the Consolidated Drug Trade Products Company in Chicago launched *Briarhopper Time*, one of WBT's most popular programs for many years. Crutchfield's announcing was a big part of the show's success. His magnetic voice, warm personal style, and comic delivery were as much a part of the show as the music.[17] In 1934, WBT started the *Crazy Barn Dance*, named after its sponsor, Crazy Water Crystals, a laxative company based in Texas. Crazy Water Crystals and similar companies also sponsored programs in the early morning and at noontime—the time slots when farmers were most likely to be listening. Soon afterward, the Monroe Brothers (Charlie on guitar and Bill on mandolin) and their announcer-manager, Byron Parker, arrived at WIS in Columbia, sponsored by a competitor, Texas Crystals. After just a few months, however, Texas Crystals ended its sponsorship of string band music, and the Monroes and Parker were hired by Crazy Water Crystals to perform on WBT in Charlotte.

Curly and his brothers, hearing these groups and such other WBT staples as Mainer's Mountaineers and the Tennessee Ramblers, were inspired to try their hands at performing in public. Marvin, the oldest, first began playing with a local musician named William Luther "Happy" Trexler in his band, the Carolina Clod Breakers, and they spent a couple of months performing on the *Crazy Barn Dance*.

Happy Trexler was a fiddler and banjo player from the Rockwell area, just east of China Grove. He made his living as a stonecutter. In 1934 Trexler decided to build a recreational lake on a forty-acre parcel of land near Rockwell. According to an article in the *Salisbury Post*, "The property originally had three small quarries on it. The lake [was] built of natural granite that was dug, shaped, and placed there, probably by horse-drawn wagons. [Happy Lake] is about 2½ to 3 acres in size and is totally spring fed."[18]

Once the lake was built, Trexler organized a band to provide entertainment for the patrons. Fourteen-year-old Curly was recruited to join the group, playing banjo in the clawhammer style. "Marvin played guitar, and Basil Barnhardt played guitar, and it seems like there was another one or two of us," Curly recalled. "[Happy Trexler] had a five-string banjo, and I took up the banjo because there wasn't nobody else to hold it. We'd go down at his lake, and we'd play while the people was swimming. We'd get to picking, and he'd get to singing, 'Gotta quit kicking my dog around, makes no difference if he's a hound, you gotta quit kicking my dog around. Arf, arf, arf, arf.'"[19]

In June 1940 Trexler was discovered dead in his car in the woods a few blocks from his home, the victim of a self-inflicted gunshot wound. His suicide made the front page of the *Salisbury Post*, which reported that Trexler "had been brooding considerably over damages to his resort lake caused by recent heavy rains which had washed out the dam, the family told officers." The article went on to say that he "won the nickname of 'Happy' by leading string bands that gave performances at numerous school, family, and public gatherings for many years throughout the county. He played a violin, but oftimes changed to a guitar or banjo and was highly proficient in musical fields. He was widely known throughout this entire area."[20]

Playing music helped Curly earn a little spending money, and he was able to purchase an old bicycle from a neighbor boy for two dollars. The neighbors lived on a hill, and Curly laughed when recalling how he climbed aboard the bike for the first time and went flying down the hill. At that time, bicycle tires were made of solid rubber, without tubes, and Curly found that his tires would not stay on the wheels. Ever resourceful like his immigrant ancestors, Curly used pieces of bailing wire to secure the tires to the wheels, solving the problem but making for a rather bumpy ride. Using a belt, he strapped a flashlight to the handlebar so he could ride at night.

Once he turned sixteen Curly bought his first car, a 1932 Ford V8, and got his first paying job at Cannon Mills in nearby Kannapolis. "Me and my cousin, we'd take turns driving each week," he noted. "There was about five of us would go down there. We charged each one twenty cents a day to ride." His first job was greasing the gears on weaving looms using a long-handled mop and a grease bucket. "My first check I got was twenty-four dollars for two weeks, and I got it all in one dollar bills at the bank and took it and counted it out on the floor. Most money I'd ever seen in my life!

"My cousin was a foreman there, and he said, 'How would you like to learn to weave, and stop sliding that bucket all over this place?' And it wasn't too long until he give me a set of looms to run. You had to watch it, and if the thread broke, the dropeye would go down and that'd kick the loom off. Then you had to take that string and put a weaver's knot in it, and pull it back through the dropeye. You'd run the loom until you'd get a roll of towels on it. Then you would take it down to the place where they inspected the cloth and towels. Then they took it to the cutting room."

Soon Curly had saved enough money to buy his own instrument, a four-string (tenor) banjo that he and Marvin picked out at a music store in Kannapolis. Marvin also bought a new Gibson guitar there. George had signed up for music lessons through the mail and had made himself a metal fiddle. Their younger brother Duard was also becoming interested in playing guitar. They recruited their friend Murray Belk to play jug and washboard, and formed a band. Influenced by the singing cowboys they saw on Saturday afternoons in the movie theaters in Kannapolis and Salisbury, the brothers wore bandanas and very large hats and called themselves the Yodeling Rangers. They adopted stage names: Marvin was called "Slim," Duard was known as "Shorty" and later "Lucky," and Murray Belk, who dressed as the rube comedian, was called "Shy Mike." Curly continued using his previously acquired nickname, and George used his given name—perhaps because he was the most serious musician and also acted as the emcee for the group.

The Yodeling Rangers began performing around the area, mostly at schoolhouses and occasionally at theaters. A show poster from 1938 indicates that admission was fifteen cents for children and twenty-five cents for adults. In the early years they were sometimes joined by the Johnson Family: "Happy" (Gidian), "Jolly" (Lillian), and "Smiley" (Hubert).

The Yodeling Rangers' big break came when Salisbury got its first radio station in January 1939. At 1500 on the AM dial, WSTP (250 watts) went on the air on Monday, January 2, 1939 at 4:00 P.M. from its studios in the downtown Yadkin Hotel. After speeches by several dignitaries, the station's president, Bryce Beard, introduced station manager John Schultz, who then introduced the staff. At 5:00 P.M. the station broadcast the Rose Bowl, which was of special interest to North Carolinians since it featured the undefeated Duke Blue Devils versus the University of Southern California Trojans.

As most stations did at that time, WSTP featured a wide variety of popular music and informational programming. Yet the station's management recognized the need to appeal to its rural "hillbilly" audience. On Saturday, January 7, just days after going on the air, WSTP launched the *Yadkin Valley Hoedown*, a two-hour barn dance program that originated from the Raney Building at the corner of Main and Liberty Streets in downtown Salisbury. The ad in the *Salisbury Post* proclaimed: "Tonight and Every Saturday Night at 9; Big 2-Hour Show; Rip-snortin' hillbillies from everywhere—really tearing loose! Admission 20 cents."[21]

Sometime in the spring of 1939 Marvin Sechler met WSTP station manager John Schultz, perhaps at the *Hoedown* or at one of the Yodeling Rangers' concerts, though no one is sure. Schultz gave the band a Monday-through-Saturday fifteen-minute radio program, which they shared with Happy Gadd, a guitarist who served as their announcer, and a couple of members of the Johnson family. They first went on the air on Monday, April 17, with Rustin's Furniture Company as their sponsor. Curly recalled that the band was paid half in cash and half in furniture. By May 21 they had become popular enough that the *Salisbury Post* ran a photo of them next to the radio listings with a caption reading "Here are the Yodeling Rangers, who fill the air with all those varied hill billy noises over WSTP every week day at 1 o'clock. The program draws a heavy fan mail at the station."[22]

Salisbury had three movie theaters, which occasionally hosted performances by well-known country music artists, as was common all around the South at that time. An artist would give as many as four performances in one day between movie showings. On June 12 Roy Rogers appeared at the State Theater, and on June 15 Uncle Dave Macon and his son Dorris were featured at the Victory Theater as part of its fifteenth anniversary celebration. Curly recalled being in the audience for their performance that night. Both Rogers and Macon stopped by WSTP to promote their performances, and Marvin Sechler remembered that Dave and Dorris Macon were guests on the Yodeling Rangers' program. The station's Ralph Roberts, who wrote a daily column in the *Salisbury Post* called "WSTParagraphics," noted, "Uncle Dave Macon, the Dixie Dewdrop, made a short but noticeable appearance on the station the other day. And Roy Rogers, star of westerns, dropped in to say 'Howdy neighbors' and play a few of the current cowboy hits. Both of these programs went over big, as could be seen by the number of listeners out in the observation room . . . seeing is believing."[23]

On June 18 WSTP joined the Mutual Broadcasting Network. This was a significant event for a station barely six months old in a small rural town in the South. The *Salisbury Post* noted: "Officials of WSTP consider themselves extremely fortunate in getting a satisfactory hookup with the Mutual, which is one of the large networks of the country. . . . There are few towns the size of Salisbury on any of the large networks. Joining the Mutual at the same time as the local station, and comprising this new southern loop within the nationwide net, are WSOC, Charlotte; WRAL, Raleigh; and WAIR, Winston-Salem."[24]

Less than three weeks later, a headline in the *Salisbury Post* read, "Radio Station WSTP Originating Daily Programs For Southern Net." The article indicated that WSTP, WSOC, WRAL, and WAIR had come together to form the Southern Broadcasting System, a southern leg of the Mutual Broadcasting System, and that WSTP would now have the ability to simulcast some of its local programs on the other three stations.[25] Ralph Roberts's "WSTParagraphics" on August 22 reported: "One of the biggest items yet is that Happy Gadd and the Original Yodeling Rangers will go on the Southern Broadcasting System soon. And with a sponsor (yessir!): the Robertson Fertilizer Co."[26]

The Yodeling Rangers were moved to the 12:30 P.M. time slot, and their music was heard throughout central North Carolina, elevating them from a local band to regional stars overnight. But the Rangers' excitement over their growing fame was tempered by the fact that they had just lost one of their most important members. In early July Curly Seckler had left to seek the big time.

CHAPTER 2

The Adventures of Smilin' Bill

1939–1944

In the spring of 1937 the Monroe Brothers and Byron Parker parted ways. Parker left WBT and returned to WIS in Columbia, forming Byron Parker and his Mountaineers. Following his departure, the Monroes stayed a few more months at WBT. By this time they were also working at WFBC in Greenville, South Carolina, sponsored by Seiberling Tires. By summer they had added a daily 7:00 A.M. show on WPTF (5,000 watts at 680 AM) in Raleigh. They soon relocated to WPTF, adding a 1:00 P.M. show on Saturdays.

The loss of Byron Parker as their manager was the beginning of the end for the Monroe Brothers as a duo. Parker had served as booking agent and emcee for the Monroes, allowing the brothers to focus mostly on their music. Without him, the proud and contentious brothers were forced to work more closely together on the business end of things. Charlie's wife Betty began to help with the business and was acting as their unofficial manager. Their success grew, but so did the hostility between them.[1] During their time in Raleigh the brothers traveled separately and rarely spoke to each other at shows or at the radio station. Entertainer Tommy Scott, who was also at WPTF in 1938, recalled, "They didn't speak to each other for a year. They'd turn their back to each other [in the studio] and sing the fool out of them songs, and one of them would get in [his] car to go to play the date and the other would get in his car to go, and they'd go on the stage and do the same thing, wouldn't speak."[2] Finally, in the summer of 1938, the Monroe Brothers parted ways.

Bill Monroe initially moved to Little Rock, Arkansas, and briefly organized a band.[3] After short stays in Memphis and Birmingham he moved on to Atlanta, where he found an apt replacement for Charlie in guitarist-singer Cleo Davis. Monroe and Davis found their first success as a duet at WWNC in Asheville, North Carolina. Monroe then decided to try again at being a bandleader, and he formed Bill Monroe and his Blue Grass Boys, adding fiddler Art Wooten and jug player Tommy Millard.

Meanwhile, Charlie Monroe took Gladys and Rusty Scott (a blackface comedian with experience in vaudeville), who had been part of the Monroe Brothers' show, and moved to WNOX in Knoxville. He also hired tenor singer Leon "Bill" Calhoun and left-handed mandolin player Lefty Frizzell (no relation to the country singer of the same name).[4] After a short stint at WNOX, Charlie moved to WDBJ in Roanoke, Virginia. By then Frizzell had been replaced by Zeke Morris.

Charlie arrived in Roanoke in October following a recording session for Bluebird/RCA in Rock Hill, South Carolina, on September 29. On these recordings Morris is listed as playing mandolin and Calhoun as playing guitar; however, photos of the trio taken about this time show both Morris and Calhoun holding mandolins. Charlie was obviously attempting to retain the guitar-mandolin brother duet sound that had brought him success with Bill. This is further confirmed by the labels on the Bluebird 78 rpm records, which listed the artists as "(Charlie) Monroe's Boys, singing with guitars and mandolin."[5]

In January 1939 Charlie moved back to WPTF in Raleigh, broadcasting Monday, Wednesday, and Friday at 1:30 P.M. and Tuesday, Thursday, and Saturday at 7:00 A.M. By that time he had added West Virginia fiddler Dale Cole and comedian Bert Stevens for live performances. A newspaper article published on January 30 in Lumberton, North Carolina, stated: "Charlie Monroe (of "Monroe Bros.") known to radio listeners, is expected at St. Pauls grammar school building on Thursday night, February 2, at 7:30, for a performance to which the public is invited. With Monroe will be Bill Calhoun, Zeke Morris and Fiddlin' Dale Cole, also 'Jolly Bert Stevens,' comedian. Admission, 15c–25c."[6]

By this time Charlie also had begun promoting his personal appearances as "Charlie Monroe and his Big Radio Show," a headline that he would continue to use on show posters for many years. An article published on Friday, February 3, stated, "Charlie Monroe and his big radio show gave a concert Thursday night at the grammar school."[7] Yet another article appeared on February 6, stating, "A large crowd attended the splendid concert put on Thursday night by Charlie Monroe of Monroe Bros. and his group of entertainers from WPTF, Raleigh."[8]

Clearly the Monroe name had become well established in North Carolina at this point, and Charlie was ready to capitalize on it. The transition from being part of a duo to being a bandleader was easier for Charlie than for Bill. Charlie had a more outgoing personality and was comfortable in the role of emcee. Audiences instantly related to his genial demeanor, and he quickly built up a loyal following. This is evidenced in a photo taken at WPTF in early 1939 that shows Charlie flanked by Dale Cole and Bill Calhoun, with a gigantic stack of fan mail in front of them.[9]

Tommy Scott had come to Raleigh in 1938 to work at WPTF with Uncle Pete and Minerva, a husband-and-wife team who acted in radio dramas and performed in theaters and schools in the evenings. Tommy was a twenty-one-year-old singer and guitarist who had performed on radio in his hometown of Toccoa, Georgia, as a youth. At seventeen he had left home to apprentice with a medicine show run by M. F. "Doc" Chamberlain. Under Doc's tutelage he learned how to charm an audience and sell a product. He also learned about the herbal remedies that Chamberlain was selling: Snake Oil, a liniment composed of camphor, menthol, benzocaine, and various oils, and Herb-O-Lac, an herbal laxative.

Medicine shows always included entertainment in order to attract and hold as large an audience as possible and thus sell more bottles of the herbal remedies. Doc Chamberlain recognized Tommy's talent as a musician but wanted him to add other skills to his repertoire. Chamberlain taught him about blackface and rube comedy, which were popular at the time. In blackface, Tommy played a character called "Peanut." As a rube, he was known as "Horsefly." Doc also taught Tommy about ventriloquism and helped him make his own doll from an oilcan and a piece of cypress wood. They dubbed the doll "Luke McLuke." When Tommy sang and performed comedy with the doll, he went by the stage name of "Texas Slim."

Tommy's talent and enthusiasm impressed Doc Chamberlain, and he began to groom Tommy to take over his business. When the time came for him to retire, Doc handed Tommy the formulas for his herbal medicines and said, "I want you to carry on the business. I think you will make a great show man."[10] He also assisted Tommy in a job search, which resulted in the offer from Pete and Minerva at WPTF in Raleigh.

On March 29, 1939, Raleigh's second radio station, WRAL (250 watts at 1210 AM), signed on the air from a small studio on Salisbury Street in downtown Raleigh. Its founder was attorney A. J. Fletcher, who went on to form Capitol Broadcasting Company, today a North Carolina broadcasting empire.[11] Pete and Minerva were hired by WRAL, and Tommy Scott went along with them. According to Tommy, "It went on the air about ten o'clock and they had the governor there, and I sung the first song that was ever sung on that station. And then I went over [from WPTF to WRAL]. They had already got me a sponsor."[12]

By this time, Charlie Monroe had been back in Raleigh for several months. Emboldened by his success as a bandleader, Charlie set his sights on moving to a bigger market with a bigger band. He pulled Tommy Scott aside one day and said, "I'm going to the *National Barn Dance* in Chicago, or I'm going to the *Wheeling Jamboree*. It looks like I'm going to the Jamboree. I want you to go up there." Tommy was interested but told him, "Now, it's going to be about two months before I can even think about going, because the new station is on the air and I've got to work out [a commitment] with [the sponsor]."[13]

Meanwhile, Charlie had become aware of a young tenor singer with an incredibly high vocal range who sounded quite similar to Bill Monroe. Curly Seckler and his brothers were performing every day on WSTP and appearing at schoolhouses all around the Carolinas in the evenings. Curly recalled how Charlie began to pursue him in the summer of 1939:

> He got to catching our [radio] program. So one day I looked up at the station, and there was Charlie Monroe. After our program was over, he come in there and was talking about hiring me to sing tenor with him. I said, "No way, no." I wasn't going to leave my brothers and I didn't want to leave home. We'd play on Saturday nights in some of the schoolhouses down there. So every time we'd play one, here would come Charlie Monroe and his wife, Betty.
>
> And he finally told me, "Well, I'll pay you eighteen dollars a week," which was a lot of money back then. And I said, "No, no, no." So it went a little

while longer, and here come Charlie again. He said, "I've just got to have you in my group. I'll give you twenty dollars [a week]." That kindly rung a bell! So I talked it over with my brothers and they said, "Well, if you want to, go ahead and try it." So I left home when I was nineteen years old and went to work with Charlie Monroe, with a tenor banjo, and we went to Wheeling, West Virginia.

The station WWVA in Wheeling first went on the air in December 1926 at 50 watts. By July 1929 it had become a 5,000-watt powerhouse that could be heard hundreds of miles away. In 1931 the station became affiliated with the CBS network and moved into modern studios in the Hawley Building in downtown Wheeling. Soon station manager George Smith conceived the idea of a regular Saturday night country music program, presumably modeled after the *Grand Ole Opry* and the *National Barn Dance*. On January 7, 1933, at 11:00 P.M., the *Wheeling Jamboree* made its debut. Listener reaction was so favorable that on April 1 the *Jamboree* was moved to the Capitol Theatre, which would accommodate a live audience of over thirty-two hundred people. In 1936, WWVA celebrated its tenth anniversary with the outdoor Centennial Jamboree, which drew over five thousand people. The following year, the Harvest Home Festival Jamboree brought in more than seven thousand people, and in April 1939 the Jamboree Tour went on the road, drawing almost twenty thousand attendees in a six-city tour.[14] Given the success of the *Wheeling Jamboree* and the reach of WWVA, it is not surprising that Charlie Monroe elected to move to that station.

On July 2, 1939, Charlie sent Tommy Scott a letter from the Hotel Matz in Bluefield, West Virginia, saying that he was forming a band and wanted the members to meet him in Bluefield on Thursday, July 6.[15] Tommy recalled, "I was the first one there. Charlie had me singing all day long, there in Bluefield, checking me out. And I went with them, in a brand new Lincoln that he had just bought, from Bluefield to Wheeling. And then Curly come in a couple of days later. He went direct to Wheeling."[16]

For Curly, the chance to work at a major radio station with a star like Charlie Monroe was a dream come true. "I had a lot of that on my mind," he recalled, "because I'd heard the Old Hired Hands, and the Monroe Brothers, and the Morris Brothers, and I knowed at that time that I could sing, so I wanted to get into it." Charlie obviously recognized Curly's talent as a singer because he was willing to offer him a significantly higher salary than anyone else in the band was making, although Curly didn't know it at the time. Not until a conversation with Tommy Scott over sixty years later did Curly learn that Tommy was only making fifteen dollars per week to Curly's twenty.

One of the first things Curly remembered on arriving at WWVA was getting a lecture from Charlie Monroe on how to dress. "Charlie was strictly business, and I admired him for that," Curly noted. "When I first went to work for him in thirty-nine, here I come in with a sports shirt on. And he says, 'Boy, ain't you got no ties and [white] shirts? If you haven't got them, I'll buy you some. Don't never let me catch you up here in the studio again without a white shirt and a tie! That's fifty percent of your show, is how you dress.' And I ain't never forgot that! Another thing I give Charlie Monroe credit for [is], when he went on the stage, everybody knowed what they was supposed to do, because you rehearsed every day, including Sunday, whether you had a show or not. That's one thing he believed in, and he put on a good show."

Tommy Scott confirmed this account: "Charlie would rehearse us four hours every day, on every song that we'd sing that night. You had to wear them hats, like him, and them boots, and a white shirt. I have to say, he made it look high-class. And he wouldn't allow us to go into the dressing room of another artist at all. He said, 'We're above them, and we're going to keep it that way.'"[17]

Charlie rounded out his new band, the Kentucky Partners (sometimes spelled "Pardners"), with mandolin player Tommy Edwards and fiddler Dale Cole, who also did blackface comedy. Although Tommy Scott had been using the stage name "Texas Slim" while in Raleigh, Charlie began calling him "Ramblin' Scotty." Tommy continued to do his ventriloquist act with Luke McLuke and to play a blackface character called Midnight. Curly Seckler was dubbed "Smilin' Bill," a ploy to lead listeners to believe that they were still hearing the singing of Charlie and Bill, the Monroe Brothers.[18] Tommy Scott recalled Charlie's telling Curly, "If you work for me, you're going to be called 'Bill.' I'm going to do that because that'll sound like you can sing like my brother, Bill Monroe. And I'll just say, 'Me and Bill's going to sing this next little song.'"[19] Tommy added, "Although we knew it wasn't exactly honest, it became a joke with us in the band, and a challenge for Curly to see how closely he could sound like Bill Monroe."[20]

Once they got to Wheeling, Charlie's wife Betty helped the new band members find a place to live. According to Tommy Scott, "Charlie didn't never stay in the hotel that his entertainers was in. He wouldn't be caught with the [band members]. He says, 'That's belittling me, the star.' Betty, she's the one who helped us get a room, and it was in a sort of a boarding house–type hotel, about two blocks down from the station. We could walk down there and back."[21] Curly recalled, "Me and Tommy Edwards stayed together in a rooming house. I think the room cost us a dollar and a half a week. And breakfast, I think, was a quarter, and leave a nickel tip." Tommy Scott added, "They fed you two big meals a day. It was boarding house style, all you could eat. Cornbread and buttermilk, and all that kind of stuff."[22]

The Kentucky Partners performed two shows each Saturday night on the *Wheeling Jamboree*. They did a daily morning radio show on WWVA and traveled up to two hundred miles from Wheeling in Charlie's Lincoln to perform concerts several evenings per week. Curly recalled that "Charlie, he'd never let anybody drive his Lincoln. He drove it in and out, always. He'd get these Moon Pies and put them in his pocket. Then he'd get some parched peanuts, and he'd sit there, driving, eating Moon Pies and peanuts, to stay awake." Tommy Scott remembered that the band would "come in a lot of times at 2:00 and 3:00 [A.M.], and then had to get up to do that early morning program. And then go rehearse for three or four hours, and then head for another town way off somewhere."[23]

The town of Wheeling borders the Ohio River, and Curly recalled that it was always foggy as they were returning from show dates. He also remarked, "You could be on the air, and you'd hear that old fog horn, down there, on one of them boats, 'Whoooo,' just like that, and they'd say, 'Oh, somebody's going through.' And us up there, broadcasting." Tommy Scott noted, "The huge building housing the radio station was situated within a few feet of a long, wide river. We were set right in the midst of the hubbub of the city. The radio station was on the sixth floor. The first floor was used completely for a food market. It was a favored place for homemakers, merchants, and restaurateurs."[24]

Tommy remembered the radio studio as being spare and not particularly comfortable. "The radio station was a very large room with two microphones in the center of the floor. The announcer would use one, and the other one would be for whatever band happened to be playing. Hard oak seats hugged three of the walls, and that was where we sat until it was our turn to do songs. Big Slim the Lone Cowboy, Doc Williams and his Border Riders, Jake Taylor and His All Girl Band, and many others would take turns playing on the air."[25]

It was while he was at WWVA that Curly first heard the song that would become his trademark, "Moonlight on My Cabin." He learned it from Harry C. McAuliffe, otherwise known as Big Slim the Lone Cowboy, who had come to WWVA in late 1937, joining Doc Williams and His Border Riders as a featured vocalist. Big Slim soon became a star in his own right, and his stage show included whip and rope tricks and a trained horse in addition to his music. He sang popular and obscure Western songs, mountain ballads, country standards, and several songs including "Moonlight on My Cabin" that he copyrighted as his own but reportedly did not write.[26] Big Slim later helped some younger artists, including Hank Snow and Hawkshaw Hawkins, get started, and in 1947, Hawkins recorded "Moonlight on My Cabin." Curly began singing the song on stage at about that time and continued to feature it for the rest of his career.

One evening in October, just a few months after they had arrived in Wheeling, Charlie Monroe came to the band with some exciting news. He had arranged for an audition at the *Grand Ole Opry*. However, Curly recalled, "about a week or two after that, after we'd done our first show at the auditorium, we was listening to the *Opry* [on the radio], and directly the Solemn Old Judge said, 'Friends, we have a new one here tonight, and he's from the state of Kentucky. It's Bill Monroe and His Blue Grass Boys!' And Charlie said, 'Good Lord a-mercy! He beat me there by just a couple of weeks!' So that was the end of that."

Bill Monroe made his *Grand Ole Opry* debut on October 28, and within a week Charlie had moved his aggregation to WHAS in Louisville. Curly explained, "WSM was a 50,000-watt station. At that time, Wheeling was only a 5,000-watt station. These Monroes was awful proud. They didn't want the other one to do something bigger. So [Charlie] said, 'He's on a 50,000-watt station, I'm not going to be outdone.' So he left WWVA in Wheeling and we went to Louisville, Kentucky, WHAS, and got on a 50,000-watt station, same as Bill was on. Gave up a good job, making good money, up in Wheeling, and went to WHAS in Louisville, an early morning program, and didn't get a nickel for it! But he was on a 50,000-watt station. Now, ain't that something? I've never seen two fellows like them in my life." Tommy Scott agreed: "I've never met two people as unusual as Charlie and Bill Monroe in my life, before or after. They both had odd ways of doing things."[27]

Like Bill, Charlie was physically strong, sometimes belligerent, and ready to take on anyone who crossed him. Curly remembered an incident at one of their shows in Bryson City, North Carolina. "We'd done went on the stage and was doing the show. Betty was looking after the door back there. Somebody come up [to Charlie] and said that somebody came in and got smart with her. Charlie looked over at me and said, 'You take the show and I'm going out there a minute.' He went out there, and he hit that guy and knocked him through two swinging doors. After the thing was over, he was going to stop at one of them cafés down there, and I said, 'Charlie, we'd better not stop or we'll get into a fight.' He cracked them knuckles, [saying,] 'I ain't scared of none of them!' We went in there, and there was the guy he hit. I thought, 'Boy, this is it.' [Charlie] walked right up over that boy and told that [waitress], 'Give me a cup of coffee.' Just dying for him to say something. That guy didn't say a word. His eye was swelled plumb shut."

Curly continued, "Oh, he'd fight a circle saw, if you messed with him. What he had, he was going to keep, and he didn't want nobody messing with it. But Charlie was a real nice fellow in a lot of ways. I remember one night we come out of a school—of course, the roads back then was mud deep. And this old car in front of us had mired down and couldn't go. Charlie says, 'There ain't no need in the rest of you getting muddy.' He got out there and [lifted up] the bumper of that car, and it went on out of there. He got back in his Lincoln and we left."

When Curly joined the Kentucky Partners he brought along the tenor banjo he had been playing with the Yodeling Rangers in North Carolina. Charlie was not entirely happy with the instrument. "It was so loud," Curly chuckled, "he took the back off of it and put rags in it, then got me a felt pick! He wanted me to trade it for a tenor guitar. Me and Tommy Scott went in this [music store] with it, and opened the case. It was a Mastertone banjo. I opened that thing up, and that fellow just laughed. I forget what he said he'd give me for it, but it wasn't nothing, so I just slammed the [lid of the] case back down, and he called me a nincompoop. I asked Tommy, 'What in the world does that mean?' Then we got into it, after I found out what it meant! But I didn't get the guitar. I kept my banjo."

The Kentucky Partners arrived in Louisville at the beginning of November 1939 and began a daily 5:30 to 6:00 A.M. radio show over WHAS (50,000 watts at 930 AM). According to Tommy, "at that time, WHAS was just about like being on the network now. We covered thirty-five, forty states, just solid. The bookings come in terrific from there."[28] Though the band went over well with radio audiences, and bookings were steady, Charlie found that, now that the Monroe Brothers were no longer together, he could not attract a sponsor. Advertisers were not fooled by Charlie's references to "Smilin' Bill." They wanted both Monroe brothers.

Sometime that winter, Curly decided to return home and rejoin his brothers in their band. According to Tommy Scott, they had been urging him to come back for a while. About that same time fiddler Paul Prince replaced Dale Cole, who had decided to return to Wheeling to work with Frankie More. A few weeks later, Tommy Scott persuaded Charlie to hire David "Stringbean" Akeman to play banjo and do blackface comedy with the group.

The Kentucky Partners remained at WHAS until the end of March 1940. Having failed to attract a sponsor in Louisville, Charlie decided to return to WFBC in Greenville, South Carolina, where he and Bill had been successful with Seiberling Tires as their sponsor. But, Tommy explained, "when he got to Greenville, that's where they really threw him out. When he went to his old sponsors back there, they said, 'You've got to be kidding. We're not going for nobody except the real thing,'" meaning the Monroe Brothers.[29]

The band had been in Greenville for just a few weeks when Charlie approached Tommy Scott, saying, "We cannot get a sponsor here. Now, I've heard you talk about that medicine Doc Chamberlain give you. Is that any good?" Tommy replied, "Well, sure it is. It'll clean your whole system out, and it's a tonic, laxative." Tommy confirmed that he owned the formula, and Charlie said, "Couldn't I sponsor myself on that? Would you be willing to go fifty-fifty on it? I've got the money, and then you go and put it in the drugstores. I'll buy you a brand new Ford car to go out and sell that medicine." Tommy replied, "OK, I'll furnish the medicine and get it in the drugstores. You pay for the time on the radio. It'll be our sponsor."[30]

Tommy wanted to maintain ownership of the patent and keep the original name, Herb-O-Lac. Charlie had other ideas. Against Tommy's protests, Charlie and Betty came up with a new name for the medicine: Man-O-Ree. They submitted it for government approval with Charlie listed as the owner. Tommy wrote a jingle that the band could sing as the sponsor's theme and arranged for the manufacturing, and they began to market the product.

By this time Charlie had moved the band to North Carolina, where he still had a loyal audience, if not loyal sponsors. He arrived at WBIG in Greensboro in the summer of 1940, broadcasting weekdays from 12:00 to 12:30 P.M. and Saturdays from 6:00 to 7:00 A.M. Charlie's idea of self-sponsorship proved to be more successful than he could have dreamed, according to

Tommy. "We went on in Greensboro," he said, "and it was unbelievable how them people started buying that stuff. We'd go out and put it in the drugstores, and they let me put it in the windows out front. Of course, Charlie Monroe's name didn't hurt it none, either. And then he said, 'Now, instead of me giving you half, let's go on another [station].' Then we went to Winston-Salem."[31] Tommy then came up with the idea of broadcasting their program on multiple stations over the telephone lines, a common practice in radio at that time. That allowed the Kentucky Partners to simulcast on fifteen stations, collectively known as the Man-O-Ree Network.

By the end of 1940 Charlie was experiencing unprecedented popularity and was selling Man-O-Ree as fast as he and his band could bottle it. Yet Tommy Scott had never seen a penny of the promised 50 percent of the profits. Finally he had had enough, and he confronted Charlie about settling up. Charlie refused to negotiate, saying, "I'll knock your head off, but I'll do what I'm going to do." Tommy replied, "You ain't going to do it with my medicine, or one or the other of us is going to go to the hospital. You get yourself another boy and I'm taking my medicine away from you right now!" Though Tommy took back the original formula, Charlie would not be deterred. According to Tommy, Charlie then "mixed up a bunch of salts and stuff and still called it Man-O-Ree, and [eventually] the federal government got him."[32]

Tommy left Charlie's band and headed home to Georgia, and before long he contacted A. P. "Doc" Durham, owner of the Herb Products Company in Anderson, South Carolina. Tommy and his high school friend Doyle Thompson had worked for Doc Durham on WAIM in Anderson in 1935–1936, prior to Tommy's joining Doc Chamberlain's medicine show. Durham had started at the Herb Juice Medicine Company of Jackson, Tennessee, in the manufacturing department. He had worked his way up to sales and advertising manager, and eventually he purchased the company. According to Tommy, Durham had become a highly successful entrepreneur, managing various businesses including a grocery store and a shopping center. He sponsored live music programs on several radio stations, including WAIM in Anderson, WSPA in Spartanburg, and WRDW in Augusta, Georgia. His laxative medicine was called Vim Herb.

Tommy called Durham and said, "I've left Charlie Monroe. I'd like to come back down there and sell some of that good old Vim Herb." Durham replied that Tommy could go on the air just as soon as he could get there.[33] Durham's *Hi Neighbor* programs aired weekdays at 7:15 A.M. and 5:00 P.M. Tommy Scott arrived at WAIM (250 watts at 1230 AM) on Monday, January 13, 1941. The listing in the *Anderson Independent* for that date read: "*Hi Neighbor* with Zeb, Art, Jay, Fiddlin' Tex, and Rambling Scotty presented by the makers of Vim Herb."[34] Zeb was guitarist and singer Zebulon Q. Turner, whose real name was William Edward Grishaw. He went on to play guitar for Red Foley and did studio work for a number of artists including Hank Williams. While they were at WAIM he would occasionally accompany Tommy on show dates.

Tommy and Curly Seckler had kept in touch following Curly's departure from the Kentucky Partners, and after Tommy had been at WAIM for a few months he decided to see if Curly would like to join him. "I began singing on the radio [at WAIM] as a single and I happened to think of Curly one day," Tommy said. "After talking to Doc Durham and getting his OK I called and asked Curly if he was interested in coming to Anderson."[35]

On leaving Charlie Monroe's band, Curly had returned to China Grove and rejoined his brothers, who by this time had changed the name of their band to the Trail Riders. During Curly's absence they had continued to broadcast over WSTP in Salisbury, along with Happy Gadd, on a daily 1:00 P.M. program called *Happy Gang*. On Monday, March 18, 1940, with their now-seasoned brother back in the ranks, the Trail Riders began their own daily program at 11:15 A.M.[36] Soon they added programs on Saturday morning at 11:15 and Sunday afternoon at 4:15. In July WSTP began a new Saturday afternoon program called the *Rail Fence Review*. The weekly "Radio Observatory" column in the *Salisbury Post* said that "the series will run through the summer and early fall. In case you missed the first show, the second session will be heard next Saturday afternoon, featuring those irrepressible Trailriders."[37]

The Trail Riders continued their daily morning programs through the rest of 1940. One morning that fall, while the band was on the air at WSTP, two young female listeners stopped by the radio station. One of them was Juanita Pate from East Spencer, just a few miles from Salisbury. Apparently it was love at first sight, and she and Curly began to date. Juanita had three sisters and at least one brother, and her father worked as a night watchman. Tommy Scott speculated that Juanita saw Curly as a glamorous, well-to-do entertainer who would enable her to live a better life. Perhaps Curly enjoyed playing that role, and so the invitation to partner with his ambitious friend Tommy Scott could not have come at a better time.

After Tommy called, Curly borrowed his brother Marvin's 1941 Ford and drove down to Anderson to visit. He observed the *Hi Neighbor* program and decided he would join Tommy in the cast. After a brief trip home to settle his affairs, Curly returned at the end of May and was first listed in the WAIM schedule on Wednesday, May 28: "7:15 A.M.—*Hi Neighbor* program (Vim Herb) featuring Tex, Blacky, Scotty and Bill."[38] Tommy believed that the name recognition he and Curly had in Charlie Monroe's band would benefit them in their new partnership, so they continued to use the names Ramblin' Scotty and Smilin' Bill. They even had these names inscribed on the license tag holders on the backs of their cars.

Curly still had his tenor banjo, but once he arrived in Anderson he decided that a mandolin would work better in the duet programs that he and Tommy would be performing. Perhaps he and Tommy also felt that having "Bill" play a mandolin would ally them with the legacy of the Monroe Brothers, thus helping them land more work. Curly explained, "One thing about that tenor banjo, it was heavy as the dickens to tote around, and it was so loud it was pitiful. I told Tommy I believed I could play a mandolin. There was a fellow on the Vim Herb program called Lonesome Luke, and he had this mandolin, an F-2 [Gibson], and he wanted to sell it. I asked him what he'd take for it, and he said, 'Forty-two dollars.' Well, I didn't have forty-two dollars, so I went to our sponsor down there, Doc Durham. He loaned me forty-two dollars to buy that first mandolin that I had. And then I laid that banjo down."

The next thing he needed was a car, and his association with Doc Durham helped him with that as well. "I decided I was going to buy me a car, and I went to this lot, and the fellow said, 'Well, I've got a Packard over there that's in good shape, and I'll guarantee it.' He said, 'Who do you work for?' I said, 'Doc Durham.' He said, 'Oh, Good Lord, Doc, yeah! Why don't you just take this Packard and try it out, and I'll get you some paperwork on it.'" Curly also bought a small trailer to live in and parked it next to Tommy's.

After getting established in South Carolina, Curly decided it was time to marry the sweetheart he had left behind in North Carolina. Following his move to Anderson, he would make the 350-mile round trip to visit Juanita as often as he could, but he soon found out that Doc Durham planned to move him and Tommy to WRDW in Augusta, Georgia. Curly and Juanita began to discuss getting married, and Tommy Scott suggested that they go to the same Methodist church in Westminster, South Carolina, where he and his wife Frankie had married in June 1940.

On Friday, July 4, 1941, Curly and Juanita were married. "I come up and got her and her mother in that Packard, and we went down there and got married in Westminster," he said. "I put her mother in the hotel, in Anderson, until she could catch the bus the next morning back to [Spencer]." Tommy and a very pregnant Frankie Scott joined them at the wedding.

Then, on the morning of July 7, while Curly and Tommy were performing on WAIM, Doc Durham came into the studio. As Tommy recalled, "Curly and I were doing our radio show as usual when Doc Durham came over and put one hand on the neck of my guitar and the other on Curly's mandolin and stopped us dead in the middle of a song. He said, 'It's a girl, six pounds and seven ounces, born at the Anderson Hospital and named Sandra. Now you boys get out of here, and I will take over.'"[39] Curly took up the story: "So we got in the car to go over and see the baby. We got over there, then they brought Frankie her breakfast, and she didn't want it. And so I said, 'Well, there's no need to let it go to waste,' so I ate it."

Curly shared many meals with Tommy and Frankie during their time together, and he remembered that Frankie was a good cook. There was at least one instance, however, when she left the cooking to the men. "Me and Tommy used to put out a trunk line in the river down there, and we caught an eel," Curly chuckled. "So we brought that thing to the house and told Frankie to cook it. She said, 'No, I'm not cooking that snake!' Wouldn't have nothing to do with it. So me and Tommy cooked that dude and eat it. Yeah, it was pretty good."

Three weeks after Sandra Scott was born, Curly and Tommy moved to WRDW in Augusta. That station (250 watts at 1480 AM) had first gone on the air in June 1930, from the fourth floor of the Masonic building at the corner of Broad and Eighth Streets. By 1941 it was a CBS affiliate owned by Augusta Broadcasting Company.[40] Curly and Juanita rented an apartment in a rooming house two blocks from the radio station, and Tommy and Frankie found a place to park their trailer. Their programs on WRDW aired Monday through Saturday at 7:15 A.M. and weekday afternoons at 5:30.[41] Tommy recalled that they also had a Sunday morning hymn program. They made transcriptions, or recordings, of their programs, which could be played on days when they could not be at the radio station because of bookings or other commitments. Tommy Scott acquired some of those transcriptions years later, and they were released as an LP on Old Homestead Records in 1980.

The songs Curly and Tommy were performing included a mix of traditional songs and a few of Tommy's originals. They opened the program with their theme, Albert E. Brumley's "Turn Your Radio On." Their gospel material included such classics as "Joy Bells," "Drifting Too Far from the Shore," and "Give Me the Roses While I Live." Secular songs and tunes included "Whoa, Mule, Whoa," "Deep Elm Blues," and "Don't Say Goodbye If You Love Me." Tommy introduced all of the songs and read the commercials for Vim Herb.

Doc Durham made sure they received regular mentions in the *Augusta Chronicle*, such as this one from August 1941:

> "The Kentucky Partners," Ramblin' Scotty and Smilin' Bill, continue their twice daily broadcasts with songs right from the hills. Ramblin' Scotty and his guitar and songs along with Smilin' Bill's singing mandolin really fill a quarter hour full of entertainment from start to finish. Listen in at 7:15 for their morning program or at 5:30 for their afternoon performance. You're also invited to come to the studio to see these entertainers in action.[42]

The Savannah River runs through downtown Augusta, and the climate there in August is hot and humid. Something in the air there triggered an allergic reaction in Curly, and he found himself once again plagued with the bronchial asthma with which he had struggled as a teenager. Curly was never one to drink, but he found that a shot of whiskey helped him sing when he was having an asthma attack. "With Tommy Scott, I'd take me a swallow of whiskey, and that would get me pepped up to where I could sing a little bit, clear your throat out a little." He also recalled that Doc Durham gave him some pills that seemed to help, although he had no idea what was in them. For a while he was even giving himself daily shots, most likely of epinephrine, which was commonly prescribed for asthma patients at that time. Epinephrine acts on the immune system, reducing inflammatory response, which helps keep airways open, but it can have serious side effects. When doctors discovered that Curly's heart was enlarged, he was advised to discontinue the shots. Luckily, Doc Durham decided to move Curly and Tommy to WSPA in Spartanburg in October 1941. The climate there was drier, and Curly's asthma subsided.

Radio station WSPA (5,000 watts at 950 AM), which signed on the air in February 1930, was the first commercial station licensed in South Carolina. In June 1940 it was purchased by the Spartanburg Advertising Company. Its studios were located at 155 South Liberty Street. By the time Curly and Tommy arrived there, it was a CBS affiliate.[43]

Tommy maintained that Durham sent them to Spartanburg to "straighten things out" at WSPA because he was not getting his allotted advertising time on the *Hi Neighbor* show there. On arriving at the station they met with the morning announcer, and Tommy repeated the message from Doc Durham. The announcer responded, "There ain't no two-bit son-of-a-bitchin' hillbilly going to come in here and tell me how to run this station!" Tommy recalled, "The words had barely come out when he lunged at me. I dodged him and busted him up the side of his nose with my fist, and Curly threw a chair at him."[44]

As Curly rcalled, "Tommy and I come in there one morning to rehearse and he wouldn't let us in a room to rehearse. We had to stand in the hall. So Scotty, he got stirred up and said a few words, and [the announcer] said us 'S.B.s' wasn't coming in here running that station. When he said that, then Tommy popped him. I know we got into a fight. And he said we'd never play there no more. And Wiley and Zeke [Morris] was doing a program at that time, and they seen it, so they come out of the studio."

According to Tommy, the station went off the air temporarily during the altercation, and Doc Durham, who was listening, drove immediately to Spartanburg and threatened to take his program off the station. Tommy recalled that the announcer refused to apologize and was fired, and Curly said that the next morning they had their rehearsal room.

Several other hillbilly bands were broadcasting on WSPA that fall, including Arthur "Guitar Boogie" Smith's Carolina Crackerjacks and the Morris Brothers. Curly stated that Wiley and Zeke Morris were "wild as guineas, but they could sing." He also remembered that a young Don Reno was playing banjo with the Morris Brothers at that time.[45] Curly laughed when he recalled driving up to the station, he in his Packard and Tommy in his Lincoln, with their names on the license tags. "I'll never forget what Don Reno said when he saw us pull up one morning down there with them cars. He said, 'Lord, they must be rich ones!'"

At 5,000 watts, WSPA had a much greater reach than did WAIM or WRDW; thus Spartanburg proved to be the most successful market for

Scotty and Bill. Their daily *Hi Neighbor* program was on from 6:45 to 7:00 A.M. They began giving daytime performances in area schools, combining music with Tommy's ventriloquist act. "We worked every schoolhouse there was," said Curly. "We called it 'educational programs.' The principal would call them all in the auditorium, and Scotty would take Luke, and he'd talk to them kids. He'd put on a whale of a good show, and it was educational. It just cost a dime to get in, and we'd work about three or four of them a day. Sometimes we'd come in with a half-gallon bucket full of dimes."

Curly, Tommy, and Frankie were also doing shows at schoolhouses, courthouses, and a few theaters in the evening. On Friday, November 28, 1941, at 7:30 P.M., they performed at Number One School near Cliffside, North Carolina. Their show poster read:

> Rambling Scotty and Smiling Bill and the Original KY. Partner Show
> Direct from Radio, Records, Screen, Stage
> Formerly with Monroe Bros. and stations WHAS, WFBC, WBIG, WWVA
>   and Networks.
> Featuring that little wise cracker LUKE McLUKE.
> Laughs and more laughs with that Black Face Comedian MIDNIGHT.
> You'll never forget seeing Horse Fly Charley, Little Miss Frankie and
>   her Magic Pistol.
> See a man escape from hand cuffs, Lock and Chain.
> Good Music and Singing from a host of other Stars.
> The show with a Thousand Laughs.

Clearly Tommy had become an expert at self-promotion. While their advertising may have stretched the truth a bit, the poster does indicate that Scotty and Bill were presenting a full evening of entertainment, not simply a musical program. Tommy was continuing to do his ventriloquist act and blackface comedy (to which Curly would play the straight man) and had added some magic tricks. Frankie had joined in the act as his assistant and was performing rope and gun tricks of her own.

Next Tommy decided to start a tent show, and they put a down payment on an old circus tent and chairs from Wallace Brothers Circus. They found a place to set it up on the outskirts of town and began presenting tent shows. They would rent Western movies from the local theaters and show them in addition to their regular stage performance. Depending on attendance, they might leave the tent up for as long as a week in one place.

Curly recalled, "We'd go on the air and advertise it for that night. And we'd run a different movie, like Tom Mix or Johnny Mack Brown, or whoever, in them old Westerns, and then we'd do our little act after the movie run. I had a big old fan, and we'd run it, and blow air through the tent."

They made a sign to put up outside the tent that read:

> In Person; Ramblin Scotty and Smiling Bill
> and the Kentucky Partners Show
> Direct from Radio, Records & Stage
> Singing Dancing Comedy
> * The Show with a Thousand Laughs *

By this time Charlie Monroe had been at WBIG in Greensboro for a year and a half and was firmly entrenched in North Carolina. At some point, while Curly and Tommy were in Spartanburg, Charlie became aware that they were using the Kentucky Partners name to promote themselves. In early 1942 he came to Spartanburg and took them to court. It is unclear exactly what happened, but in a 1972 interview Charlie said, cryptically, "Curly Seckler went down to Spartanburg, South Carolina, and Tommy Scott worked with me, we named him Ramblin' Scotty. His name was Texas Slim when he come with me. Took them to court down there, cost $163 in court costs, and they lost the name."[46] Tommy recalled that they went to magistrate's court, "and they had a hearing, and the judge throwed it out."[47] Curly said, "I know it didn't amount to nothing. We just had to quit using the names. Had to quit using 'Smilin' Bill.'"

The issue with the names turned out to be moot, for the adventures of Scotty and Bill would soon come to an end. On Monday, March 2, 1942, a major snowstorm struck the Carolinas. The headline in the *Spartanburg Herald* on Tuesday read: "Heavy Snowfall Blankets Entire Piedmont; Wire Services and Travel Are Halted By Snow."[48] Tommy and Curly had left their tent set up after their Saturday night show, since they were planning to do additional shows in the same location. As Curly remembered it, they went to try to secure the tent from the winds of the storm. "When the snowstorm came, we were doing an early morning program, and then we went down there and we tied one of the guy ropes to my trailer. When the snow got on [the tent], it pulled my trailer off in a ditch. It destroyed the tent, practically." Tommy agreed, saying, "It was just ruined. It had fold-up chairs [under the tent], and as it got fuller of snow, it just eased on down, and everywhere that one of them chairs was, punched a hole in the tent, and it was totally full of holes. We called the people we got it from. We told them that we didn't have no money and the snow had ruined the tent, and to just come and take it, and they come and got it."[49]

The loss of the tent and trailer led Curly to decide he'd had enough, and he elected to return to North Carolina. He and Tommy parted the best of friends and continued to stay in touch. Curly and Juanita returned to Spencer, where they rented a house not far from her family, and Curly went back to work in a cotton mill. By this time, Juanita was pregnant with their first child. Ray Allen Sechler was born on June 6, 1942, in the Salisbury hospital.

Just a few months later, Curly had a surprise visit from guitarist and singer Leonard Stokes. Stokes had worked with Mitchell Parker as the Dixie Melody Boys on WMFR radio in High Point in 1936. He then joined J. E. Mainer and George Morris (brother of Wiley and Zeke) in a band that eventually became Mainer's Mountaineers. Stokes, Mainer, and Morris worked with Byron Parker's Hillbillies in 1937, and they recorded twenty-six songs with Parker as Byron Parker's Mountaineers in 1940, while working at WIS in Columbia.

Curly recalled, "Ray was about three months old, I guess, when Leonard come up [to visit], and I thought he was still working with the Old Hired Hand [Parker]. All at once, here he was beating on my door, wanting to take me and join up and we'd do some singing." It was Leonard's idea for them to call themselves the Melody Boys, apparently a throwback to his duo with Mitchell Parker in High Point.

Leonard had his sights set on Knoxville, which had a vibrant hillbilly music scene at that time, thanks in large part to two influential radio announcers: Cas Walker of WROL and Lowell Blanchard of WNOX. Walker was a highly successful businessman, politician, and radio personality. Beginning in 1941, he served for thirty years in Knoxville as city councilman, vice-mayor, and mayor. Walker was a self-made man who worked hard at any job he undertook. He had cut timber, threshed wheat, dug potatoes, herded cattle, and mined coal before settling in Knoxville in 1923 at age twenty-one and purchasing his first grocery store. He eventually built a chain of supermarkets in eastern Tennessee, Kentucky, and Virginia.[50]

Station WROL first went on the air in February 1927 as WNBJ, broadcasting religious programming. The station was sold to Stuart Broadcasting Corporation, and the call letters were changed to WROL. By 1941 it had arrived at 620 AM, broadcasting at 1,000 watts, and was an NBC affiliate. Its studios were at 524 South Gay Street, on the third floor of the Hamilton Bank building in downtown Knoxville.[51] In 1929 Cas Walker created a live music variety program called the *Farm and Home Hour*, which aired daily on WROL. His grocery chain sponsored the program, and Walker did the announcing.

On arriving in Knoxville in the fall of 1942, Leonard and Curly headed for WROL to check out Walker's program. Curly recalled,

> We pulled up to the station, there. We was going to listen to the Brewster Brothers pick their early morning program with Cas. We got on the elevator, and here comes a fellow in, and he says, "Who are you boys?" We told him who we was, and he says, "I'm Cas Walker." Leonard spoke up and said, "Well, we are entertainers. We're coming up to see your show." And [Cas] said, "Well, how would you like to do my show this morning? My boys ain't going to be here." Leonard said, "Well, we've got our instruments out there in the car." He said, "Get them and come on up," and we did, and that's how we met Cas Walker. We went on the air and done the show, and he kept saying on the air, "Now, if you like these boys, Leonard and Curly, the Melody Boys, write or call in and I'll see about keeping them here." And, Lord, the phone lit up, and in just a few days you couldn't even get the mail in that box they had, we just drawed so much mail. So then we went to work for Cas Walker. He paid us ten dollars a week, apiece, which was pretty good money. Then we wrote a little songbook, and he said take so many to all his grocery stores, and we sold no telling how many of them things, at fifty cents apiece.

The songbook, titled *Favorite Melodies, as sung by The Melody Boys, Leonard and Curly*, contained twenty songs, including Leonard's composition "We Can't Be Darlings Any More." This was a song that Curly was later to bring to the attention of Lester Flatt when the Foggy Mountain Boys were preparing to record in 1950. Lester liked the song and suggested that they approach Stokes about buying it from him. Curly contacted Leonard and he agreed to sell it for twenty dollars; Lester and Curly each paid ten dollars. Flatt and Scruggs recorded the song in November 1950, and it became one of the most popular Flatt-Seckler duets.

The Melody Boys' songbook also included such classics as "Don't Let Your Sweet Love Die" (later popularized by Reno and Smiley), "Little Paper Boy" (recorded by Johnnie and Jack), and "When My Blue Moon Turns to Gold Again." Among the many gospel titles were "Turn Your Radio On" and "Give Me the Roses While I Live" (which Curly brought from his time with Tommy Scott), "Kneel at the Cross," and "You Can Be a Millionaire with Me." Also included was the obscure story song "The Letter That Went to God," which Curly finally recorded for the first time in 2004. According to Curly, the Melody Boys sold hundreds of the songbooks in Cas Walker's stores, and Walker never took a cent of the profits.

Curly remembered Walker as a proud and powerful man, who was always ready to help those in need. "Cas was in on a lot of things to help people," he said. "If somebody's house burned down, he'd get on the air and start advertising, 'Needs this, and needs that,' and he'd get everything them people ever needed. People believed in Cas Walker over there. He just ruled that town. And some of them'd get mad and want to whoop him. He'd get on the air and say, 'I'll be at such-and-such a store, and you just come on over there and I'll be waiting on you. I'll take you one at a time.' He'd take them in a cooler back there and whoop their tails! He wasn't no big man, but he was just muscled.

"But Cas was a good-natured fellow," Curly continued. "He'd help you any way he could. He sure helped me and Leonard, because I didn't have no money when I went over there. He paid us right on the ball. When we was working with Cas, you had to have gas stamps to get gas. That was [during] the war. He'd say, 'Go back behind a certain store. There's a drum back there with gas in it. Get it.' And a lot of entertainers worked for Cas Walker, because Cas would give them a job when nobody else would."

It wasn't long before the Melody Boys' popularity at WROL caught the attention of Lowell Blanchard, who had a daily music program of his own on the competing station, WNOX. Blanchard offered them twelve dollars a week, and they made the move.

Station WNOX originally went on the air in November 1921 as WNAV. It was the first radio station in Tennessee and the eighth in the United States. In 1928 it was sold to Sterchi Brothers and was moved from the St. James Hotel on Wall Avenue to the Andrew Johnson Hotel on Gay Street. In December 1935 it was purchased by Scripps Howard Radio, Inc., which also owned the *Knoxville News-Sentinel* daily newspaper. In the spring of 1942, WNOX (990 AM) added three new towers and doubled its power to 10,000 watts, thus increasing its coverage area by an estimated 40 percent.[52]

The station hired Illinois broadcaster Lowell Blanchard in 1935 as an announcer and talent scout. He soon created two groundbreaking live hillbilly music programs: the *Mid-Day Merry-Go-Round*, which aired weekdays from 12:15 to 1:45 P.M., and Saturday night's *Tennessee Barn Dance*, which ran from 8:30 to 11:00 P.M. and was broadcast on WNOX from 9:45 to 11:00. These shows became so popular that hundreds of curious onlookers packed the Andrew Johnson Hotel, and management asked the station to leave. The studios were then moved to 110 South Gay Street, the site of an abandoned tabernacle with an auditorium that could accommodate the growing crowds.

According to the historian Ed Hooper, "Blanchard was not only selling WNOX, he was selling radio to people who were just discovering it. Blanchard was a phenomenal voice on radio and an astounding master of ceremonies. He wrote his own scripts, did comedy, and mastered stagecraft. His good natured approach and on-stage sales ability allowed him to put acts on the stage that could not have made it anywhere else, and it paid off big."[53]

Blanchard was to become a legend among Tennessee broadcasters. He helped launch the careers of many musicians who went on to be major country music stars. Roy Acuff, Chet Atkins, Don Gibson, Archie Campbell, Homer and Jethro, Kitty Wells, the Louvin Brothers, and Carl Smith are just a few of the artists who got their start on the *Tennessee Barn Dance*.

Among the musicians who worked at WNOX when Curly and Leonard were there was Bill Carlisle, who also played a comedic character called "Hot Shot Elmer." Carlisle was originally from Kentucky and had begun his music career in the 1920s. He began recording in the 1930s and had performed on a number of radio stations before landing at WNOX. Carlisle and his brother Cliff were among the first musicians Curly met when he arrived in Knoxville. He recalled that when they were all working at WNOX, Bill invited Curly and Leonard to his house for breakfast one morning in order to show off his new son Bill Junior, who had been born in August.

Curly also remembered that Carlisle was quite an entertainer. When it was Carlisle's turn to perform on the *Tennessee Barn Dance* or the *Mid-Day Merry-Go-Round*, he would make a flamboyant entrance. "They had a banister [at WNOX], from up in the office," Curly said, "and when he'd come on [stage], he'd come sliding down that railing, right down into the audience. Of course, he did a lot of comedy. He'd get on the buses [dressed as Hot Shot Elmer] with a skunk that he had fixed to where it couldn't spray. He pulled a lot of things there in Knoxville, but people really appreciated Bill Carlisle, and Hot Shot Elmer. He was just down to earth good, in every way."

Curly recalled, "When I was in Knoxville, playing the *Merry-Go-Round*, me and Bill Carlisle got to talking one day, and he said, 'You know, I believe we could rent one of those buildings across the railroad tracks' and teach what we called the 'ear method' of [playing music]. We didn't know no notes, you know, just play it by ear. And so we rented this building. There was three rooms in it. We charged a dollar a head to teach them. Leonard played the guitar. I was trying to teach them to play the mandolin. Bill was teaching guitar, well as I remember. You'd pay about a dollar and a half a week [rent] for a room."

Although Cas Walker and Lowell Blanchard were associated with competing radio stations, they sometimes worked together on community service events. After all, Walker was a city councilman, so his first responsibility was to the people of Knoxville. In December 1942 the Melody Boys took part in two fundraising events for a children's charity called the Empty Stocking Fund. The first took place at the WNOX studios on Thursday, December 10, and was broadcast live from 7:00 to 9:00 P.M. Lowell Blanchard was the master of ceremonies. An ad in the *Knoxville News-Sentinel* touted the benefit as an "ALL STAR SHOW for the benefit of the Empty Stocking Fund! Two Solid Hours of Gala Music and Riotous Fun! See 'em in person! Hear 'em at home! Listen! Have a Good Time . . . Help Others Have a Good Time!" Performers listed included the Melody Boys, Cas Walker, Hotshot Elmer, Cowboy Copas, the Tennessee Valley Players, Bill Lawson's Commanders, the Dixieland Swingsters, and others.[54]

Then, on Saturday, December 12, Cas Walker presented his annual Mile o' Dimes program, also benefiting the Empty Stocking Fund. A photo on the front page of Sunday's *News-Sentinel* showed Walker at the microphone with several children and a crowd behind him, including Hot Shot Elmer and Curly Seckler. The headline read: "Cas Walker, Entertainers Set All-Time 'Mile' Record—$1240." According to the article:

Up went a new all-time Mile o' Dimes record when Cas Walker and his hill-billy entertainers called it a day last night.

The tide of giving he and his entertainers set in motion added the record-breaking total of $1240.10 to the Empty Stocking Fund—that's 722 feet of dimes.

All day long crowds jam-packed both sections of the Mile, tossing on coins and folding money to the lively tunes, jokes and patter of Councilman Walker's troupe of entertainers.

The crowds never seemed to thin out much and the shows never stopped. Hot Shot Elmer was there; Leonard and Curly, the Melody Boys; the Murphy Sisters from Wyboy, Ky.; Cas Walker's Smoky Mountain Hillbillies; the Blount County Ramblers; the Cowgirls; Marshall and Luther Whaley, midget father and son.[55]

The Mile was a section of downtown Knoxville with an outdoor stage on each end. Performing outdoors in Knoxville on a chilly December day was challenging, and Curly recalled wearing an overcoat. He remembered that Junior Huskey, who was a member of Cas Walker's Smoky Mountain Hillbillies, was playing bass wearing gloves with the fingers cut off. Huskey, who was from the Knoxville area, played with several different bands in the 1940s and 1950s including the Brewster Brothers and the Bailey Brothers. He was a regular on the *Tennessee Barn Dance*, often filling in with guest bands that were without a regular bass player. He went on to become a highly respected studio bass player in Nashville. Apparently Huskey was creative in other areas as well. In 1942 he made Curly the mandolin strap that he continued to use on his Gibson F-2 for the entire time he owned it.

Another colorful person that Curly first met in Knoxville was Arthur Q. Smith, whose real name was James Arthur Pritchett. Smith arrived in Knoxville in 1936 and was hired as a rhythm guitarist in the WNOX house band for the *Mid Day Merry-Go-Round* and *Tennessee Barn Dance* programs. He also had his own fifteen-minute program, dubbed *The Tennessee Corn-shucker Show*.[56] Smith soon gained a reputation as a prolific and skilled songwriter. He also was known to have a serious drinking habit, however. Curly recalled that Smith often sold his songs to other musicians for a few dollars or even a bottle of whiskey. Among those who bought or popularized Smith's songs were Bill Monroe, Don Gibson, Ernest Tubb, Kitty Wells, and Hank Williams.

By early 1943, with World War II in progress and rationing in effect, it was becoming difficult for musicians to obtain gas for travel. Many were being drafted and sent overseas. Leonard and Curly, both of whom suffered from bronchial asthma, received a 4-F rating from the draft board and so were not called for active duty. But they decided they would give up music and seek employment in a defense plant until the war ended. They left for Ohio, where there were a number of defense plants, but ended up enlisting in the army reserve. They were stationed at a base near Gallipolis, a small town in southern Ohio, just across the Ohio River from Point Pleasant, West Virginia.

At some point Juanita's parents and two of her sisters, Pauline and Christine, and their husbands also moved to Gallipolis. Her parents managed a diner called the Windmill Restaurant, and the sisters worked there as well. Curly remembered sometimes helping out by peeling potatoes. But most of his time was spent in strenuous training at the army base.

"We didn't stay there long," he said, "because I couldn't take it. They'd get you out every morning and run you up and down a creek, and I couldn't get my breath, because I had bronchial asthma. They'd run you, and they'd come and pick you up and take you back, and you'd get back in line and go again. And they had this big plant up there, had a big fence around it, and they had these tires that [we] would have to stay in all night, and had a beacon light there, you'd shine it around to see if anybody was trying to crawl the fence. And they had a telephone, and you had to report in every hour, that you hadn't gone to sleep."

After about three months, when it became clear that Curly and Leonard were in no condition to withstand the rigorous training, they were able to be discharged. They decided to go to Columbus, the state capital, where it might be easier to find steady work. Juanita and little Ray stayed behind with her family, and Curly rode with Leonard to Columbus. He left his cherished 1937 Packard with Pauline's husband so that he would have a vehicle to drive to work.

Leonard found work at the Timken Roller Bearing Company, which made bearings for the automotive, agricultural, and mining industries. During the war, Timken also made bearings, gun barrels, and steel tubing for the military. Curly got a job in the main post office in downtown Columbus. Once he got settled, he planned to return to Gallipolis to retrieve his Packard and bring Juanita and Ray back with him; however, he soon received word that his brother-in-law had wrecked the car and it was beyond repair.

Curly found a small second-floor apartment in a building just behind the hospital, and soon Juanita and one-year-old Ray took the bus to Columbus. By the summer of 1943 Juanita was pregnant again, and on January 15, 1944, Monnie Lee Sechler was born. The family moved to a larger apartment, and Curly got an occasional second job loading freight to help pay the bills. After working all day at the post office and loading dock, Curly would arrive home to help with domestic chores. "I went out and got me a big tin tub, and a scrub board," he recalled, "and when I'd come home from work, then I'd scrub diapers. Back then you couldn't throw them away."

There wasn't much time for recreation, but sometimes Curly and Juanita would pass the time by singing together. "Juanita was a good singer," Curly said. "She could play the piano and the guitar. I come in one evening, and she says, 'I'm writing a song.' She was a pretty good songwriter. So then I picked it up and we completed it, in forty-three, 'Traveling Down This Lonesome Road.' And me and Mac [Wiseman], when we went together [in 1947], we sung it."

It wasn't long before Curly was supporting an even bigger household. Juanita's sister Christine and her two young children arrived in Columbus in the summer of 1944, after Christine's husband was drafted into the military. "She come to live with us, with her two kids," Curly said. "We only had one bed downstairs, and there she was, with her kids, all piled in the bed. [Juanita] was sleeping with her feet up this way, and I was sleeping with my head up that way, and there's the kids in between us. Here I was working at the post office eight hours, and then sometimes I'd go over and load freight for four hours, to make enough money to take care of everything and pay the rent. It was rough."

Juanita's sister and the brother-in-law who wrecked the Packard were not the only ones to take advantage of Curly's generosity. "Her daddy and mother come to me about, would I get the money together to send them to Washington State; that he had a job, but he had to have the money to get there. And so I gave him the money to go out there to go to work."

If that wasn't enough, Juanita and her sister began taking turns partying with the servicemen that were stationed in Columbus. While Juanita would stay home and watch the four children, Christine would go out on the town. Then, when she returned, Juanita would head out. For Curly, that was the last straw in a marriage that had already been rocky. "I just told her that was it and I was getting out, and she said, 'You'll never leave me. My looks will hold you.' I said, 'Honey, it's only skin deep,' and that's the last words I ever said to her. Out the door I went with my kids."

Curly had been planning his exit and had already reserved his train ticket. In October 1944 he boarded the train with baby Monnie, who was just nine months old, and two-year-old Ray, and headed home to China Grove. "I'd set it up to where I could get on a [train] car and not even have to get off, clear to China Grove," he said. "And I bought up milk, and they had this dry ice, that wouldn't melt, and that's what I took on there."

Curly's sister Mary speculated that Juanita's wild streak was a rebellion against her restrictive upbringing: "Her mama and daddy had this religion that they wouldn't let [their daughters] go anywhere, they wouldn't let them wear makeup, they wouldn't let them do anything. When she got loose from mama and daddy, she went crazy."[57]

Carrie Sechler welcomed her son and grandchildren with open arms. They joined the household, which at that time also included Mary and her young son Jerry. (Mary's husband, Walter Freeze, was overseas in the service.) Mary recalled taking all of the children to church each Sunday. "Jerry would sit on one side and Ray would be on the other, and I'd be holding Monnie." She also recalled that Ray was suffering from separation anxiety, having been taken from his mother at such a vulnerable age. "The house was pretty big, and if you started to go out of the room where he was, he'd start crying and say, 'Aunt Mary, don't leave me, don't leave me.'"[58]

It must have been especially difficult for Ray and Monnie, because as soon as Curly returned to the old homeplace he began suffering from bronchial asthma again. In addition, the emotional toll of the unraveling of his marriage caused him to experience a bout of depression. He spent several months recuperating and unable to work. As luck would have it, a call would soon come that would lift him out of his malaise and return him to the musical stage.

CHAPTER 3

Don't This Road Look Rough and Rocky

1945–1949

Curly had been out of the music business during his two years in Ohio, but he had not been forgotten. He had rubbed elbows with a number of up-and-coming musicians while in Knoxville, including Danny Bailey of the Bailey Brothers. Danny and Charles Bailey grew up in East Tennessee and began playing music together professionally in 1937 on WOPI in Bristol, Virginia, as the Happy Valley Boys. In 1940 they arrived at WROL in Knoxville, but after a few months moved to WNOX. Then, in March 1941, they were hired by Cas Walker and returned to WROL. A few months later, the Baileys were offered a job at WSM's *Grand Ole Opry* in Nashville, but before they could accept the invitation Charles Bailey was drafted into the army. Danny remained in Knoxville for several years with a band that included Willie and Ray Brewster and Junior Huskey. In the fall of 1944, with Charles Bailey still stationed in the Pacific and no end to the war in sight, Danny finally decided to accept the job at WSM. At age twenty-four, he was the youngest member of the Grand Ole Opry at that time.

A few months after the Happy Valley Boys moved to Nashville, Ray Brewster was drafted into the army. Willie Brewster and Junior Huskey then returned to Knoxville, and Danny Bailey hired the Cope Brothers, Lester and Charles, to replace them. The Copes were also from East Tennessee. Like the Baileys, the Copes eventually settled in Knoxville, and by the early forties they were regulars on WNOX. They joined Danny Bailey at WSM in early 1945, and Bailey also hired a fiddler from Missouri named Curly King.

It was then that Bailey contacted Curly Seckler and asked him to join the band. Because Charles Cope was already playing mandolin, Curly brought a guitar to Nashville and left his Gibson F-2 in China Grove. He sang duets with Danny Bailey, and the Cope Brothers were also featured as a duo on shows. The Happy Valley Boys played at schoolhouses and theaters during the week, performed on the *Opry* on Saturday nights, and began an early morning program over WSM in March 1945.[1] Radio listings in the *Nashville Tennessean* during that time indicate that early mornings were loosely organized. The Happy Valley Boys appeared several days a week for fifteen to thirty minutes starting as early as 5:30 or as late as 6:15. They shared these time slots with artists such as Ernest Tubb, Lew Childre, Pete Pyle, and the Bailes Brothers.

Curly didn't remember much from his short stint with Danny Bailey, but he did recall that the fiddle player would often find clever ways to conceal liquor and was frequently inebriated on the job. He also remembered admiring Charlie Cope's mandolin playing, as well as that of Ernest Ferguson, who was working at the *Opry* with the Bailes Brothers. Though Curly enjoyed his time with the Happy Valley Boys and appreciated the opportunity to perform on the *Opry*, by summer he had made up his mind to leave the band. Ironically, Danny Bailey called one morning and asked Curly to meet him so they could talk, and it turned out that Bailey wanted to offer Curly a partnership in the band. Curly considered the offer but stuck to his decision and gave Bailey his two weeks' notice.

At that time, Curly's old friend Tommy Scott was also based in Nashville. He was performing on the *Opry* and also booking, managing, and appearing on package shows with several acts including Danny Bailey, as well as Curley Williams and his Georgia Peach Pickers. After leaving Bailey, Curly Seckler went on several road trips with Tommy Scott and Curley Williams. He recalled being with them in Shelby, North Carolina, and buying a newspaper on August 15, 1945, the day World War II ended. Soon after that, he returned home to China Grove, only to be called out again by his old boss, Charlie Monroe.

Charlie had spent most of the early forties based at WBIG in Greensboro, North Carolina, where he appeared daily on the highly successful *Noonday*

Jamboree and packed audiences into area schoolhouses, courthouses, and theaters at night. He spent much of 1944 and 1945 based at WSJS in Winston-Salem. Since Curly's departure from the original Kentucky Partners, Charlie had employed several tenor singers including Lavelle "Bill" Coy, who came and went several times, and Lester Flatt. Flatt joined the band in 1943 and stayed for about a year before heading to Nashville to work with Bill Monroe's Blue Grass Boys. Apparently Lavelle Coy replaced Lester in the Kentucky Partners; he was mentioned in several ads for show dates in 1945. Also in the band at that time were North Carolinians Jimmy "Slim" Martin, who played fiddle and harmonica, and his wife Wilma ("Little Wilma"), who sometimes played bass. By this time electric guitarist Larry "Tex" Isley had also joined the Partners.

Curly retrieved his mandolin and joined Charlie Monroe at WSJS in Winston-Salem, which was still broadcasting through telephone hookups on the multi-station Man-O-Ree Network. Curly remembered the jingle that he helped Charlie sing as they signed on each day:

> Man-O-Ree is on the air, we hope that you are there,
> We try our best to please you one and all.
> If you're feeling down and out, try without a doubt,
> What you need right now is Man-O-Ree.

Charlie would then laugh his distinctive laugh and greet listeners by saying, "How you do, everybody, how *do* you do?" At the end of the program they would sign off singing: "It is time for us to go, and we want you all to know/ We try our best to please you one and all," followed by the rest of the Man-O-Ree jingle. At that time Charlie was being managed and booked by Charlie Arnett, who later would form a band with his wife Ethel ("Daisy Mae") working on stations in West Virginia and Florida. Arnett acted as the announcer for Charlie Monroe's radio programs in Winston-Salem, introducing Monroe and reading the Man-O-Ree commercials.

Charlie, who was also doing tent shows, had an entourage of performers who traveled with him, including "Jasper, 'The Clown' Tight Wire Walker, who does many seemingly impossible feats on a Tight Wire in Mid-Air" and "'Smokey' Strickland, Magic Escape Artist."[2] Curly remembered Jasper as being quite a showman. "That boy was really good," he marveled. "He could get on there and dance and carry on, and then he'd walk that wire that was across the stage. He did some blackface comedy. He was from over around Mount Airy."

Charlie's tent could seat two thousand people, and he would fill it twice every night. He had a staff of workers who would set up the tent and chairs, and he would leave the tent in place for at least three days before moving it to another location. The tent was transported on a truck that also carried a generator to supply power for lights and sound.

About a month after Curly joined the band, Charlie relocated to WBT in Charlotte. Perhaps this was when the government cracked down on him for marketing medicine illegally, as Tommy Scott maintained. In any case, Curly stated that once they moved to Charlotte, Charlie stopped selling Man-O-Ree and they never sang the jingle again. Charlie also gave up doing the tent shows at that time.

Charlie's move to Charlotte coincided with the purchase of WBT by the Southeastern Broadcasting System, a subsidiary of Jefferson Standard Life Insurance Company, which also owned WBIG in Greensboro. The negotiations resulting in the sale were handled for Jefferson Standard by J. M. Bryan, vice president of the company, and Edney Ridge, manager of WBIG. Ridge, who was also secretary of Southeastern Broadcasting, was awarded a 10 percent ownership interest in the company in recognition of his services during the transaction.[3]

The deal was finalized and ownership was transferred at the end of September. Given Charlie Monroe's tremendous popularity on WBIG, it is possible that Ridge may have recommended him for the newly acquired WBT. The order files of Hatch Show Print reveal that Charlie ordered five hundred posters and five hundred window cards (for advertising show dates) on September 19, to be sent to Charlotte.[4] On Friday, September 28, he began a daily 6:00 A.M. program on WBT.[5]

Although Charlie's show was only fifteen minutes long, it fell right in the middle of the prime time slot commanded by one of WBT's most popular air personalities. Grady Cole, known as "Mr. Dixie," had joined the staff of WBT in 1930. By 1945 he was dominating the airways with a three-hour daily morning news, talk, and variety program. Loyal listeners would set their alarm clocks or even leave their radios on all night in order to wake up with Cole when he signed on at 5:00 A.M.

Charles Crutchfield, who by this time had been promoted to station manager at WBT, attributed Cole's popularity to his friendly personality and sincere delivery. "He talked with people, not at them," said Crutchfield, "and listeners believed in him and what he was selling."[6] Curly remembered

Grady Cole as a zany character who liked to pull pranks. "He was always doing something silly," Curly chuckled. "He would try to break us up while we was singing [on the air]. I remember one time we was in there singing, and he was jumping around and dropped his britches clear to his ankles. There he was in his shorts! Just stuff like that. He was a comical guy."

Their advantageous time slot notwithstanding, when the Kentucky Partners arrived at WBT they were dismayed to find that an obscure union regulation required a waiting period before they would be allowed to play their instruments over the air. There has been speculation that guitarist Arthur Smith, who was on the board of directors of the American Federation of Musicians, called for the enforcement of this regulation in an attempt to keep Monroe from infringing on his territory. Smith and his band, the Crackerjacks, who had moved from WSPA in Spartanburg to WBT in 1943, were emerging as one of the station's most popular acts. "He didn't want Charlie Monroe in there, because it was ruining some of his business," Curly maintained.

Charlie was able to get around the delay of instrument use by calling his group the "Monroe Quartet" during his first month on WBT.[7] Roy "Whitey" Grant, who was a member of the Briarhoppers, was recruited to accompany the quartet on guitar. Curly recalled that "they wouldn't let us take our instruments in, and they made Whitey come in and play the guitar. Well, he couldn't play it like we wanted. Charlie said, 'He just can't pick the guitar to where we can sing.' So then Charlie got it fixed to where he [Charlie] could just come in with his guitar. And we'd sing quartets and duets with just his guitar. And Whitey would still have to come up there and sit in a chair while we did our program every morning. But we finally got to take our instruments in there." By October 30 "Monroe Quartet" had been replaced by "Kentucky Partners" in the WBT radio listings, so presumably that was the date the restriction was lifted.[8]

The Kentucky Partners remained at WBT for the rest of the year. Hatch Show Print files indicate that the last show date for which Charlie ordered window cards was on Saturday, January 12, 1946, at the high school in Galax, Virginia.[9] The last day the Kentucky Partners appeared in the WBT radio listings was January 16. At that point, as had become his habit, Charlie ceased touring for the winter and headed back to his farm at Beaver Dam, Kentucky.

Curly took a job at Air Engineering in Charlotte, where he worked for the next six months. Then, in August 1946, Charlie beckoned again. "I was on a job in Opalaka, Alabama," Curly recalled. "We was putting up humidifiers for this weaving room in a cotton mill, and I was the foreman on that job. That's when Charlie called me and I left for Beaver Dam.

"Charlie would quit when it come wintertime," Curly explained. "Then, when it come summertime he'd start calling and hunting these entertainers. When he'd get ready to start again, he'd get us to come to Beaver Dam, stay there in the hotel, and we'd rehearse for a week before we'd go back on the road. Some of his cousins, I think, ran the café, there in town, and we could go over there when we wanted to eat, and just sign the ticket, and he picked up the tab."

In early September 1946, Charlie took the band to WNOX in Knoxville. This time the Kentucky Partners included Curly on mandolin, Paul Prince on fiddle, Tex Isley on guitar, and Robert "Pickles" Lambert on bass. On Monday, September 30, they went to Atlanta to record four songs for RCA Victor. It was Charlie's first session since May 1939, and his first with the Kentucky Partners. Government restrictions imposed during World War II, along with the recording ban in force during the musicians' union strike in 1944, likely had prevented him from getting into the studio earlier. The songs recorded in this session included "Who's Calling You Sweetheart Tonight," "Rubber Neck Blues," "There's No Depression in Heaven," and "Mother's Not Dead, She's Only Sleeping," the latter two of which featured Curly's tenor harmony.

Charlie listed himself as the writer of "Rubber Neck Blues," but according to Curly, this song, and a number of others that Charlie claimed, were actually written by Arthur Q. Smith. "Charlie bought a lot of them," Curly said. "Over in Kentucky he could get a fifth of whiskey for about six or seven dollars. He'd bring it there to Arthur Q. Smith and give it to him [in exchange for a song.]" Though Charlie also claimed authorship of "Mother's Not Dead," it was actually composed by the Spencer Brothers, who had worked for Charlie in the early 1940s.

The session, which took place in the Piedmont Hotel, was conducted by RCA's Steve Sholes. Curly recalled that the band was in one hotel room and the engineer was in another. The band was instructed, "When the red light comes on, start singing." There were only two microphones, and recording technology at that time did not allow for overdubs, so if anyone made a mistake the band would have to perform the whole song again. Thanks to

Charlie's obsession with rehearsing, however, they breezed through the session in less than two hours—a miraculous feat by today's standards.

Curly still remembered Charlie's words of advice as they were preparing to record: "Curly, we may not be the two best singers on earth, but I'll tell you one thing. If we sing it long enough and loud enough, our way, somebody's going to like it." One song that did require a second take was "Mother's Not Dead, She's Only Sleeping." Charlie "stopped and said I wasn't saying 'sleeping' right," Curly explained. "I'd been saying 'sleepin' all the time. He wanted the 'ing' on it. And so, you listen to that record, and the 'ing' is on it."

These recordings were Charlie's first with a full band. They retained the old-timey feel of his earlier records, but the music was more dynamic and was clearly the work of a polished ensemble. Tex Isley's electric guitar was tastefully understated, overshadowed sometimes by Paul Prince's lilting fiddle and at other times by Curly's bluesy, driving mandolin. Although Curly was playing mostly tremolos and chords, the occasional single-note fills were perfectly placed, and his playing was highly rhythmic throughout. In these, his first recordings ever, Curly was already demonstrating his skill at matching a lead singer note for note, breath for breath, as well as his soaring vocal range and power—talents that would be his trademarks for the rest of his career.

Knoxville was a good market for Charlie, and the band stayed busy during their time at WNOX. According to Hatch Show Print order files, in the months of October and November alone, the Kentucky Partners worked forty-five show dates,[10] *in addition* to their regular Saturday night appearances on the *Tennessee Barn Dance*.

It was at WNOX that fall that Curly first met a young musician from Virginia named Mac Wiseman, who had joined Molly O'Day's band there. Mac recalled seeing Curly there with Charlie but said they didn't get to know each other well at that time. "Charlie was pretty aloof," Mac explained. "He'd do all his rehearsing at his hotel, and come over [to WNOX] just in time to go on the air, and then make the guys leave after, so we didn't get acquainted with his boys very much. He'd bring them home at night and drop them at their house and forbid them to go out anywhere. He was tough."[11]

Not only did Charlie restrict his band members' social lives, but he also had exacting standards when it came to their appearance. Curly had already learned how to dress neatly from his first stint with Charlie. In Knoxville he witnessed Tex Isley being chastised for the appearance of his guitar case. Tex had a case that opened at the back end, rather than on the side, with a clasp that secured it. The clasp was broken and could not be secured properly. "He was walking along, carrying that thing, and the guitar fell out the back," Curly chuckled. "He went down to the station and was talking about it, and Charlie said, 'Let me tell you one thing. You go get you another case. Don't you never come back down here with a case looking like that!' Tex said, 'I can't afford it.' Charlie said, 'Can you afford this job?' So Tex got him a new case."

The Kentucky Partners had not been in Knoxville long when Curly came down with a sore throat and was told his tonsils would have to be removed. He had the surgery and spent a few weeks recovering back in China Grove before he could sing again. He remembered sitting at home, listening to the Kentucky Partners' radio broadcasts over WNOX. Then, within weeks of his return to work, he was stricken with a more serious illness. He was diagnosed with an enlarged heart, and the doctors at Baptist Hospital in Knoxville told him that he wouldn't live to see his next birthday in December. Once he told his mother about the symptoms and the diagnosis, however, she was convinced that he was suffering from pleurisy, a respiratory ailment, rather than a heart condition.

"She said, 'Good Lord, young 'un, they're going to kill you!'" Curly recalled. "I told them I was getting out of there. They said, 'Well, you'll never make it.' So she sent my brothers up there, and they come and got me in the car. When I got down [to China Grove], we went to our family doctor, Dr. Whitaker, and he said, 'I can tell you right quick what's wrong with you. I don't care what kind of medicine you've got, you throw it all away. You're anemic.' And so he put me on Vitamin A, fifty thousand units. I've been taking them every day since then."

Curly spent the winter of 1946–1947 recuperating. It is possible that he was actually suffering from a different kind of heart trouble caused by the dissolution of his marriage two years earlier. Looking back, he referred to this period as a "nervous breakdown," saying, "I couldn't even stand to ride in a car, I was in such shape. I just couldn't make it. I couldn't stand no rackets, I couldn't stand nothing. And I couldn't stay down home, because I had bronchial asthma [there]. So I went to the Empire Hotel in Salisbury and rented a room in the back, and I was in there about four or five months.

I had a friend, E. P. Williams, he would bring me my meals. I'll tell you, it was rough. I just went all to pieces."

For the first month or two, Curly rarely left his hotel room. Once he began to regain his strength, he ventured out to the café across the street for his meals. He and E. P. Williams began doing musical programs in schools around the area. They would perform at as many as four different schools on a given day, collecting nickels and dimes from the students, just as Curly had done several years earlier with Tommy Scott.[12]

While staying at the Empire Hotel, Curly wrote a song titled "I Can't Help but Cry over You." He never recorded it or performed it in public, but he kept it all through the years with his collection of handwritten song lyrics. Though he eventually regained his health, he never forgot that painful period in his personal life. It was the inspiration for several other songs, including "I Miss You So Tonight," written in 2004 for his last recording session, and "That Old Book of Mine," which he first recorded with Flatt and Scruggs.

Since Curly was unable to rejoin the Kentucky Partners in Knoxville that winter, Charlie replaced him, possibly with Lavelle Coy or with Slim Martin, who was listed as the tenor singer on Charlie's next recording session, on March 24, 1947. By that time Ira Louvin had also joined the band on mandolin.[13] Ira had moved to Knoxville from Chattanooga in the summer of 1945, after his brother Charlie's enlistment in the army interrupted their career as a singing duo.[14] Not long after Ira recorded with Charlie Monroe, Charlie Louvin was discharged from the army, and the brothers reunited in Knoxville. Charlie Monroe apparently disbanded his group and returned to Beaver Dam at the end of March; at least, he placed no more window card orders with Hatch Show Print until August.

In the spring of 1947 Mac Wiseman was still in Knoxville working with Molly O'Day. His friend Leslie Keith was playing fiddle with the Stanley Brothers, who were based at WCYB in Bristol, Virginia. Keith contacted Wiseman, saying that WCYB needed another band for its popular *Farm and Fun Time* program and suggested that Wiseman put together a group and audition for the slot.

Station WCYB (10,000 watts at 690 AM) had first signed on the air on December 13, 1946, from its studios on the ground floor of the General Shelby Hotel in downtown Bristol.[15] Curly King and the Tennessee Hilltoppers[16] began a daily late afternoon program on WCYB that day, and they soon joined the cast of *Farm and Fun Time*, which initially ran from 12:30 to 1:30 P.M. Monday through Saturday. By the end of December, Carter and Ralph Stanley and their band, the Clinch Mountain Boys, had joined the cast. The program was designed to appeal to farmers who were on their lunch break. It became one of WCYB's most successful shows, thus prompting the station to seek a third band to participate.

"So I made an audition [disc] with Tex Isley, Ira and Charlie Louvin, and L. E. White on fiddle," Wiseman recalled. "And I thought this was a knockout outfit. I took it up to the program director and he hired us immediately, but on opening day, the only guy that showed up was Tex Isley!"[17] Mac persuaded WCYB to allow him time to regroup, and he immediately contacted Curly Seckler. By this time, Curly had recovered his strength and was ready to hit the road again. He recommended that Mac also recruit fiddler Paul Prince, who was living in southwest Virginia. Mac dubbed his band the Country Boys, and they joined the Stanley Brothers and the Tennessee Hilltoppers on WCYB's *Farm and Fun Time* in late spring.

According to Wiseman, when Charlie Monroe heard that Wiseman was essentially using Charlie's former band members—Tex Isley on guitar and autoharp, Curly Seckler on mandolin, and Paul Prince on fiddle—he was furious, and came to WCYB to try to get them back. Mac recalled, "He walked in there and talked through the studio window, and they just fell apart, because he was so domineering. He went to the station to try to have me thrown off, but the station was loyal to me. They told him I meant as much to their station as he did, so that kind of hurt his feelings and he left."[18]

By the end of June, Mac had become important enough to WCYB that he was given a daily fifteen-minute 6:00 A.M. program of his own, on which he performed solo. After their mid-day performance on *Farm and Fun Time*, the Country Boys would travel up to two hundred miles in Mac's 1939 Studebaker for show dates in Kentucky, Tennessee, Virginia, and North Carolina. They performed at schoolhouses, theaters, grange halls, and courthouses, as well as at a lucrative Saturday night square dance at the Burley Tobacco Warehouse in Abingdon, Virginia.

Jesse McReynolds, who grew up in southwestern Virginia near Coeburn, was working with Roy Sykes and the Blue Ridge Mountain Boys on WFHG in Bristol in 1947. He remembered first having seen Curly perform with the Kentucky Partners when Charlie Monroe brought his tent show to

Coeburn in 1945. Jesse, who often listened to the Country Boys on WCYB, remembered the first time he saw Curly sing with Mac Wiseman. It was at a theater in St. Paul, Virginia. On this particular show, Jesse recalled, "there was just the two of them. Curly played mandolin and Mac played guitar. They had one microphone and one little amplifier for the sound system."[19]

Though Wiseman, Seckler, Isley, and Prince formed the core of the Country Boys, on occasion they were joined by Clarence "Tom" Ashley, who lived nearby in the little town of Shouns. Ashley went by the stage name of "Rastus" and did blackface comedy. Curly's friend E. P. Williams, who had followed Curly from Salisbury to Bristol in the hope of opening a barbecue restaurant, also played with the band for a while. Fiddler Jimmy Vance worked with them sometimes as well. After a few months, Tex Isley left the band, and at Curly's recommendation Mac hired Curly's brother Duard ("Lucky") to replace Tex on guitar.

The Country Boys mostly performed popular songs of the day and gospel quartets. Mac recalled, "I had plenty of old story songs to do, and they seemed to be big favorites, and I did some songs of the day—'A Big Rock in the Road,' a Bob Wills tune, and 'Detour,' which was written by Wesley Tuttle, and 'No Children Allowed.'" Curly would sing tenor harmony and also would contribute a few solos of his own, accompanying himself on guitar. "He had one I remember he featured called 'Moonlight on My Cabin,'" Mac said, "because he beat me to it. It had just come out by Hawkshaw [Hawkins], and he learned it and featured it, so I laid off it."[20] Curly confirmed that he first began performing "Moonlight" while with Mac, and it was so well received that he continued to feature it with every subsequent group. They also featured the song that Curly and Juanita had written in 1943, "Traveling Down This Lonesome Road," which Wiseman later recorded with Bill Monroe. "I started singing it with Mac," Curly said, "and, of course, we put our songs together there, and when Mac got ready to leave he had that song. I didn't have it copyrighted, so him and Bill recorded it."[21]

While working with Wiseman, Curly was once again struck with a serious illness. "We was playing one night on the stage somewhere," Curly recalled, "and I got the awfullest pains in my back. Mac says, 'Well, you'd better go to a doctor in the morning.' So I went to the doctor and he said, 'You've got appendix problems. You're going to have to have [it] took out of there.' And after he got done it looked like he took [it] out with a spoon," he chuckled, referring to the large scar which was still visible on his abdomen.

Under doctor's orders, Curly spent the next two weeks in bed recovering in his room at Lou Smith's boarding house on State Street, just a few blocks from the radio station. A number of the musicians from WCYB lived there, including Ralph and Carter Stanley, fiddlers Ralph Mayo and Chubby Collier, and Curly's brother Lucky. Lou Smith made sure Curly stayed in bed and brought him his meals until he was able to get up.

In Curly's treasure trove of memorabilia is a hand-written get-well poem sent to him at WCYB by an admiring female fan after his appendectomy. Although her spelling and grammar were not the best, she made up for it with sincerity and humor. The poem referenced many of the songs that Curly was singing with the Country Boys, several of which ("Hannah," "Moonlight on My Cabin," "Sign Upon the Dotted Line," and "What's the Matter With You Darling") he would carry with him throughout his career. A note at the top of the page said, "Please give to Curley when able to laugh."

> He is that Curley Scheler Boy,
> From North Carolina's pines
> He's the one that always bring us joy,
> We think his singing fine.
>
> He took that common "Hannah" and
> He made her especially fine
> We shall miss her Curley dear,
> Untill your're back in line
>
> "With Moonlight on My Cabin,"
> That moon no longer shine,
> Because your'er in the hospital,
> I hope you'll soon be fine.
>
> "Like Poor Old Johnny Lawson,"
> I've a notion to run amuck,
> Till those pretty sweet nurses,
> Sends you back with best of luck.
>
> "I'd love to smooth that yellow curl,"
> With a kind and loving hand,
> I'm jealous of your best girl,
> As she loves her ailing man.
>
> "Are We tired of you, My Darling,"
> No never till life is over.

I'd love to smooth your pillows.
And maybe straighten your covers.

"In My Lonely broken heart"
Again for you I pine.
"I want to be Loved, but only by you"
I know that you'll be fine.

"You're my flower,"
I hope you don't droop and fade,
"For I'll be waiting"
In a cabin neath the shade.

"Last night I heard you crying in your sleep,"
For me today sun won't shine,
I hope I'll soon hear you or better
"Sign on the Dotted Line."

"What the Matter With you Darling."
I know that you'll be fine,
"You took My sunshine with you,"
"Give me your love and I'll Give you Mine."

"Oh Why Should I Wonder."
The Lily of the Valley there.
"To Give you a kiss, but only by her lip, Dear,"
And lovingly curl your hair.

I cannot be your sweetheart
I would not be you're wife
"I'll be around if you need me"
All the rest of your natural life.

The 1947 configuration of the Country Boys never recorded, but Mac Wiseman did put out a songbook, which he sold on shows. Curly, Tex Isley, and Paul Prince were not pictured in the songbook but had a photo of the three of them that they were able to sell to make some spending money.

Mac's early morning program ended on September 30, and as the winter approached, bookings became sparse. "Most of our dates were in the mountain area of Kentucky and southwestern Virginia, and I could see the writing on the wall," Mac said. "It was going to dry up. We didn't have any money from the station. They gave us [air] time, and we didn't have any records, so we depended on the airplay to get us known enough to draw a crowd. I stayed until the weather got cold and just forced us out of business."[22]

Mac noted that before he left Bristol, he had a visit from Earl Scruggs. "Earl had come up in the fall and asked for a job, because he and Chubby [Wise] were wanting to leave [Bill] Monroe and come to work for me, which was flattering. But I was getting ready to go back to Virginia, so I just had to be honest with him. I couldn't offer him a job, so he went back to work with Monroe, and then in the spring, when Lester [Flatt] decided to leave, too, that's when they pulled out."[23]

Curly recalled that Wiseman left Bristol rather abruptly in mid-December. "Mac just up and left, and we didn't know what was going on," he maintained. "All at once he just vanished." According to Mac, he went back home to Waynesboro for the winter, although Jesse McReynolds remembered that by early 1948 Mac was trying to organize a band again. "Mac did come down and meet with Jim and me and tried to get us to work with him," Jesse said, but "it never did work out. I think he was just trying to get something together and wasn't sure where he was going."[24]

Following Mac's precipitous departure, Curly and Lucky decided to regroup and continue using Country Boys as their band name. They recruited guitarist and lead vocalist Bob Oaks from Newland, North Carolina, and fiddler Ralph Mayo, who had been working with Curly King. Ralph was also living in Lou Smith's boarding house, and Curly was rudely awakened early one morning when Ralph and Lucky came in from a night of duck hunting. "They'd been out drinking," he chuckled, "and they come in with some ducks, flapping me in the head with them. Said, 'You ever eat any duck?' They got Lou Smith to cook them ducks. Seems like the meat was pretty good."

Curly called his old friend Cas Walker in Knoxville, and by early 1948 the Country Boys had a slot on Walker's program on WROL, which paid them a regular salary. While in Knoxville, the band worked mostly schoolhouses in the evenings, although Curly did recall once playing a nightclub called Dead Horse Lake. Once was enough. "I didn't like the thoughts of working clubs," he said, "because they's always getting drunk and this and that. We got up there and got to picking, and some of them got into a fight and got to throwing beer bottles, and Lucky got down behind the bass. They wanted us to play it every week, but when they got to throwing beer bottles, that was enough. We never did go back."

In March 1948, while they were based at WROL, Curly received a telegram from Bill Monroe. Lester Flatt had left the Blue Grass Boys and Bill wanted Curly to come to Nashville for an audition. Curly had no interest in being a lead singer, nor in working for Bill Monroe, so he never responded. The Country Boys remained in Knoxville until that summer, when Cas Walker replaced them with the Bailey Brothers, who had worked repeatedly for Walker during the forties. "They come back to work for Cas, and then Cas let us go," Curly explained, "which I didn't blame him, because the Baileys made Cas Walker, just about."

Bereft of a home on radio, Curly and Lucky decided they would buy a vehicle and go out on tour. In an interview he gave in the 1970s, Ralph Mayo remembered that Curly had talked about how Tommy Scott was constantly touring and that the Country Boys should follow his example.[25] Curly and Lucky went to an auto dealer on the Clinton Highway and paid $1,000 down on a four-seat Packard limousine. Then the Country Boys took off for points west. No one in the band had any management experience, however, and their big dreams were soon dashed. Mayo recalled, "That was a wild trip. We'd play one town one night, and then go on to the next town and book it and ballyhoo it and play it. That just didn't work."[26]

On Thursday, July 15, the Country Boys played at a campaign rally in Selmer, Tennessee, for Estes Kefauver, who was running for the United States Senate. (He won the election.) "He was barnstorming the state," Mayo said. "If we'd have stuck with Kefauver, we'd have had it made. I know he paid us well; more than we'd been making playing these courthouses."[27]

Those courthouse shows were always a gamble. The band would rent the building, drive around town ballyhooing (advertising the show), and sell the tickets. They often had to pay a custodian to open the building and clean up afterwards. They were lucky to break even. Of the tour Curly said, "We didn't do no good. We played quite a few places, but we never did get nobody [to come]. We just took a wild tour and thought we could do something, but it failed. I remember one time we was in Memphis, and we hadn't eat—we'd been eating out of cornfields, to tell you the truth. We was parked at a place there overnight, and everyone had a seat to sleep in. There was a bakery just a short ways from where we were parked, and the aroma was blowing this-a-way. Somebody said something about moving the bus, and Lucky said, 'Over my dead body!' He was smelling that bakery."

The tour wound up in Corinth, Mississippi, where the Country Boys were booked at the courthouse and the only person who showed up for the concert was the janitor. Curly recalled that they had to pawn the bass fiddle and a valuable Parker pen set in order to buy gas to get home to

Knoxville. Once they made it back, Bob Oaks returned to North Carolina and became a preacher. Ralph Mayo joined the Bailey Brothers at WROL. Curly and Lucky ended up back at Lou Smith's boarding house in Bristol, hoping to find work.

As fate would have it, soon after they arrived Curly received a call from Charlie Monroe, who was ready to regroup. "He called me from [Beaver Dam], and wanted to know if I would go back to work with him," Curly said. "Then he said, 'I don't have no bus. Do you know where I could get one?' Well, that hit my hole card. I said, 'Well, I've got one here that we ain't going to be able to pay off.' He said, 'All right, me and Betty'll be up there in the morning to see it.' So he bought the bus. Me and Lucky had paid a thousand on it to start with, and he said he would pay us back. Then I went to work with Charlie again." Curly recalled that Charlie went to the auto dealership in Knoxville and paid the balance of what was owed on the Packard with a one-thousand-dollar bill. Having had his fill of the musician's life, Lucky decided to return home to North Carolina and got a job in a restaurant in Charlotte.

The job with Monroe was a godsend in a number of ways. It relieved Curly of the responsibilities of paying off the Packard and supporting a band of his own, and it gave him the security of a regular paycheck when he needed it most. Back home in China Grove, his sons Ray and Monnie were growing older. Curly's nomadic life as a musician made it impossible for him to keep them with him, and it was becoming clear that his extended family would not have the resources to continue to care for them. Carrie Sechler had her hands full with maintaining the farm. Mary's husband Walter needed special care, having returned from World War II with malaria and probably with what is now known as post-traumatic stress disorder. The decision was made to enroll Ray and Monnie in an orphanage in nearby Rockwell, North Carolina.

Alhough its mission has changed dramatically in recent years, during the time that the Sechler boys were there, this particular children's home was operated as a traditional orphanage, housing disadvantaged or orphaned children until they finished school or reached adulthood. Ray and Monnie lived upstairs in a big rock building that served as the boys' dormitory. The home's facilities included a dining hall, a playground, a swimming pool, and a three-hundred-acre working farm. Children were taken by bus to local schools and to occasional recreational outings sponsored by charitable organizations. They wore clothes that were donated by various church organizations.

Mary explained that Ray went first because children had to be of school age in order to be enrolled. "Ray begged me to take him, and not put him in no home," she recalled. "Walter was sick at the time, and I said, 'Ray, I just can't do it.' I said, 'They'll be good to you down there if you be good.' And so he went, and we kept Monnie until he was old enough to go."[28]

Ray Seckler still remembered the day he arrived there. "When I was six years old, they took me to the orphanage. I didn't realize what they were doing. They enticed me by the playground there. I thought, 'This is going to be neat. I'm going to get to play on this playground all day, and nothing else to worry about.' I thought I was in heaven, until I looked up and they were gone. The next day it was raining. They had me out there pulling Johnson grass!"[29]

Although he laughed when he thought back on his days at the orphanage, Ray's recollections paint a distressing picture.

> Our day started at 4:30 in the morning. [They] had corn and vegetable fields, and we had to hoe [them]. If you missed and chopped up a plant, that old man [might] just knock you in the head with that hoe handle. He broke a handle over one boy's back. We marched from one building to the next, when we went to eat, just like in the military. And after every meal they'd dump the slop in this big old barrel, and I'd have to roll that thing down a hill [to the hog pen]. The hogs would be jumping and hollering and carrying on, and they scared the crap out of me! We used to kill our own hogs, too, in the slaughterhouse. They'd shoot them in the head first, and then they'd cut their throat and let them bleed to death. I mean, here we was, seven, eight years old. We didn't need to be seeing some of that stuff. But we done it all.[30]

Ray recalled being attacked by one of his grandmother's roosters when he was only four or five years old, and how that experience came back to haunt him at the children's home. "[Roosters] will flap them wings and they'll jump on you and try to peck you. It scared me to death. So when I got in that orphanage, the first job that I had was feeding the chickens and gathering the eggs. If an old hen would try to peck at me when I'd reach to get them eggs, I'd just let it go. The egg production got to going down, and the superintendent went behind me one day, and he gathered dozens of eggs. He said, 'Now, everybody's going swimming tonight except Ray. Ray's got to sit on the side and watch, while he holds a rooster.' Well, I about had a heart attack. So they made me sit and hold that rooster while everybody else swam and had a good time."[31]

Ray always looked forward to the Sunday afternoon visits from his grandmother, who would come whenever she could get someone to drive her there. At Christmas, the boys would get to spend a week with her at home on the farm. Visits from Curly, who was continually on the road, were few and far between. Ray suffered through humiliation and loneliness during his eight years in the orphanage, but he later understood that his father was doing the best he could under the circumstances. As a child, Ray seemed to have vacillated between feeling abandoned and viewing his father as an elusive and mysterious hero figure. "I had a picture of him in his big hat sitting on my dresser," he said. "Grandmother helped more than anything. We'd go to her house, and he'd be on the radio, and she'd say, 'Come here, boys. I want y'all to hear this. Can y'all hear him talking to you?' He was just singing, but she would try to build us up."[32]

At the time Ray Seckler entered the orphanage, Curly was without a car and thus unable to visit, having just sold his Packard to Charlie Monroe. Curly's recollection was that Monroe went to work immediately at WCYB, but the Hatch Show Print order files indicate that the Kentucky Partners spent several weeks at WNOX in Knoxville before arriving in Bristol.[33] This information is supported by a newspaper article from September 27, 1948, which likely would not have pleased Charlie with its multiple references to his brother:

> Charlie Monroe, brother of the famous Bill Monroe, became so popular he organized his own string band and has already reached the top in his particular field of the entertainment world. He now threatens to even surpass his brother. . . . Charlie was associated with Bill Monroe and his Bluegrass Boys for more than seven years before forming his own band. He has been heard many times on the *Grand Ole Opry* at Nashville, Tennessee, and is currently heard over Station WNOX, Knoxville.[34]

According to Hatch order files, Charlie arrived at WCYB in early October.[35] By this time the Stanley Brothers had relocated to WPTF in Raleigh, so there was an open slot on *Farm and Fun Time*. An ad for a show date in Rogersville, Tennessee on October 11 indicated that the Kentucky Partners included "Jimmy Martin [Slim Martin], Curly Sechler, Little Wilma, Buddy

Osborne, Murphy Slim and Others."[36] Also based at WCYB at that time was a hot new band called the Foggy Mountain Boys, which included Lester Flatt, Earl Scruggs, Mac Wiseman, Jim Shumate, and Howard Watts. They had arrived in Bristol in May and were already making their mark.

Lester Flatt was born in 1914 in Overton County, Tennessee, the seventh of nine children born to Isaac and Nancy Flatt. As a youngster he took up the guitar and began singing at home and at social gatherings. In 1931 he married Gladys Stacy, and the two of them worked in the Sparta Silk Mill. In 1935 they moved to Covington, Virginia, to work in a textile mill. Gladys was also a proficient singer and guitarist, and they sometimes performed together in the area. While they were in Covington, Lester suffered a debilitating bout of rheumatoid arthritis that left him emaciated and nearly paralyzed, until he found an herbal medicine that helped him regain his health.

Lester's first professional job in music came in 1939, when he joined Charlie Scott's Harmonizers, appearing on WDBJ radio in Roanoke. Then Lester and Gladys moved to Burlington, North Carolina, in 1941 to work at Burlington Industries, and Lester teamed with Clyde Moody to perform on WBBB. In 1943 the Flatts both signed on with Charlie Monroe's Kentucky Partners. Lester sang tenor and played mandolin, and Gladys, who went by the stage name Bobbie Jean, sang and played guitar. By this time, Charlie Monroe was well established in North Carolina via his Man-O-Ree Radio Network. He was touring constantly, often selling out several tent shows each day. Lester and Gladys grew tired of the grueling schedule, and in the latter part of 1944 they left the band.

Soon afterward, Lester received an offer to play guitar with Bill Monroe's Blue Grass Boys. It is unclear exactly when Flatt joined the band. In several different interviews Flatt stated that he joined Bill Monroe's band in 1944. This is repeated in biographies of Flatt and also in a Flatt and Scruggs songbook from 1948. However Flatt was not present on Monroe's February 13, 1945 Columbia recording session,[37] so it is possible that he joined soon after those recordings were made.

For that session Monroe's band included guitarist Tex Willis, banjo player David "Stringbean" Akeman, fiddler Robert "Chubby" Wise, Wilene "Sally Ann" Forrester on accordion, and Howard Watts ("Cedric Rainwater") on bass. A few weeks after that session, Watts went on leave from the band to spend time with his family in Florida after the death of his father. Willis and Wise went along, leaving several vacant positions in the Blue Grass Boys.

Lester Flatt replaced Willis, and Andy Boyette replaced Watts, playing bass and performing comedy.[38] Soon afterward, twenty-three-year-old fiddler Jim Shumate, from Hickory, North Carolina, joined the band. While driving through North Carolina, Monroe had heard Shumate playing onWHKY in Hickory with Don Walker and the Blue Ridge Boys. Monroe had been impressed with Shumate's fiddling and, when Wise left the Blue Grass Boys, Monroe had given Shumate a call.

Shumate joined the band in March and stayed until the end of November, when Howard "Howdy" Forrester returned home from serving in the navy during World War II. Forrester had been the Blue Grass Boys' fiddler in 1943 before his induction, and the law required employers to allow a returning veteran to reclaim the job he'd had prior to joining the war effort. While Jim Shumate was still in the band, he had arranged an audition for a young banjo player from North Carolina named Earl Scruggs.

Scruggs was born in 1924 in Cleveland County, North Carolina, near the town of Shelby. Almost everyone in his family played a musical instrument, and by the time he was four Earl was learning to play banjo, guitar, and fiddle. He entered and won second or third place in his first banjo contest at age six, and not long after that he began playing with his brothers on WSPA in Spartanburg, South Carolina. Earl first learned to pick the banjo in the two-finger style (thumb and index finger) common at that time, but at age ten he discovered a three-finger style, which opened up a new musical world for him.

When he was fifteen Earl played with a group called the Carolina Wildcats on a radio station in Gastonia. He also worked with the Morris Brothers onWSPA in Spartanburg. About this time (1939–1940) Earl first met Jim Shumate in Hickory. Shumate was a regular on a Saturday night barn dance program called the *Carolina Jamboree*, broadcast over WHKY, and he often had guests perform on his portion of the show. Shumate recalled, "One night Earl and a fellow by the name of Grady Wilkie come by there, and I let them pick a little bit to see what they could do. I realized [Earl] was an awful good banjo picker, so I gave him a spot on the show, and I took some notes, to see, maybe, I might want to use him again sometime."[39]

During the summer of 1945 Bill Monroe hired entertainer Lew Childre to work the tent show circuit with the Blue Grass Boys. Toward the end of the season Stringbean and Childre had become fishing friends, and they decided to form a partnership. Stringbean turned in his notice, and Monroe asked

Shumate if he knew of a good banjo player to replace him. "Yeah, I know where the best one in the country is," Shumate told him. He then called Earl's home and was told that Earl was touring with Lost John Miller, who was based in Knoxville. Shumate discovered that Lost John had an early morning program scheduled the next day on WSM, so he set his alarm for 5:00 A.M. and went to the radio station to find Earl. He brought Earl back to his hotel room and Monroe joined them there for an impromptu audition, after which Monroe offered Earl the job.[40]

Earl remembered things a bit differently. According to his book *Earl Scruggs and the 5-String Banjo*, "Jim asked me several times to audition for Bill's band. I always told him I was happy working with Lost John and I didn't want to leave his band. On December 1, 1945, John told the band he was going to quit working the road full time . . . so I called Jim and told him I would like to try out for Bill's group. Jim arranged for an audition, and Bill hired me at a salary of sixty dollars a week."[41]

Scruggs made his *Grand Ole Opry* debut with the Blue Grass Boys on Saturday, December 8, 1945, to a thunderous ovation. By then, Shumate had returned home to Hickory to work in the furniture business, but he made a point of listening to the show, and attested that "when Earl hit the stage, he really tore that place up."[42]

Earl Scruggs was not the inventor of the three-finger style of banjo playing, but he was the first to bring it to the national spotlight and is considered to be its definitive proponent. Earl's playing revolutionized Bill Monroe's music, and the configuration of the Blue Grass Boys that recorded on Monroe's next Columbia session in September 1946—Bill Monroe, Lester Flatt, Earl Scruggs, Chubby Wise, and Howard Watts—is considered to have been the "original bluegrass band." This group remained intact for the next year and a half, recording such Monroe classics as "Blue Moon of Kentucky," "Little Cabin Home on the Hill," "Molly and Tenbrooks," and "Blue Grass Breakdown." They kept a full touring schedule, which often meant sleeping in the car while traveling from one show to another, with very few days off. Lester did most of the emcee work on stage and contributed a number of original songs to the group's repertoire. Earl, who was the only band member with a high school education, was in charge of the money.

By the end of 1947, Flatt and Scruggs had become seasoned professionals and were weary of their roles as sidemen under the domineering Monroe. There have been varying accounts of their departure from the Blue Grass

Boys, but according to Scruggs, he was burned out and ready to move back to North Carolina. In February 1948 he gave Monroe his two weeks' notice. At the end of those two weeks, Monroe asked him to stay another two weeks, and he did. As Earl was leaving the band, presumably in early March, Lester confided that he, too, was preparing to give notice. A few days after Earl arrived home in North Carolina, Lester called and proposed that they form a band together.[43]

In an autobiographical booklet published in the late 1970s, banjo player Don Reno recalled hearing Monroe perform without Scruggs on the *Opry* over WSM on the first weekend in March 1948. Monroe had offered Reno a job in late 1943, but Reno was joining the army and declined the offer, so Monroe had hired Stringbean. Then Scruggs had joined the band while Reno was still stationed overseas. After being discharged, Reno was working at WSPA in Spartanburg. When he realized that Scruggs had left Monroe, he immediately drove to Nashville, only to discover that Monroe was on tour in North Carolina and would be playing in Taylorsville on Tuesday, March 9.[44] He drove to Taylorsville, and Monroe hired him immediately. Reno said that Lester Flatt was still in the band at that time and that he stayed on for "three or four weeks," although it most likely was closer to two weeks.[45]

Howard Watts had also departed from the Blue Grass Boys by the time Reno joined the band. In a 1978 interview, Flatt told writer Don Rhodes, "Before my notice was up, Cedric Rainwater turned in his notice with Monroe and proposed that Scruggs and I start our own group."[46] According to Flatt's biographer, Jake Lambert, Flatt and Scruggs had held several meetings in late December to discuss striking out on their own, and Watts had been present at some of them.[47]

On February 27, 1948, the Blue Grass Boys played at the Armory in Danville, Virginia.[48] At that time, Flatt apparently approached singer and guitarist Jim Eanes, who lived in nearby Martinsville, about the possibility of working together in a band.[49] A few weeks later, Eanes recalled, "Lester and Earl and Cedric . . . called me from Shelby, North Carolina, and I went and picked them up. We all came back to Martinsville and decided to start a program in Danville on WDVA. This was the original Foggy Mountain Boys. About two weeks later Bill (Monroe) sent me a telegram and I went to work with him."[50]

When Eanes left, Flatt, Scruggs, and Watts decided to go to Hickory, North Carolina, and recruit fiddler Jim Shumate to join the new band.

According to Shumate, they just showed up at his house one day. "They said they'd pulled out from Bill and were organizing their own show and were going to call it the Foggy Mountain Boys. They said they were going to use 'Foggy Mountain Top' as the theme song and they needed me to play fiddle."[51] By this time Shumate had four young daughters, and he initially was reluctant to join the band because going on the road would mean giving up his secure job in a furniture store. But he agreed to give it a try.

Since Shumate was already an established performer at WHKY radio, the band was able to start its own daily program almost immediately, on Thursday, April 1, from 1:15 to 1:30 P.M.[52] On Saturday, April 3, they also took over Shumate's spot on the station's weekly barn dance, which was held at the Hickory Opera House. The *Blue Ridge Jamboree*, sponsored by Longview Flour and Feed Mill, was broadcast live from 8:00 to 9:30 P.M., and its cast included Jean and Glenn—Radio Sweethearts, Doyle Fox and his Talking Guitar, and Toots Crisp.[53]

Once the Foggy Mountain Boys were established on WHKY, they got in touch with Mac Wiseman. Lester and Earl had heard Mac's early morning program over WCYB when they were traveling in the area with Bill Monroe. Monroe liked Mac's singing and always wanted to be awakened if his program was on when they passed through. Earl had met with Mac in the fall of 1947 when he was thinking of leaving Monroe's band. Mac was at home in Virginia when they called, but he was contemplating heading to Bristol to form a new band, so he readily agreed to join the Foggy Mountain Boys.[54]

It is unclear whether Flatt and Scruggs recruited Wiseman specifically because of his ties to Bristol, but within a couple of weeks of his joining the band they auditioned and were hired at WCYB. According to Earl, Hickory was not a particularly good market. He recalled the band playing at a small theater there—possibly the Rivoli, where they played on Tuesday, April 13[55]—at a percentage date: "After advertising expenses were taken out of the gate receipts, our grand total profit for the night was seventeen cents each."[56]

"We weren't doing a bit of good in Hickory," Wiseman confirmed. "The station was too small. By this time, Jim felt like we did have a good unit together, enough that he decided he would quit [his furniture job] and join us. So I suggested we go to Bristol, and took them over there for the audition, because I knew the territory. I did all the booking the whole time we were there."[57]

The band's last program on WHKY was on Thursday, April 29.[58] According to Shumate, "We went from there to WCYB in Bristol, and there we set the woods on fire. We had no trouble at all getting work. We played everywhere—at schoolhouses, ball parks, auditoriums, and airports."[59] Shumate proudly recalled winning a fiddle contest in Richlands, Virginia, that was attended by twelve thousand people that summer.

Jesse McReynolds, who was working at WFHG in Bristol, remembered hearing the Foggy Mountain Boys play their first program at WCYB. "I'll tell you, they had a knocked out band," he attested. "I was right there across the street when they was doing their audition at WCYB. And Pee Wee Lambert [who was playing with the Stanley Brothers], he walked out on the street and started talking to me. He said, 'You reckon they'll get on?' And they did get on, and that changed a lot of things around there. After they was on about a week, things started moving for them. They'd go out and do two or three shows a night."[60]

The Foggy Mountain Boys signed a recording contract with Mercury Records, and in the fall of 1948 they cut four songs: "God Loves His Children," "I'm Going to Make Heaven My Home," "We'll Meet Again, Sweetheart," and "My Cabin in Caroline." These recordings show that Flatt and Scruggs were already carving out a distinctive sound for themselves and distancing themselves from Bill Monroe. The mandolin is conspicuously absent, and Wiseman's tenor vocals do not have the "high lonesome" edge of Monroe's. Earl's finger-style lead guitar is prominent in the two gospel numbers, while the secular tracks are punctuated by Wiseman's guitar runs on the lower strings, giving the music a more mellow feel than Monroe's.

Flatt and Scruggs made a point of recording their own original material in this first session. Wiseman noted that "Lester was writing, any minute he was free, the new songs that we would do that wouldn't be like Monroe's." Yet the band did continue to perform some of the Blue Grass Boys' material on show dates, with Howard Watts singing the tenor parts. According to Wiseman, "Cedric sang those because he already knew them, and I just didn't bother to learn them."[61]

The Foggy Mountain Boys' first songbook, printed about the time they moved to Bristol, confirms that they were performing the Flatt-Monroe favorites "Sweetheart, You Done Me Wrong," "Little Cabin Home on the Hill," and "Will You Be Loving Another Man?" They had also introduced originals by Howard Watts ("Remember the Cross," "Church Upon the Hill of Clay") and Lester Flatt ("We'll Meet Again, Sweetheart," "Brother, I'm Getting Ready to Go," "I'll Never Shed Another Tear"). They rounded out their repertoire with material by other writers of the day, including Jimmie Davis, Ervin Rouse, and Carl Story.

Their second songbook, published in the fall of 1948, contained only one Flatt-Monroe original: "When You're Lonely." It included the newly recorded "My Cabin in Caroline," which was called "Cabin in Carolina" in the songbook—likely an indication that it was recently written. Several other unrecorded Flatt and Scruggs originals appeared, including "Darling, Is It Too Late Now?," "So Happy I'll Be," and "Why Did You Wander?," suggesting that the band was not yet well enough known to be concerned about other musicians' stealing their new material.

Wiseman described the way the live shows went: "We'd all go out together on stage and do a couple of fast tunes. Then Lester and Cedric would leave and Cedric would change into his comedy clothes. Shumate and Earl and I would do about fifteen, maybe twenty minutes, just me singing. I was what they call today an 'opening act.' And then they'd come back and we all stayed out there for the rest of the show."[62]

He and Lester would take turns driving the band to show dates, Mac in his 1939 Studebaker and Lester in a 1939 woody station wagon. "I'd drive one week and he'd drive the next," Mac chuckled. "Well, he was always joking about my car. I'd have it lined up, and hit a little pothole, and the wheel would squat out. So it was a running joke. The lights on it weren't very bright, so Scruggs said, 'Want me to get a lantern to hold out there, so you can see where you're going?' And so one week I was driving, and Flatt's station wagon was sitting up in the yard. He had the windows raised up, and we had a lot of rain and then hot summer days. It had a canvas-top roof on it, and those wood slats, you know. We got in Lester's car the next week and I was in the back seat and happened to look up. Mushrooms were growing in one of those slats! Well, boys, if I didn't hush his mouth! Anytime he'd criticize my car I said, 'Well, it ain't got no mushrooms in it!'"[63]

It was probably about this time that Curly Seckler first met Flatt and Scruggs. In August 1948, after he and Lucky had returned from their ill-fated tour, the Foggy Mountain Boys were booked at a schoolhouse in southwest Virginia. Curly and Lucky decided to attend the show. "We drove that big Packard down there," he laughed, "and not a cracker in it! And Lester was driving a Mercury Ford. I went down there and was talking to him, and we caught their show." Curly may have been trying to impress Lester and Earl, but the impression he made was not what he had intended. Years later, Earl told him that, on the ride back to Bristol after the show, Lester had remarked, "If there's ever been a smart aleck on this earth, he [Curly] is number one!"

Once Curly was working with Charlie Monroe at WCYB on *Farm and Fun Time*, Lester and Earl became aware of his vocal abilities. They still didn't fraternize, however, because Charlie didn't allow his band members to speak to other musicians. "Lester and Earl would do their program in Bristol," Curly said, "then we'd go right in. Soon as they'd come off the air, [Charlie would say], 'No one speaks to them!'" Apparently Lester took Charlie's bravado seriously. He told Curly confidentially that he was carrying a small gun in his pocket and said, "If that big scrapper jumps on me, I'm going to shoot him!" Luckily it never came to that, but Curly said, "I wouldn't have blamed him. As far as fighting Charlie Monroe, Good Lord, Charlie could pick [Lester] up and throw him across the hotel!"

The Kentucky Partners stayed busy that fall, working theaters, parks, courthouses, and schools in Virginia, West Virginia, Kentucky, Tennessee, and North Carolina. They worked forty-five dates between October 1 and December 4.[64] Then, as was his custom, Charlie disbanded them and returned to Beaver Dam for the winter, leaving Curly to search for a new job.

According to Jesse McReynolds, a number of musicians were looking for work in the Bristol area at that time. Jesse and his brother Jim met with Curly and Roy Sykes, and perhaps one or two others, to discuss the possibility of forming a band. "They was trying to figure out what to name the band," Jesse recalled. "Curly said, 'Well, as much publicity as I've had on the radio, with Charlie Monroe and everybody, we [could] just call it the Curly Seckler Radio Show,' or something like that. I don't think Roy liked that too well. Anyway, it never did develop."[65] What did develop, however, was a friendship between Curly and the McReynolds brothers that brought them together several times during their musical careers.

Curly's next offer of work came from Hoke Jenkins, who fronted a band called the Smoky Mountaineers, at WGAC in Augusta, Georgia. Jenkins, who grew up in Harris, North Carolina, and was the nephew of banjo player Snuffy Jenkins, had played banjo in various bands before being drafted into the army in 1941. Upon his discharge in 1945 he joined Carl Story and his Rambling Mountaineers at WNOX. About a year later, Hoke formed the Smoky Mountaineers and moved to WWNC in Asheville, North Carolina. Band members initially included Jack and Curly Shelton, Skeets Williamson (brother of Molly O'Day), and Carl Smith, all of whom had been working at WNOX. After a couple of years in Asheville, Jenkins and Smith moved to WGAC in Augusta in 1948. Wiley Morris joined them there, and for a short time the Murphy brothers—Dewey, Fred, and John—were in the band. Later in the year, Carl Smith moved back to WNOX before joining the *Grand Ole Opry* in Nashville in 1950, and the Murphy brothers returned home to North Carolina. Once they left, Hoke called Curly about joining the group. He agreed to come if he could bring Jim and Jesse McReynolds along.[66]

After making a special trip to Bristol to check out the McReynolds brothers, Hoke agreed, so Curly, Jim, and Jesse rode together to Augusta in December 1948 or January 1949. As Jesse remembered it, the three of them rented one large room in an old rooming house near the radio station. At age twenty-nine, with a decade of professional experience under his belt, Curly served as a mentor for the young brothers (Jim was twenty-one and Jesse nineteen), who had never been that far from home before. "Of course, [the other band members] all dressed up, wore white shirts and ties," Jesse recalled. "Me and Jim had never wore a necktie before, so Curly went and got us both a necktie and put these ties on us, and showed us how to tie it and everything. I'm always reminded that he was the first to put a necktie on us!" he laughed.[67]

The Smoky Mountaineers had a daily noontime show on WGAC and played evening shows around Georgia and South Carolina. Curly recalled that everyone in the Smoky Mountaineers received an equal cut of the earnings, even though Hoke was the bandleader. On February 4, 1949, they played at the Estill Theatre in Estill, South Carolina, about seventy-five miles from Augusta. The show poster gave an indication of the various band members' roles:

HOKE JENKINS and his SMOKY MOUNTAINEERS
Direct from WGAC Augusta, Ga
Featuring

Wiley Morris	Radios Finest Soloist
Reynolds Bros.	South's Best Duet
Curley Sechler	radio's gift to women
Sleepy Brainstorm	Goes Political

Mountaineers Quartette
A Clean Show for the Whole Family Starting at 8 P.M.
Admission 25c & 50c Tax Included

Curly recalled that "Sleepy Brainstorm" was a character played by Hoke, who had a pair of large, floppy clown shoes that he would don for his comedic routines. At that time, comedy was still an important part of hillbilly entertainment, and Jim McReynolds remembered that "Hoke was always doing comedy. To really entertain an audience, you make 'em feel sad one minute and then . . . you get 'em hollerin' and laughin' with you and that sort of rounds out the show."[68] One of the skits that the Smoky Mountaineers used prior to Curly's tenure involved Wiley Morris's chasing one of the other band members, dubbed "Highpockets," around the auditorium and hitting him on the head with a guitar. Apparently Morris was prone to using his guitar as a weapon. "We'd go in them schoolhouses, and it'd be warm in there, and these old wasps would get to flying around," Curly chuckled. "He'd take his old Gibson guitar and hit at the wasps."

Curly enjoyed his time with the Smoky Mountaineers, but he was not particularly fond of the climate in Augusta. As the weather grew warmer, his asthma threatened to return. In mid-March, he received a phone call that would provide him with an escape from his breathing problems. It was also to change his life in ways he never could have anticipated.

CHAPTER 4

Creating the Foggy Mountain Sound

1949–1952

By the late 1940s radio had become an established medium. Most large towns had at least one station. Television was in its infancy and most households did not yet have a set, so radio was still the standard delivery system for instant news and entertainment, especially in rural areas. Radio was the primary way for hillbilly bands to connect to their audience. Although most stations did not compensate musicians for their on-air performances, the entertainers were able to use the airwaves to promote their show dates and to sell songbooks, photos, and other items. Bands relied heavily on letters from radio listeners as a gauge of their popularity, and the stations took note of which groups were drawing the most mail.

Because they were doing live daily radio programs, the bands could only travel a limited distance for show dates and still get to the station in time for their program the next morning. This meant playing many of the same towns and venues on a regular basis, and eventually the band would become overexposed and attendance would diminish. This was called "playing out" an area. Once a band had played out an area, it would be time to move on to a radio station in another area where the band could find new fans. Musicians would keep tabs on where other bands were based and, when one band left a radio station, another would see an opening to move in. Likewise, bandleaders kept track of where various sidemen were, so that they could find a replacement quickly if a band member left.

Despite his first impression of Curly Seckler as a smart aleck, Lester Flatt had taken note when he heard Curly singing with Charlie Monroe at WCYB. When the Foggy Mountain Boys needed a new tenor singer in March 1949, Flatt tracked Curly down in Augusta and offered him the job. Given the opportunity to join an increasingly successful young band and earn $50 per week (good money in those days), Curly readily accepted, gave notice to Hoke Jenkins, and caught a bus to Bristol.

The Foggy Mountain Boys had been in Bristol for almost a year at that point. The group had made a name for itself on *Farm and Fun Time*, but they had played out the area, and the local economy was suffering because of a coal miners' strike. Mac Wiseman had stayed with the band until Christmas, but when the weather turned he was ready to move on. He went home briefly and then went to WSB in Atlanta to perform with Bill Carlisle. Soon afterward, Jim Shumate decided he had had enough of life on the road and returned to his furniture job in Hickory. His replacement was fiddler Art Wooten from Sparta, North Carolina. Art had worked previously with Bill Monroe and with the Stanley Brothers.

Although the Foggy Mountain Boys had begun as an equal partnership, Flatt and Scruggs had established themselves as the band's leaders. As the original partners dropped out, beginning with Mac Wiseman and Jim Shumate, their replacements were hired as salaried employees. It is unclear why Flatt and Scruggs waited until March to find a replacement for Wiseman. Perhaps it was simply a matter of economics: they could not afford to support an additional musician during the lean winter months. Perhaps Curly Seckler was hired in response to Mercury Records's desire for the band to record again. Transcriptions from a Flatt and Scruggs appearance on *Farm and Fun Time* after Wiseman's departure indicate that Howard Watts was singing the tenor harmony. He had an extensive vocal range and was able to handle any part, but Watts could never match the power and edge of Curly's natural tenor voice. Curly did remember that, nonetheless, on some of the first programs he played with the band, they performed the song "Summertime Is Past and Gone" with Watts singing the tenor part and Curly singing bass.

When Curly joined the band, he discovered that Lester Flatt expected him to step into the role that Mac Wiseman had vacated, that of assistant master of ceremonies for the band's stage shows. It was a baptism by fire, but he quickly adapted, and the experience would serve him well over the years. "I'd never did no commercial emcee work until I went to work with Lester," Curly said. "And the first night I went to work with them, we got halfway through the show and he walked off. He said, 'Seck, take over.' And he did that from then on. He'd walk off the stage and I did half of the show. And that's how I learned, was with Lester, because to me he was one of the greater emcees that's ever been in bluegrass music." Another thing Curly discovered was that the band members kept their instruments tuned a half step higher than standard tuning. As Curly understood it, this was because Earl felt that it made his banjo sound better.

Within days of Curly's arrival in Bristol, the Foggy Mountain Boys pulled up stakes and moved to WROL in Knoxville. Curly did not own a car, so he rode along with Earl and Louise Scruggs in Earl's 1941 Buick. Louise, who was pregnant at the time, would give birth to their first son, Gary, on May 18.

While it was not as powerful and influential as WNOX, WROL was still an important station for hillbilly musicians. Its power had increased to 5,000 watts in 1947. It was an NBC affiliate, and it carried the *Grand Ole Opry* on Saturday nights. Cas Walker continued to sponsor his early morning music programs. In the spring of 1949, WROL began broadcasting a daily 8:15 to 10:00 A.M. musical variety show called *Country Playhouse*, hosted by Archie Campbell, whose radio name was "Grandpappy."

It seems likely that Mercury Records A&R man Murray Nash was responsible for the Foggy Mountain Boys' move to WROL and that he helped them obtain a spot on the *Country Playhouse* program. Nash was living in Knoxville and, after signing the band in the fall of 1948, he had taken them to record their first Mercury session in the WROL studios. A number of other Mercury artists were based in Knoxville at that time. On April 9, 1949, *Billboard* reported that "Archie (Grandpappy) Campbell, for years a feature at WNOX, Knoxville, has moved to WROL in the same city, where the Mercury artist will direct an expanded hillbilly policy. Other artists on the station are Lester Flatt, Earl Scruggs and the Foggy Mountain Boys and Carl Sauceman, all Mercury diskers."[1]

The Foggy Mountain Boys' arrival in Knoxville coincided with the debut of their second Mercury single, "We'll Meet Again, Sweetheart" backed with "My Cabin in Caroline," which was released on 78 rpm on April 1. Their first single, "God Loves His Children" backed with "I'm Going to Make Heaven My Home," had been released on January 15.

Soon after they arrived at WROL, Murray Nash had the band in the recording studio again. This time they went to Cincinnati and cut four sides at Herzog Recording Company, on the second floor of a building at 811 Race Street. The first commercial studio in Cincinnati, it was just around the corner from radio station WLW. Herzog Recording was started in 1945 by WLW engineer Earl "Bucky" Herzog and his brother Charles. According to *Grand Ole Opry* announcer Eddie Stubbs, who did extensive interviews with Murray Nash, the Herzog studio was popular with country singers and producers because of its first-rate session band, the Pleasant Valley Boys. Originally the band of *Grand Ole Opry* star Red Foley, the group included Tommy Jackson on fiddle, Louis Ennis on rhythm guitar, Zeke Turner on electric guitar, and Jerry Byrd on steel guitar. They also worked as the house band for WLW's *Midwestern Hayride*. Nash knew the Herzog studio well and used it for a number of Mercury sessions over the years.[2]

In April or May 1949 the Foggy Mountain Boys cut four tracks at Herzog: the originals "Bouquet in Heaven" (called "Decoration Day in Heaven" in the second Foggy Mountain Boys' songbook, from the fall of 1948), "Down the Road," and "Why Don't You Tell Me So?," along with Jim Eanes's "Baby Blue Eyes." There are a number of things worth noting about this session. Curly was hired for his skills as a singer rather than as an instrumentalist, yet his mandolin playing was featured in breaks on all of the tracks except "Down the Road." Though the inclusion of mandolin as a lead instrument brought the band's sound closer to that of Bill Monroe, there was no attempt by Curly to copy Monroe's style. The breaks were very straightforward tremolos punctuated by simple tags at the end. Mandolin expert Tony Williamson pointed out that Curly's choice of an F-2 model mandolin rather than an F-5 was a further departure from Monroe's sound. "[The F-2] gives it more of an old-time feel," Tony said. "I think Curly sort of paved a certain niche for that instrument in bluegrass."[3] Conspicuously absent (or at least inaudible) in these first four recordings was Curly's trademark rhythm "chop," which would later become an important element of the Foggy Mountain Boys' sound.

"Why Don't You Tell Me So?" was noteworthy as the first bluegrass recording to feature a banjo break in F, a challenging key for banjo players. It was also the first recorded Flatt and Seckler duet, and it demonstrates the immediate chemistry between the two singers. It is surprising that Earl Scruggs did not sing in these sessions. Instead, the baritone harmony on "Bouquet in Heaven" was handled by Howard Watts.

After a couple of months on WROL's *Country Playhouse*, Flatt and Scruggs were apparently popular enough in Knoxville that they were chosen to headline a brand new program. Monday, May 30, 1949, at 12:15 P.M., was the debut of the *Dinner Bell* program, hosted by Archie Campbell and starring "Molly O'Day, with Lester Flatt & Earl Scruggs' Foggy Mountain Boys, plus radio's tallest singing cowboy, 6 ft. 7 inch Bob Mason and his Cowboys."[4] The show was in direct competition with WNOX's popular *Mid-Day Merry-Go-Round*, which aired from 12:15 to 1:45 each day. The *Merry-Go-Round* cast at that time included Mercury artists Carl Story and Bonnie Lou and Buster.

Even after relocating to Knoxville, the Foggy Mountain Boys returned often to the Bristol area for show dates. They played at schools in Kingsport at least twice in May. They continued to be regulars on the popular Saturday night *Burley Jamboree*, a square dance held at the Burley Tobacco Warehouse in Abingdon. Curly had first played it with Mac Wiseman in 1947, and Mac had booked the Foggy Mountain Boys there once they arrived in Bristol. Curly recalled that this was strictly a square dance and that the Foggy Mountain Boys performed only instrumentals for the whole evening.

Photos of the Foggy Mountain Boys from 1948 indicate that, although they had not done so in Hickory, in Bristol Lester and Earl were dressing in jodhpur riding pants and boots for personal appearances. This garb was a holdover from their days with Bill Monroe, who sometimes dressed his band in the riding attire of his home state of Kentucky (the Blue Grass State). Perhaps Flatt and Scruggs felt that dressing that way might legitimize them by reminding audiences of their previous association with Monroe. They were still wearing the jodhpurs and boots when Curly joined them, and he was required to follow suit. Photos from WROL indicate, however, that they soon abandoned the riding attire in favor of the dress pants, white shirts, and stylish wide neckties they had worn in their earliest days in Hickory.

In mid-June 1949 the band made its longest road trip to date. Murray Nash had helped arrange a big show in Tampa–St. Petersburg, with a number of Mercury artists on the bill. Charlie Arnett and his wife, who performed as Daisy Mae and Old Brother Charlie, had signed with Mercury in the summer of 1948 after moving from West Virginia to WDAE in Tampa. This was the same Charlie Arnett who had managed Charlie Monroe for a time in 1945. By the winter of 1948 Arnett was managing Radio Ranch, a ten-acre "folk music center" near Tampa with a thirteen-hundred-seat performance venue, picnic grounds, and rodeo facilities.[5] According to Nash, "It was my idea to put on this show down in Tampa. So we had all these artists from the Knoxville area that went down, combined with the artists from Florida, on Mercury. These artists were more or less made in the business from the promotion of this one week. Flatt and Scruggs got a lot of attention on it. It was the first attention that they had had outside of the Knoxville area, and it resulted in an offer to them to move to Florida."[6]

The concert, which took place on June 17 at the Playhouse Theatre, was billed as a "Round-up of Stars." The cast included Nelson King from WCKY in Cincinnati, Flatt and Scruggs and the Foggy Mountain Boys, Molly O'Day and the Cumberland Mountain Folks, Bob Mason and his Swing Billies, and Daisy Mae and Brother Charlie. There were shows at 2:00, 7:00, and 9:00 P.M. The ad in the *St. Petersburg Times* said, "Only once in a lifetime is it possible to see and hear so many famous radio and recording artists in one great show."[7]

A similar concert had been held in Augusta, Georgia, on June 16. According to the *Augusta Chronicle*:

> There'll be a hot time in the municipal auditorium tonight when 20 big-time hillbillies put on a personal appearance to benefit the Augusta Junior Chamber of Commerce. The "Radio Jamboree," which begins at 8 o'clock, stars such entertainers as Molly O'Day, Archie (Grandpappy) Campbell, Red Kirk, Bob Mason, Lester Flatt and Earl Scruggs. They come direct from Station WROL in Knoxville, Tenn.[8]

The Foggy Mountain Boys and Molly O'Day continued to headline the *Dinner Bell* at least through September 2, 1949.[9] It is not clear how much longer they remained at WROL, because after that date program listings did not give specific band names. On October 22 *Billboard* reported that "Lester Flatt, Earl Scruggs and the Foggy Mountain Boys (Mercury) and Molly O'Day and Lynn Davis have . . . left WNOX."[10] This is a mistake; the radio station they left was actually WROL. A week earlier *Billboard* had noted that "Cousin Harry Moreland of WROL reports that Molly O'Day and Lynn Davis have purchased a drive-in in West Virginia and plan to take over in November."[11]

On September 4, an ad for a new barn dance show ran in the Lexington, Kentucky, newspaper. The *Kentucky Mountain Barn Dance* was to be held every Saturday night at the Clay-Gentry Livestock Arena at the corner of Anglin Avenue and Versailles Road. The debut would be on Saturday, September 10, with shows at 7:00 and 9:00 P.M. The Kentucky Mountain Barn Dance Gang would be featured in a broadcast over WVLK radio in

Versailles from 6:00 to 7:00 P.M. The headliner would be Molly O'Day, and the large cast of performers would include Chuck Fallis, the Wanderers, the Sizemores, and others.[12] As it turned out, construction on the Clay-Gentry Auditorium was not completed in time, so the September 10 show was moved to Woodland Auditorium at East High and Kentucky Avenues.[13]

It seems likely that Molly O'Day told Flatt and Scruggs about her booking at the *Barn Dance* and even recommended that they make an appearance there. A week later, on September 17, the Foggy Mountain Boys did just that. Although they were not advertised (the Stanley Brothers were the headliners), J. D. Crowe, who was twelve years old at the time and lived just outside Lexington, recalled seeing them perform that night. "It was like an audition," he said. "They did it as a guest, to see how the crowd liked them. I think it was a fifteen- or twenty-minute spot. They walked out and just blew everybody away, including me!"[14]

By this time, WVLK radio was broadcasting portions of the live *Barn Dance* performances from 7:30 to 8:00 and 9:30 to 10:00 P.M. each week. The hosts of the *Barn Dance* were Mickey Stewart and Don Horton. Horton, the program director of WVLK, was involved in hiring the performers for the *Barn Dance*. A Kentucky native, Stewart got his start in broadcasting while in the military during World War II. He later toured as an entertainer with the USO and worked as an army recruiter. He returned to Lexington to work in the tobacco warehouse business before joining a group of businessmen who purchased Gentry Stockyards, the first livestock auction marketplace in the United States and the oldest facility of its kind in operation.

Clay-Gentry Pavilion was constructed in 1949 as a modern multi-purpose building. Although the complex was primarily a livestock sales arena, the pavilion was constructed so that it could be converted into a climate-controlled theater with a kitchen area for concessions.[15] Photos indicate that the stage was semicircular, with a barnyard backdrop. Cast members who were waiting their turns to perform sat on a row of hay bales that ran along the back of the stage. The audience seating area wrapped around the stage and was steeply tiered, allowing good visibility. The sections, with wooden theater-style seats, were separated by steep sets of concrete stairs. Seating capacity was about eight hundred but, according to the *Barn Dance Songbook*, it was not unusual for as many as fourteen hundred people to pack the arena. The *Barn Dance* was sponsored by Burley Tobacco Warehouses, most likely through the influence of Mickey Stewart.

On September 24 the Foggy Mountain Boys returned for their first advertised appearance at the *Barn Dance*. The newspaper ad read: "FEATURING The Original FOGGY MOUNTAIN BOYS, Formerly with Bill Monroe and his Blue Grass Band, WSM, Nashville, Tenn."[16] The band did not appear at the *Barn Dance* in October, but they were back on November 5. This time the ad read: "FEATURING LESTER FLATT and EARL SCRUGGS, Originally with Bill Monroe and the Blue Grass Boys, Stars of WSM's *Grand Ole Opry*."[17] A photo taken in December and included in their next songbook shows them wearing boots and jodhpurs, likely to enhance their appeal to the Kentucky audience.

By this time Don Horton apparently had realized that the Foggy Mountain Boys were a big draw, and on November 14 he signed them to a six-month contract. They were paid $150 per week, plus a bonus for the radio broadcasts of their performances.[18] The *Barn Dance* ad on November 19 referred to them as "LESTER FLATT and FOGGY MOUNTAIN BOYS, The Original Band of Bill Monroe and The BLUEGRASS BOYS from WSM *Grand Ole Opry*, Nashville, Tenn."[19] The next week, November 26, a photo of the Foggy Mountain Boys appeared at the top of the ad, and they were referred to as "LESTER FLATT and The Foggy Mountain Boys, The Original Band of BILL MONROE."[20] This was the last time Bill Monroe's name was mentioned, and most future ads referred to them as "LESTER FLATT, EARL SCRUGGS And The Foggy Mountain Boys."

Around the time that the band began appearing at the *Kentucky Mountain Barn Dance*, Art Wooten left the band and was replaced by Benny Sims, who was from Sevier County, Tennessee. Earl Scruggs had become acquainted with Sims through the Morris Brothers, with whom Sims worked in the mid-forties. In an interview, Wiley Morris recalled playing at the *Kentucky Barn Dance* with the Shelton Brothers and Benny Sims. Flatt and Scruggs were also on the bill, and Morris said that Lester and Earl approached Benny that night about working for them.[21]

Although they were now regulars at the *Barn Dance*, the Foggy Mountain Boys apparently remained based in Knoxville through the end of 1949. Curly recalled that they were still living in Knoxville when they went to Cincinnati for their next Mercury recording sessions, which were in December. The two sessions on December 11 at Herzog Recording produced eight sides for Mercury. The first session included two Flatt-Seckler duets, "I'll Never Shed Another Tear" and "No Mother or Dad," one Flatt solo, "Is It Too Late

Now?," and one of the most popular and well-known bluegrass instrumentals of all time, Scruggs's "Foggy Mountain Breakdown." The second session produced two gospel quartets featuring Scruggs's lead guitar work, Howard Watts's "I'll Be Going to Heaven Sometime" and the Flatt-Scruggs original "So Happy I'll Be," as well as the driving Flatt-Seckler duet "My Little Girl in Tennessee," and the Flatt solo "I'll Never Love Another."

Sometime that fall, after the band had finished its program on WROL, Curly had returned to his hotel room inspired to write a song. "No Mother or Dad," written from the perspective of a son whose parents have passed on, would turn out to be one of his most popular originals. It was not unusual at that time for a bandleader to share songwriting credit with a sideman who brought an original song to the band. Thus "No Mother or Dad" was credited to Flatt and Seckler, although Curly was actually the sole composer. "I wrote that song in about an hour's time, one morning," he said. "I was thinking a lot about my dad. He died when I was just nine years old. I got in there with the guitar and just started writing it, thinking about home. And I took it over and said, 'Lester, here's a song that I just wrote.' And we got to singing it. And so, the next time we went to record he said, 'Let's record that thing. That's a good number.' So we did." The recording shows how adept the band had become at arranging and interpreting. Benny Sims's mournful fiddle kickoff set the tone, and the soaring Flatt and Seckler vocal harmonies are infused with loneliness.

In general, the music from these sessions reflects how the Foggy Mountain Boys' sound was maturing. The springtime session had had a more old-timey feel, as the musicians tended to all play at once, both behind the singers and during instrumental breaks. In the December sessions, there was more space and less clutter in the arrangements. Although Benny Sims was more aggressive in his playing than was Art Wooten, he backed off during the vocal segments, whereas Wooten tended to continue playing. Curly now was rarely playing tremolos on the mandolin behind the lead instruments and vocals, but clearly had developed, and was very effectively using, his trademark percussive rhythm chop. His one instrumental break, on "I'll Never Love Another," was played entirely tremolo, but with more authority than in previous efforts.

The first single from these sessions was "I'll Never Shed Another Tear" backed with "I'll Be Going to Heaven Sometime," released on January 15, 1950. Next came "No Mother or Dad" backed with "Foggy Mountain

Breakdown," on March 15, 1950. By this time the Foggy Mountain Boys had relocated to Versailles, Kentucky, just outside Lexington. But before they moved, Curly made good on a promise he had made when they first arrived in Knoxville.

"Right after I joined them, they went to Knoxville, and I told them that I'd been over there and hadn't made no money," Curly said. "And so I told Lester, 'The day you leave Knoxville, I'm going to burn my hat.'" When Curly joined the band, the members were wearing round-brimmed hats, and the hat that Curly had been wearing with Charlie Monroe did not match. Lester had an extra hat of the same type, and he offered to let Curly use it. Lester's head was larger than Curly's, but he was able to cut a strip of cardboard to insert in the hatband so that the hat would fit.

It was a chilly, rainy winter day as they prepared to leave Knoxville. The band members were wearing their hats as they dismantled their trailers and packed the cars. And so, Curly said, when it came time to leave, "Lester said, 'Well, Seck, it's time for you to burn your hat.' Well, we tried to burn it, and it wouldn't burn because it was wet. Cedric Rainwater said, 'Well, I've got a can of gas back here,' so we poured gas on that hat and set the thing afire, and [the flames] just stretched up [there]. I've got a picture of all of us, warming our hands on that thing. And Lester told this quite a bit on the stage. He said, 'I was really enjoying Seck burning that hat, and I got to thinking . . . whose hat is he burning?'"

Soon after the Foggy Mountain Boys moved to Lexington, Curly met a beautiful brunette at one of their road shows in West Virginia. Her name was Mable Virginia Sowards, and she was from the tiny town of Ranger, West Virginia, about twenty miles southeast of Huntington. They struck up a friendship, and Curly would visit her whenever he was in the area. They would often go to Camden Park in Huntington to ride the roller coaster. Curly was smitten, but he had to be content with a long-distance relationship for the time being, since he had no car and Ranger was nearly 150 miles from Lexington.

On Monday, February 6, 1950, the Foggy Mountain Boys began a daily radio show from 12:15 to 12:30 P.M. over WVLK (1000 watts at 590 AM) in Versailles.[22] On Saturdays J. D. Crowe's father would occasionally take him to the radio station to see them. He recalled that the station was in the basement of the old Logan-Helm Library building and that the band's Saturday program aired from 11:45 to 12:00 noon. "They'd come in there about an hour early and rehearse their show, and [then] do the show live," he said. "And they'd advertise the *Barn Dance*. The little room they were in was like a cubicle. They had a couple or three chairs in there, and that's where me and my dad would sit while they were doing it. I was right [up] on them, you know.

"While they were doing it, they'd try to get somebody to laugh," he chuckled. "You know, start talking behind them, and they'd get tickled and start laughing. But when that engineer pointed to them and that light come on, they hit it. And it was all business. I mean, they'd still have a good time, but in the music it was serious. It was all business."[23]

Curly recollected seeing J. D. come to the radio station. "I remember the first time I saw him," Curly said. "His daddy was leading him into the studio at the radio station, and he sat down in a chair, and he took Earl's banjo and played it. He was just a little bitty young 'un. He played pretty good. I remember Earl telling him, 'You stick with that like you're doing it, one of these days you're going to be a big man with a banjo,' or something on that order. And look where he went."

Jesse McReynolds recalled making a guest appearance on the Flatt and Scruggs program around this time. "Jim and I went to Wheeling and tried to get a job at the station there," he said, "and we came back through Lexington, Kentucky, and we was guests on their radio show one day. They were working on 'Head Over Heels in Love,' and Benny Sims was playing the fiddle. They were practicing before the radio show, and Earl took the fiddle and showed Benny how to play that tune. We told Earl that we were trying to find a job somewhere. He said Asher Sizemore, in Waterloo, Iowa, tried to get them to come up there for a show he had. He gave us the address and everything, so we called [Sizemore], and that's how we went to Iowa."[24]

By early 1950 the Foggy Mountain Boys had become the star attraction of the *Kentucky Mountain Barn Dance* and were pictured at the top of almost all of the *Barn Dance* newspaper ads. There would often be a well-known guest star such as Grandpa Jones, Jimmie Skinner, Pee Wee King, George Morgan, the Delmore Brothers, or Bradley Kincaid. The *Barn Dance* regulars included Casey Clark, Chuck Fallis, the Sizemores, Oscar the Funnyman, Barefoot Brownie, and others.

In the spring of 1950 Esco Hankins and his Tennesseans joined the cast, replacing Casey Clark and the Lazy Ranch Boys, who made their final appearance on March 18.[25] Like the Foggy Mountain Boys, Hankins came up from WROL in Knoxville. He grew up in the same Union County, Tennessee, town as Roy Acuff had and was sometimes referred to as an Acuff sound-alike. His band in 1950 included fiddler Curly Farmer, vocalist Elizabeth "Aunt Liz" Miles, bass player Mike Martin (known as "Uncle Jake"), and a young slide guitar player named Burkett Graves (known as "Uncle Josh").

Graves remembered the first time he saw the Foggy Mountain Boys at the Barn Dance, when Esco Hankins made a guest appearance in December 1949. "I thought it was the greatest-looking outfit I'd ever seen. They had on those riding boots, and roll-brim hats. Lester looked like a jaybird standing in a shotgun shell. That belly, you know, and them little legs," he laughed. "I stayed in Lester and Earl's dressing room every night, just listening to [them], and we got to be good friends."[26]

Josh was also studying Earl's picking and developing a new style of play-ing the resonator guitar. "I started off on the Dobro with two fingers: a thumb and one finger with a pick," Josh said. "The best thing that happened to me is when I met Earl Scruggs. He taught me that roll. That got me into three picks. Scruggs taught me timing and when to play and when not to play."[27] Jody Rainwater, who joined the band that spring, remembered Lester Flatt telling Josh, "Keep in touch. I'm going to hire you later."[28]

On April 1, Clay-Gentry switched the broadcast of the *Kentucky Moun-tain Barn Dance* from Mutual affiliate WVLK in Versailles to WKLX (1,000 watts at 1300 AM) in downtown Lexington. With studios in the Phoenix Hotel, WKLX was part of the Eureka Network, sponsored by the Eureka Flour Company of Beaver Dam. After the switch, WVLK decided to produce its own version of *Kentucky Barn Dance* at Woodland Auditorium. This cre-ated a dilemma for Flatt and Scruggs. Since they had signed a contract in November with Don Horton of WVLK, were they still under contract with WVLK radio, where they had a daily show, or was their contract with Clay-Gentry? On Monday, April 3, Clay-Gentry filed a petition with the Fayette County Circuit Court seeking an injunction against the Foggy Mountain Boys, and individually against Lester Flatt, Earl Scruggs, Benny Sims, Curly Seckler, and Cedric Rainwater, preventing them from performing anywhere other than the *Kentucky Mountain Barn Dance* on Saturday nights between 7:00 and 11:00 P.M. until the expiration of their contract on May 14. At is-sue was whether the *Kentucky Mountain Barn Dance* name referred to the concert held at Clay-Gentry arena or the radio broadcast over WVLK.[29]

On Saturday, April 8, while awaiting the judge's decision, the Foggy Mountain Boys did not appear at the *Kentucky Mountain Barn Dance*. The featured acts that night were Esco Hankins and the Sauceman Brothers. The show was broadcast at 7:30 to 8:00 and 9:30 to 10:00 over WKLX. On Wednesday, April 12, Judge Chester Adams handed down his decision: "Clay-Gentry Stockyards Company is the originator and owner of the *Kentucky Mountain Barn Dance*, and Radio Station WVLK cannot produce a similar show under the same name. Furthermore, the Foggy Mountain Boys . . . cannot perform on Saturday nights from now until May 15 for anyone except Clay-Gentry."[30]

Station WVLK did make a short-lived attempt to present its own barn dance, called "*WVLK's ORIGINAL KY. BARN DANCE Show*," at Woodland Auditorium.[31] It is unclear whether the *WVLK Barn Dance* was held on Saturday, April 8, or whether the Foggy Mountain Boys performed on it. In any case, on April 15, Flatt and Scruggs were back in their starring role at Clay-Gentry's *Barn Dance* and a supplemental newspaper ad stated, "Notice: *Kentucky Mountain Barn Dance* Broadcast over WKLX 7:30 and 9:30, Clay-Gentry Arena."[32] On Friday, April 21 the Foggy Mountain Boys broadcast their last daily radio show over WVLK and made their first appearance in their new time slot from 11:45 to 12:00 noon on WKLX.[33] Esco Hankins also began a daily program on WKLX that week. Once Clay-Gentry switched radio stations, Randall Parker, who had several mid-day programs on WKLX, joined the *Barn Dance* cast. Parker had come to WKLX from the *Renfro Valley Barn Dance* in 1948.

When they had moved to Lexington, Flatt and Scruggs had decided to take on a booking agent and promoter to help with the band's business. Flatt had first met Chuck Johnson in 1946 or 1947, when Flatt and Scruggs were with Bill Monroe. Johnson was playing mandolin and doing comedy under the stage name "Little Jody" with the Blue Ridge Mountain Boys at WTOB in Winston-Salem, North Carolina. When the Blue Grass Boys went to nearby Lexington, North Carolina, for a show, Flatt and Johnson met and struck up a friendship. In early 1948, Little Jody joined Smokey Graves and his Blue Star Boys at WDBJ in Roanoke, Virginia, playing mandolin and bass, doing comedy, and handling the band's bookings. Soon afterward, Flatt, Scruggs, and Watts left Monroe's band and formed the Foggy Mountain Boys. According to Jody, when the Foggy Mountain Boys moved to WCYB in Bristol, they wanted to hire him to handle bookings and advertising. But things were going well for the Blue Star Boys in Roanoke, so he elected to stay with them.[34]

In the fall of 1949 WCYB offered the Blue Star Boys a slot on *Farm and Fun Time*, and they moved to Bristol. Jody recalled that the band almost starved because of the economic impact of a coal miners' strike (the third walkout of the year engineered by John L. Lewis, head of the United Mine Workers union). So, when Flatt called again in early 1950, Jody immediately accepted the job and moved to Lexington, Kentucky. He began handling the Foggy Mountain Boys' bookings and would drive his own car to promote the shows ahead of the band's arrival. "The first four or five weeks, I was just at their show on Saturday night," Jody said. "I'd double back and come in, if I was out. I had them booked up solid for almost two months."[35]

Knowing of Jody's background as a comic, Flatt came up with an idea. "One Saturday night," Jody recalled, "backstage, they were tuning up. Lester says, 'Jody, how about billing you as Cedric's brother, and you're going to be with him next Saturday, here on the [*Barn Dance*].'" Jody's debut was a rousing success, and he immediately took his place as the Foggy Mountain Boys' second comedian. To keep things interesting, Jody and Cedric would take turns coming up with the punch lines, and Curly, Lester, and Earl would take turns playing the straight man. "And we had them roaring, I'll tell you!" Jody said. "And this is where I took the name Jody Rainwater."[36]

In addition to the band performances, the *Kentucky Mountain Barn Dance* would present various other forms of entertainment, including beauty contests, skits, and comedic boxing or wrestling matches. One week it would be "Jodie [*sic*] Rainwater vs Uncle Josh" (Graves), and the next week it might be "Jodie Rainwater vs Uncle Jake the Tennessean" or "Uncle Jake vs Oscar Gooblertooth Shagnasty" (another *Barn Dance* regular).

On May 13, 1950, the newspaper ad for the *Barn Dance* included a photo of Cedric Rainwater and mentioned his name in the copy (for the first time), above Flatt's and Scruggs's.[37] This was most likely because it was Cedric's last appearance on the show with the Foggy Mountain Boys. He left at about this time to return to Nashville, perhaps with the idea of rejoining Bill Monroe's band. The *Kentucky Mountain Barn Dance Songbook*, published in 1950, had the same photo of Cedric with a caption reading: "CEDRIC RAINWATER—A star of the *Barn Dance* Group. At the time he appeared here, he was part of the Foggy Mountain Boys and did a comedy and tap-dancing routine that kept many an audience hysterical all through the performance. Cedric has since moved on to Nashville where he is again associated with Bill Monroe and the Bluegrass [*sic*] Boys."[38] As it turned out, Cedric did not go back to work with Monroe, but, after a couple of months of freelancing, was hired by Hank Williams.

Jody Rainwater remembered that it was only a few weeks after he began doing comedy with Cedric that the latter left the band. Perhaps Cedric was simply waiting for the Foggy Mountain Boys' Clay-Gentry contract to expire on May 14. Another factor in his departure may have been that Flatt and Scruggs had decided to return to Bristol once the contract expired. A poster for their show on Tuesday, May 23, at the Towne Theatre in Hillsville, Virginia, read: "Direct from WCYB, Bristol, VA, *Farm and Fun Time*" and included the same picture of Lester and Earl standing at the WCYB microphone that was in their songbook from the fall of 1948. It appears that they had not actually arrived at WCYB at the time of the May 23 show, however, because they were still listed as having a daily program at 11:45 A.M. on WKLX in Lexington through Friday, June 2.[39]

Once Cedric left the band, Jody's previous experience made it easy for him to move into the role of bass player and bass singer, while continuing as comedian and booking agent. When doing comedy, he dressed in baggy cutoff pants with suspenders and a floppy hat. Curly remembered Jody as a good entertainer and a hard worker. Because Jody was still booking and promoting the band's shows, he continued to drive ahead in his own car and sometimes would even sleep in his car if he couldn't make it back to Lexington. Curly recalled that, when Jody did get to sleep in his own bed, he slept so soundly that he kept an alarm clock in a bucket on each side of his bed in order to ensure that he didn't oversleep.

After moving to Bristol, the Foggy Mountain Boys continued to make the 230-mile trip on winding mountain roads to Lexington each Saturday to perform on the *Kentucky Mountain Barn Dance*. Lester and Earl would take turns driving the band to show dates, and each had a car with the band name emblazoned on the side. As most bands did, they would put their instruments and baggage in the trunk and tie the bass to the top of the car. This was a precarious way to travel, and Curly remembered at least one occasion when Cedric Rainwater had failed to secure his bass properly. "The strap broke, and the bass flew off, and broke the neck out of it," Curly said.

"Cedric had a DeSoto," he continued. "Me and Lester was with him one day, when he was out trying to book a thing or two. The hood flew up on that thing and blinded us. We had to stop, and he got him some wire and tied the hood down to where it would stay. It had a door that wouldn't stay shut, and he had a belt around it, to keep it shut. He said he might not be able to keep the doors or the hood shut, but he could stop it 'on a dime.' We topped a hill, and he run up under a truck! He didn't have time [to stop]. He went right up under that truck, and the headlights flew everywhere, and we just flat died laughing!"

Curly also recalled a funny incident involving Jody and his car. "We was in Bristol, and we was taking off to play a show that night, and Jody [drove] his car, because he would stay [over] and then go on and book shows. Earl said, 'You think you can keep up with us, with that little old car of yours?' [Jody] said, 'Don't worry, I'll keep up.' And we got into some of them curves, and Jody was behind us, and Earl said, 'Look at that white church yonder. Watch me duck in behind that.' And he run in behind it. Here come Jody down the road, just a-flying. We sat there laughing, and we pulled out and got behind Jody. Jody thought we'd really left him, sure enough. Earl was always getting into something like that."

By early June the Foggy Mountain Boys were back at WCYB in Bristol. On June 23, 1950, they headlined on the Frank and Mack Show at the annual American Legion Carnival in Kingsport.[40] Frank and Mack were the comedy team of Frank Taylor and Mack Riddle. They became so popular in the 1930s that they were given their own stage at the carnival and would feature a variety of musical guests during the two-week event. Flatt and Scruggs had first performed there when they arrived in Bristol in 1948, and it became a regular stop for them for several years. They were so well received that they would perform on multiple nights each year. The ad for their return appearances on Thursday, July 6, and Friday, July 7, read: "They're Coming Back, Your Favorites, FOGGY MOUNTAIN BOYS."[41]

Another Bristol-area venue where the Foggy Mountain Boys played at least twice that summer was the Moonlite Drive-in Theatre, on the Bristol-Abingdon Highway (U.S. Route 11). The Moonlite was one of the larger drive-ins in the area, with parking space for up to seven hundred cars, a playground, and a brand-new restaurant. There were two movie showings each night. On Wednesday, August 9, Flatt and Scruggs performed before each showing of *Last of the Wild Horses*, a western starring James Ellison.[42] They were back on Wednesday, September 20, for two shows, along with the movie *Frontier Marshall*, starring Randolph Scott.[43]

Performances at drive-ins were to become more and more common for the band in the following years. From 1948 to 1950 the number of drive-in theaters across the country doubled from just under one thousand to almost two thousand. By 1954 there were nearly four thousand,[44] and drive-ins had become a staple of the Foggy Mountain Boys' touring schedule. The band would usually perform standing on the flat roof of the concession stand, and their microphones would be plugged into the theater's sound system so that patrons could listen over the speakers that could be attached to their car windows. Patrons would honk their car horns at the end of each song rather than applaud.

Another burgeoning source of work for the band was a new type of venue, the country music theme park. On Sunday, September 17, 1950, the Foggy Mountain Boys performed for the first time at one of the best: Sunset Park in West Grove, Pennsylvania.[45] Sunset Park was founded in 1940 by dairy farmer Roy Waltman. Every Sunday afternoon from spring to fall, the park would present some of the biggest names in hillbilly music along with various dancers, comedians, magicians, and a baseball game. Families brought their picnics and settled in for an entire day of entertainment. Sunset Park, which would continue to operate for more than forty-five years, was a regular stop for generations of country and bluegrass artists. Flatt and Scruggs performed there annually for the duration of their partnership.

On Saturday, September 23, 1950, the *Kentucky Mountain Barn Dance* ad featured a large picture of Flatt and Scruggs with a caption stating: "MAKING THEIR FINAL APPEARANCE FOR SOME WEEKS."[46] Lester and Earl had accepted an offer to move to WDAE in Tampa, Florida, to appear with Daisy Mae and "Old Brother" Charlie Arnett on their daily program (Monday–Friday) from 8:15 to 9:00 A.M. Arnett had been impressed with the Foggy Mountain Boys when they had played on the package show that Murray Nash had put together in the summer of 1949.

The move turned out to be a mistake. Earl Scruggs explained, "Old Brother Charlie, he'd buy an hour of radio time for x number of dollars, and then he'd sell his own sponsors, and he was taking in more than he was spending out, so he was making a good living. We went down there and weren't doing any good, because we had to go out and play a schoolhouse or something and get a percentage. And we got to investigating, and the dang radio station was directional. That meant it went out across the ocean, where no people lived, and nobody was hearing us. So we had a lot of fans, but they were fish! They didn't buy tickets."[47]

In the summer of 1950 Columbia Records, a major label, had offered Flatt and Scruggs a recording contract. Recording with Columbia would be a step up, and Lester and Earl wanted to accept the offer, but they were still under contract with Mercury. After moving to Tampa they approached Murray Nash about their desire to leave Mercury. Nash recalled, "They thought they had a better offer, but they didn't want to tell me what it [was]. I had my own philosophy of how to handle these things. We had Flatt and Scruggs on a three-year contract. So I went to Lester and Earl, and I said, 'All right, I'll release you from Mercury, providing you fulfill your three-year contract as far as the number of sides are concerned.'"[48] Lester and Earl agreed, and Nash made arrangements to drive from Knoxville to Tampa and record them in the studios of WDAE. Earl recalled, "Murray Nash drove a one-seater Studebaker car, and he'd just bring his portable things into the studio and set them up, and we just did it right there where you'd do a radio program."[49]

Nash drove all night and met the Foggy Mountain Boys at WDAE during their morning program on Friday, October 20. There was just one problem. A hurricane in the Gulf of Mexico had taken a surprise turn on Thursday night and was heading right toward Tampa. Warnings had been issued, and the band members wanted to join the evacuation and head inland. Nash convinced them they would be better off staying at the radio station. "I talked them into staying there, getting their families, and bringing them into the studio there," he said. "They were living out on the edge of town somewhere. [The station] was a solid brick building."[50] As it turned out, Nash's advice was sound, because the hurricane skirted the Tampa Bay area and made landfall further north, close to where the band had planned to take refuge.

Nash set up his equipment, and the band recorded eight songs on October 20 and four more on October 21. Nash used a two-piece portable Magnacorder tape recorder, which at that time was fairly new technology. "We were about the first at Mercury to record on tape," he noted.[51] In a 1983 interview, Nash recalled recording with four microphones. "We had to have one for fiddle. We had to have one for banjo. We had to have vocal. Lester and Earl would play close together, so we'd get enough of Lester's guitar in the banjo mic. Then one for the bass, and that was about what we had."[52] Nash had a trick for getting a better sound from the banjo: "I used a little old fourteen-dollar microphone on Earl Scruggs's banjo," he said, "and we would put a light bulb in his banjo to heat the head. They were not nylon heads back then. These were all gut heads, and we put a light bulb in there to heat it up and give it that good string sound that we wanted."[53]

It has often been said that the Foggy Mountain Boys' Mercury sessions are some of the best recordings they ever made. There may be many reasons, including the band's skill at vocal harmonies and ensemble playing, the group dynamic of the members at that time, and the type of equipment used. Much of the credit should also go to Murray Nash, however, for his skills as an engineer. Because he was using a single-track tape recorder, unlike today's multi-track technology, he was an active participant in the recording process. He explained:

> I usually liked to use the station's board mixer, and I would plug my tape recorder into the output of that. I think there's a lot in microphone placement and engineering, as to what sound you come up with. Back in that period, that was the biggest value of an A&R man, was knowing what to do to get this feel, understanding these singers and these musicians, their volume, their tendencies, the whole thing, and then being able to control the mixing panel from your knowledge of that. On low notes, the singer had one volume. On high notes, he had a different volume, so you had to know something about the song he was singing. You were sitting there riding his voice to go into this tape, because there was no way of changing it after it got on the tape."[54]

Flatt and Scruggs chose to record all covers for these sessions, saving their original material for the upcoming Columbia recordings. These were songs they had been performing at their personal appearances, so very little rehearsal was required. According to Nash, the only issue was the length of the songs. For radio airplay, a song needed to be less than three minutes long. "When they got going, sometimes they'd go for three and a half minutes, and then we'd have to figure out how we could cut forty-five seconds out of it in order to get it down below three minutes," Nash explained. "We'd figure out leaving a verse out or leaving [an] instrumental out or whatever it took to get it down to record time and just do it again, but there was very little repeated takes because of the musical end of it."[55]

The sessions are interesting in part because the band members traded roles on several of the songs. Jody Rainwater, who was a skilled multi-instrumentalist, played the mandolin on the duets "Will the Roses Bloom Where She Lies Sleeping?" and "Back to the Cross." Benny Sims played the bass rather than the fiddle, giving these tracks a more old-timey feel. On "Back to the Cross," surprisingly, Curly sang the lead vocal on the chorus and Lester sang tenor harmony (Curly didn't remember why). "Old Salty Dog Blues" was a song Benny Sims had learned from Wiley and Zeke Morris, and he often sang it (with Curly and Earl harmonizing) in the portion of the Foggy Mountain Boys' shows when Lester would leave the stage. The band recorded it in that configuration, with Curly playing the rhythm guitar and Lester sitting one out. The gospel quartet "Preaching, Praying, Singing" featured Earl's guitar as the only lead instrument, and no fiddle or mandolin. The bass vocal was handled by Benny Sims, even though Jody Rainwater normally sang the bass part at shows.

That final Mercury recording session was practically the only good thing that came out of the band's time in Florida. Curly remembered that they spent much of their time fishing. Curly and Benny would cast their lines from the beach, catching fish barely big enough to eat, while Earl went out on a boat and came back with whoppers. "Scruggs bugged me about that a lot," Curly laughed. "He said, 'How big was that fish you caught in Florida, Seck?'"

Curly also recalled that when interviewers asked Lester about their time in Florida his response would be, "We'd go out of a night to play schoolhouses, and if you left your window halfway down, the big mosquitoes couldn't get in." Curly added, "They're the only thing that ever come out to our shows down there." If that wasn't enough, in the Florida humidity Curly's bronchial asthma returned with a vengeance. "One morning I told Flatt, 'I want a two weeks' notice. I'm leaving.' He said, 'What's wrong?' I said, 'I can't get my breath.' He talked to Earl, and a day or so after, he said, 'Now, Seck, if you'll stay just another week, we're going to go with you.' So we all left."

On Monday, November 6, the Foggy Mountain Boys made their last personal appearance in Florida. They were the featured entertainers for a political caravan designed to stir up votes for the November 7 election. A newspaper article read: "Accompanying the motorcade of candidates making their final plea for votes will be 'Old Brother Charlie and Daisy Mae' and the Foggy Mountain Boys, a hillbilly aggregation. They will present a concert at each stop on the tour."[56]

By Saturday, November 11, Flatt and Scruggs were back in Lexington. The *Kentucky Mountain Barn Dance* ad included a large photo of Lester and Earl with the caption "BACK AGAIN!"[57] Also on the show were the Stanley Brothers, Esco Hankins and his Tennesseans, Randall Parker, and the Powell County Boys. A few weeks later the *Barn Dance* moved to Woodland Auditorium, where it would remain for the next year and a half. Once it moved to Woodland, WKLX appears to have stopped broadcasting from the *Barn Dance* because the station was no longer mentioned in the ads.

After leaving Florida, Flatt and Scruggs signed with Columbia Records, and on November 21 they were in Nashville to record six songs at Castle Studio in the Tulane Hotel. Troy Martin, who had arrived in Nashville in 1949 to work for Peer International Publishing Company, may have been responsible for bringing Flatt and Scruggs to the attention of Columbia's A&R man, Don Law. Martin assisted Law in producing recording sessions and finding new performers for the label. He also was involved in publishing the songs that Lester and Earl were writing and recording.

At the November 21 session, they recorded four Flatt originals: the solos "I'm Head Over Heels in Love" and "The Old Home Town" and the Flatt-Seckler duets "Come Back, Darling" and "I'll Stay Around." The third duet of the session, "We Can't Be Darlings Anymore," is credited to Flatt and Seckler but was actually written by Leonard Stokes and purchased from him by Lester and Curly, as mentioned above. The one trio of the session, "I'm Waiting to Hear You Call Me Darling," was written by Jody Rainwater. This song is of special note because it was the first time the Foggy Mountain Boys recorded a trio with both harmony parts above the lead—a practice used more commonly by Bill Monroe and by the Stanley Brothers. For the chorus of "I'm Waiting to Hear You Call Me Darling," Earl sang the lead, Lester sang tenor, and Curly sang high baritone. This was the only time they ever recorded in that specific configuration while Curly was in the band, and they would not record with high baritone again until Jake Tullock joined the band in 1954.

Curly contributed mandolin breaks to "We Can't Be Darlings Anymore" and "I'm Waiting to Hear You Call Me Darling." In each case he played mostly double-stop tremolos punctuated by single-string licks at the end, and he threw in some nice fills behind the vocals as well. While most mandolin players today use a rhythm chop only on the off beat, Curly sometimes chopped both on and off the beat, providing a more urgent drive to the music. His work on "I'm Waiting to Hear You Call Me Darling" was a good example of this technique, especially as he played behind Benny Sims's fiddle break.

On Monday, December 4, the Foggy Mountain Boys were back on WVLK in Versailles, with daily fifteen-minute programs at 12:30 and 1:15 P.M. At about this time Benny Sims decided to return to Knoxville to accept a position as a staff musician for WNOX's *Mid-Day Merry-Go-Round* and *Tennessee Barn Dance* programs. He was replaced by Chubby Wise, who had been working with the York Brothers in Detroit.

On returning to Lexington from Florida Curly had renewed his acquaintance with Mable Sowards, and he decided it was time to propose marriage. They were wed on December 29, 1950, at Mable's aunt's house in Huntington, and they moved into a rooming house in Lexington. The rest of the band lived in a trailer park, and they would pick Curly up each day on their way to the radio station. "It was about thirteen miles from Lexington to Versailles, and we'd play poker on the way," he recalled

In the winter of 1950–1951 a seventeen-year-old from Liberty, Kentucky, moved with her older sister to the big city of Lexington. Sixty years later, Jewel Russell recalled seeing the Foggy Mountain Boys at the *Kentucky Mountain Barn Dance*. "That was who everybody went to see," she confirmed. "They were the big ones." Jewel and her sister Rose attended the *Barn Dance* as often as they could, and they would often speak to Curly during intermission. "Curly was so good to us," Jewel recalled. "He was just like a brother or an uncle, friendly and down to earth. Seemed like Lester never was as friendly. He was more serious, and older. Earl Scruggs was just a real gentleman. His wife was so pretty and black-headed. He'd carry his little boy around at intermission, and I just thought they was so cute. The bass fiddler was Little Jody Rainwater. He'd always come and talk to us. He was funny." Jewel, who admitted to being a "cut-up" herself, recalled that sometimes Curly would take her and Rose backstage to get autographs and that on one such occasion, "Lester Flatt's hat was hanging on a hat rack and [I] tried it on!"[58]

On January 13, 1951, comic and dancer "Kentucky Slim" (Charles Elza) made his first advertised appearance at the *Barn Dance*.[59] By March he was a regular cast member, working with Esco Hankins. Elza grew up in Harlan County, Kentucky, and learned to dance as a teenager. At seventeen he befriended Cas Walker while they were both working in the coal mines. The two of them traveled to Knoxville, where Walker opened his first grocery store and Elza performed on Walker's radio programs on WROL. Early in his career Elza did blackface comedy and worked with a medicine show. He worked briefly with Roy Acuff, the Cope Brothers, and Carl Story at WNOX before joining Esco Hankins. Flatt and Scruggs took note of Elza's skills as an entertainer and kept him in mind for future reference, just as they had with Josh Graves.

Lester and Earl had also been impressed by mandolin-playing tenor singer Everett Lilly, whom they first encountered during their time touring with Bill Monroe. Everett and his brother Bea grew up near Beckley, West Virginia, and began singing together as teenagers. They worked early in their careers on a number of radio stations, including WJLS in Beckley, WCHS in Charleston, WWVA in Wheeling, and WMMN in Fairmont.

In March 1951, after a disagreement that no one seemed to remember, Curly Seckler left the Foggy Mountain Boys. As it happened, the Lilly Brothers were between radio jobs, so Everett Lilly was hired as Curly's replacement. Following the personnel change, Flatt and Scruggs returned to the studio, and on May 9, 1951, they recorded six songs for Columbia at Castle Studio in Nashville.

Meanwhile, Curly returned to WCYB in Bristol to work with the Sauceman Brothers. Carl and J. P. (John Paul) Sauceman were from Greeneville, Tennessee, about sixty miles southwest of Bristol. Curly had first met them when he was in Bristol with Mac Wiseman in 1947. Carl Sauceman, who was four years older than J. P., had worked in bands at WISE in Asheville and WHKY in Hickory before his brother joined him at WWNC in Asheville in 1944. Carl spent two years in the navy, and on his return the brothers formed the Hillbilly Ramblers, working at WGRV in Greeneville. From there they moved to WROL in Knoxville, working an early morning program for Cas Walker, as well as Archie Campbell's *Dinner Bell* program at noon. Band members included Ralph Mayo on fiddle, Wiley Birchfield on banjo, Junior Huskey on bass, and for a short time in late 1948, Carl Smith, who had just returned from working with Hoke Jenkins and the Smoky Mountaineers at WGAC in Augusta, Georgia. While the Saucemans were at WROL, Cas Walker advised them to change the name of their band because he didn't like the connotations of the word *hillbilly*. Since they were from Greene County, they chose the name Green Valley Boys.

In late 1950 Carl and J. P. went to Detroit, to play in clubs on the advice of Chubby Wise, who had made a good living there with the York Brothers.

After enduring a harsh winter with disappointing financial return, the brothers went home in February 1951. Their younger brother Jim recalled, "They got in touch with Lester [Flatt] and he said, 'Yeah, I'll give you a good recommendation.' And they got [a] spot on WCYB."[60]

When Curly joined them in the spring of 1951, the band included Carl on guitar, J. P. on guitar or mandolin, Arvil Freeman on fiddle, Carmon Freeman on bass, and multi-instrumentalist Joe Stuart, who would play mandolin, fiddle, bass, or guitar, depending on what was needed. The "Green Valley Quartet," which was featured on gospel material, included Carl on lead vocal, Curly on tenor, J. P. on baritone, and Joe Stuart on bass vocal and finger-style guitar. A few months after Curly arrived, banjo player Larry Richardson joined the group and Carmon Freeman left. At that time, Joe Stuart took over as bassist. He also played a comic character called Uncle Duddie.

Since there were already two capable mandolin players in the band, Curly abandoned his Gibson F-2 for a Martin D-18 guitar that he bought from Carmon Freeman. In addition to singing harmony parts, Curly was often featured performing his trademark solos such as "Moonlight on My Cabin," "You Took My Sunshine," and the novelty tune "Hannah." The Sauceman Brothers' songbook, published that year, included the words to "Hannah" along with a full-page photo of Curly holding his mandolin. That seems to indicate that Curly was a highly regarded band member, and this was confirmed by Arvil Freeman. "He was a welcome addition to the band," Freeman said. "It kind of helped us, because of him being with Flatt and Scruggs. They were getting very well known [at that time]."[61]

Carl and J. P. both contributed original songs to the band, and the songbook indicates that they were also singing material written by the Delmore Brothers, Carl Smith, Johnnie and Jack, Larry Richardson and Bobby Osborne, and Arthur Smith. Curly sang several of his originals, as well as standards like "Jimmy Brown, the Newsboy." Frequently J. P. sang a song he had written called "I Love You Until I Am Dizzy," and one day he offered to sell it to Curly. "We was in the studio at WCYB," Curly recalled, "and we got through singing it, and he said, 'How would you like to own that number? I need ten dollars.'" So I give him ten dollars and took it and sent it to Southern Publishing Company, and that's how I got that number."

As the older and more experienced brother, Carl Sauceman acted as the bandleader. "Carl did most of the emceeing in the band," Jim Sauceman said, "and Carl really had a wonderful personality on the stage. He could make you think he was a whole lot better singer and entertainer than he was."[62] Arvil Freeman confirmed that Carl was an excellent emcee and bandleader, and added that he also drove the band to their shows in his Pontiac: "Two in the front, three in the back, instruments in the trunk, and bass on the top. It wasn't the most comfortable way to travel, I'll tell you that," Arvil laughed.[63]

In an interview with Hilary Dirlam, Freeman recalled, "We played four or five live shows a week, along with the radio shows. We mostly played movie theaters. They'd show the movie, then we'd come out and do a 45-minute set. We always had a full house—standing room only."[64] For instance, on April 5 they played at the Carolina Theatre in Spruce Pine, along with the Marx Brothers movie *Love Happy*. On May 30 they were at the Taylor Theatre in Gate City, Virginia, along with *Heritage of the Desert*, and on June 7 they were at the Fox Theatre in Kingsport with *All About Eve*, starring Bette Davis. On July 11 they joined Wilma Lee and Stoney Cooper for a "double-header stage show" at the Moonlite Drive-in.

On June 2 the band performed for the Hawkins County American Legion Day celebration in Rogersville, and on June 22 and 23 they were featured in the Frank and Mack Show at the American Legion Carnival in Kingsport. *Billboard* reported that "the Sauceman Brothers and their Green Valley Boys, WCYB, Bristol, TN, topped all records for Airport Grove, Richlands, VA when they did 10,000 payees recently."[65] Arvil Freeman recalled, "That was a double bill with Flatt and Scruggs. That was the biggest crowd we'd ever even thought about playing to. It was sort of like a little fairgrounds that they had out there."[66]

Freeman, who was only seventeen at the time, soon grew tired of the band's grueling schedule. "Our radio shows was at 12:05 to 12:30, and 1:15 to 1:30. Then right after that we'd pile in the car and here we'd go [to a show], and we wouldn't get back until sometimes one or two o'clock in the morning, and then our rehearsal time was from 10:00 to 10:30 at the radio station."[67] In the fall of 1951, weary of the road and anticipating that he would be drafted, Freeman left the band and returned home to North Carolina. He was replaced by Clarence Tate.

Tate had worked with the Sauceman Brothers in the late 1940s at WROL in Knoxville, and it was their sponsor, Cas Walker, who gave him the nickname "Tater." Though they only worked together briefly in 1951, Tater and Curly developed a life-long friendship and would cross paths many times.

On November 10, 1951, the Sauceman Brothers traveled to Lexington to perform on the *Kentucky Barn Dance*. The newspaper ad mentioned all of the Green Valley Boys by name except for Joe Stuart, who was referred to as "Uncle Duddie, the Old Maid's Heartthrob."[68] By this time the *Barn Dance*, still held at Woodland Auditorium, was back on WVLK, the word *Mountain* dropped from its name. So it appears that Don Horton and WVLK had the last laugh in the dispute with Clay-Gentry that began in the spring of 1950. Curly renewed his acquaintance with Don Horton that night, and it would prove to be a serendipitous encounter.

A number of changes came to the Sauceman Brothers band soon after that show. Carl had just signed a contract with Capitol Records and was eager to record. He had also made arrangements to move to a radio station in Carrollton, Alabama. Tater Tate and J. P. Sauceman both were drafted in early December, however, and the band began to fall apart. Joe Stuart joined the Bailey Brothers, and Larry Richardson was recruited by Bill Monroe.[69]

Bobby Osborne had come to Bristol that fall with Jimmy Martin after they both left the Lonesome Pine Fiddlers. (Martin had replaced Larry Richardson in the Lonesome Pine Fiddlers when he left to join the Sauceman Brothers.) Martin and Osborne played for a month on WCYB before Martin took a job at WROL in Knoxville. Osborne then joined the Stanley Brothers, but after only about three weeks, he joined the marines and was sent to Korea, leaving the Stanleys without a mandolin player.[70] Carter Stanley had tried to recruit Curly several times, but Curly had always been otherwise committed. Following the breakup of the Sauceman band Curly was available, and he readily accepted when Carter called this time.

Carter and Ralph recognized that Curly could not only help their band musically but also could provide valuable business knowledge and experience. "Curly Seckler had been with Flatt and Scruggs," Ralph said. "Curly was great on the harmony singing, and he didn't sound nothing like [Bill] Monroe. He was a little older than us, and he knew people in the business, and he was in good standing."[71]

Meanwhile, Flatt and Scruggs had moved to WDBJ in Roanoke, Virginia, where they had early morning and noontime shows beginning on Monday, August 27, 1951.[72] After just a few months there, they moved back to Lexington. On November 16 the ad for the *Kentucky Barn Dance* read "COMING BACK, Lester Flatt & Earl Scruggs and Foggy Mountain Boys," with a photo of Lester and Earl.[73] On Saturday, December 1, the Foggy Mountain Boys began a 12:30 to 12:45 P.M. program Monday through Saturday on WVLK. They appeared on the *Barn Dance* for four weeks, but the ad for their December 8 performance said, "Final Appearance."[74] They continued the daily radio show until Saturday, December 29, after which they moved to WPTF in Raleigh, North Carolina.

Soon after joining the Stanley Brothers, Curly received a call from Don Horton of WVLK. "He called down there and wanted to know, was I working with the Sauceman Brothers, or who was I working with," Curly recalled. "He said, 'That's the group I want, whoever you're working with.' I said, 'Well, at this time I'm working with the Stanley Brothers. I just recently went over with them.' He said, 'Reckon they'd come up here?'" The Stanley Brothers immediately made the trip to Lexington to perform at the *Kentucky Barn Dance* on Saturday, December 15, and Horton hired them to return as regulars, taking over the slot vacated by the Foggy Mountain Boys.

"So I took Carter and Ralph up there," Curly continued, "and I guess that's the first paid job they ever had on a radio station. We had a [radio] program five days a week, and then we had the *Kentucky Barn Dance*, which paid us a little salary. Bristol never did pay nobody nothing." Ralph Stanley confirmed this account, stating, "Curly helped us get a job at WVLK, in Kentucky. This was the first radio program where we got a salary. We worked a morning program every day for WVLK, and got us a sponsor, a tobacco warehouse out of Versailles. We'd play personal appearances five or six days a week, and on Saturdays we'd work the *Kentucky Barn Dance*. Curly had helped get the barn dance going with Flatt and Scruggs, and it was real popular. So we were getting two regular salaries."[75]

When the Stanleys got ready to move to Lexington, they switched Charlie Cline (who had been playing bass) to the fiddle slot, and called George Shuffler to play bass. According to Shuffler, "[My wife] Sue and I were in Hickory at her parents' home when Carter Stanley called me from Bristol on December 28, and said they were going to WVLK to replace Flatt and Scruggs. Carter said they were leaving WCYB in Bristol and that they had Curly Seckler with them."[76] George agreed to join the band and met them in Abingdon, Virginia, on the way to Lexington. Once they arrived, Jody Rainwater, who had been booking Flatt and Scruggs, gave the Stanleys his date book as he was leaving town, so they had a ready-made list of contacts in the area.

Shuffler recalled that they played mainly at theaters and courthouses. "There was one man that had a little chain of theaters, five or six of them, and we'd call him and book a week there. [At] the courthouses, you had to find the janitor, and give him five dollars to turn on the lights and build a fire in a big pot-bellied stove, and unlock everything, [then] turn the lights out and clean up after we left."[77]

Although the bookings were good, Carter Stanley was already plagued by a well-documented drinking problem and was sometimes unable to perform. While Curly got along well with Ralph and the other band members, he was uncomfortable with Carter's erratic behavior. After about six weeks Curly went to Don Horton and told him he was planning to leave the band. "[Don] said, 'I want you to stay, regardless. You helped build this thing, and I want you to stay here.' And Don asked me who I could bring in in their place. I said, 'Well, Jim and Jesse, who I've worked with before.' So I called Jim and he said, 'How soon do you want us there?'"

Curly gave two weeks' notice to the Stanley Brothers, and the McReynolds Brothers joined him in Lexington in late February. They brought along Hoke Jenkins to play banjo, and Curly went back to playing guitar. Jesse McReynolds and Hoke Jenkins would take turns playing a comic character called Sparkplug. By this time they were calling the band the McReynolds Brothers and the Cumberland Mountain Boys. Their first appearances on WVLK were on Thursday, February 28, at 12:15 to 12:30 and 1:00 to 1:15 P.M.[78] The Stanley Brothers retained their 12:30 to 12:45 P.M. radio slot until early April, when they left the area. During that time, both bands appeared at the *Barn Dance*, though they seldom interacted. Jesse McReynolds recalled that the Stanleys "didn't want their band members to mingle with anybody else in any other band," although George Shuffler would come and socialize when Carter and Ralph were not around.[79]

The McReynolds Brothers' first appearance at the *Barn Dance* was on February 23. March 1 happened to be when WVLK had scheduled a hillbilly "beauty contest," in which all of the musicians were to dress like women. The newspaper ad read: "WHO are Kentucky's most beautiful hill billies? You pick 'em! Beauty Contest, plus WVLK'S BIG KENTUCKY BARN DANCE SHOW. Your Favorite Radio Stars IN PERSON! Girls? Girls? Girls? Girls?" The performers were listed with their special stage names for the evening, including "Merry McReynolds 'Sisters,' Baby Doll 'Blondie' Sechler, Jumpin' 'Josephine' Jenkins [Hoke Jenkins], The Gorgeous Stanley 'Sisters,' Alluring 'Alice' Allen [Red Allen], and Beautiful 'Beulah' Butler [Carl Butler]."[80] Curly had a photo of the contestants on stage, and he recalled that Carl Butler, who had recently joined the *Barn Dance* cast, won the contest, wearing a mop on his head.

Jewel Russell, who was still living in Lexington, attended the show and took photos. She remembered that the musicians dressed in shorts and the announcer (presumably Mickey Stewart) wore "long-handle underwear." She recalled going to pick up her photos and running into Curly. "I went to Walgreen's, and he was there!" she laughed. "He was getting pictures, too, and I give him some of mine. I think we had a cup of coffee, and we laughed at all these pictures."[81]

The Stanley Brothers once performed at the *Barn Dance* with Harley "Red" Allen playing bass, according to J. D. Crowe. Allen's name was listed next to theirs in the *Barn Dance's* beauty contest ad, so it is possible that this was the occasion. Allen was living nearby, and soon after that he began showing up occasionally to perform with the McReynolds Brothers. "Red was a pretty good singer," Curly said, "but he was just bumming around. If I went in [a restaurant] and ordered a steak, that's exactly what he'd order. I said, 'Red, you ain't got no money.' He'd say, 'Dad, you'll pay for it.' Ain't no telling how many meals I bought that young 'un!"

"Red Allen was sort of a hang-out," Jesse McReynolds laughed. "He lived in Jackson, Kentucky. He and his wife had separated, so he came up to Lexington, and he wasn't a member of our group, but he'd travel with us some. He stayed with us in the hotel, there in Versailles, which was a different county from Lexington. The law people came up to arrest him, because his wife had put a warrant out for him, for child support or something. They came to arrest him and he reminded them that they was out of their jurisdiction, because it was a different county. After this happened, we took him out on Highway 25 and he flagged a Greyhound bus and went to Dayton, Ohio."[82]

Then, on April 1, the McReynolds Brothers played a show at the courthouse in Richmond, Kentucky. The police assumed that Red was still working with them and arrived at the show with a new warrant; however, they mistook Curly for Red. "That night, when the [show] was over, here they come and were going to arrest me for non-support!" Curly said. "They said, 'We have a warrant here to pick up the boy that plays the guitar.'" Curly initially thought that Hoke Jenkins was playing an April Fool's joke on him, but the officers were not amused. Curly explained that he was not Red Allen and showed them his driver's license, but they were adamant that he must come with them. "They took me over to the jailhouse," Curly continued. "They got on the phone in there, and after a while they let me go. I got on the air the next day and said a word or two about what the policemen down there had done. And then Red, about a week later, he'd heard what happened and he called me: 'How ya doing, Dad? I heard you about got locked up.' I said, 'You dirty rat. If you were down here, I'd kill you with a dry stick.'"

Saturday, April 5, was the last time a newspaper ad appeared for the *Kentucky Barn Dance* at Woodland Auditorium. By May 3 it had moved to Joyland Amusement Park on the Paris Pike. Joyland had the typical rides and games, a penny arcade, a swimming pool, a "kiddieland," and a casino that hosted events such as dog shows and weekly dances. The park's Country Barn was the new venue for the *Barn Dance*, which took place from 8:00 until midnight, featuring "Mike Martin, Tip Sharp, Rainy Mountain Boys, The McReynolds Bros., The Cumberland Mt. Boys."[83] Perhaps the *Barn Dance* was moved to Joyland in order to encourage audience participation, since the May 3 ad announced, "SQUARE DANCE TONIGHT." Perhaps Don Horton felt that the program would attract a broader audience if it were held at the larger Joyland facility. There was no mention of a radio broadcast in the Joyland ads, however, so it is unclear whether WVLK was still involved. In any case, J. D. Crowe said, "After that it went down. When it left Woodland Auditorium, then I really didn't go out there that much after that. And I don't think it lasted very long at Joyland."[84]

While based at WVLK, Curly received a fan letter containing a poem about the war in Korea that inspired him to write a song called "A Purple Heart." He began singing it as a solo on show dates. Jim and Jesse were writing songs as well. They would sing brother duets, with Jesse taking the lead and Jim singing tenor. They often sang trios, in which Jim would sing lead, Curly tenor, and Jesse baritone. "We had a pretty good blend with the trio, there," Jesse said. "We were singing a lot of old songs. Things we'd learned from listening to records, like Mainer's Mountaineers, the Monroe Brothers, and the Blue Sky Boys. We did a lot of Bill Monroe songs. Curly was a great entertainer, and he still is. He knows how to put on a good show, and he communicates good with an audience. We learned a lot from him. Of course, I never could handle it like he did, but he did teach us quite a bit."[85]

Jesse decided the band was ready to record, and he began contacting record labels. He set up an audition with King Records in Cincinnati, but nothing came of it. Then he heard that an A&R man for Capitol Records, Ken

Nelson, was in town. "He worked with Jimmie Skinner, who had a music store up there, and we met Ken at the music store," Jesse explained. "He listened to our music, and he was interested in it. So he called us a week after that, and wanted us to come to Nashville and record. Ken Nelson wanted us to [shorten our name], so we turned it around and used 'Jim and Jesse' at that time."[86]

On Friday, June 13, 1952, Jim, Jesse, Curly, and Hoke were at Castle Studio in the Tulane Hotel in Nashville to record for Capitol. They recruited Sonny James, who had just signed with Capitol, to play fiddle, and Bob Moore, who was becoming a much-sought-after Nashville session musician, to play bass. They recorded eight songs, including six McReynolds Brothers originals, the Louvin Brothers' "Are You Missing Me?," and Curly's "A Purple Heart." Five of the tracks were duets by Jim and Jesse, and Curly sang tenor harmony on two gospel trios: "Are You Lost in Sin?" and "Look for Me, I'll Be There." For the recording they arranged "A Purple Heart" as a trio, with Curly singing lead, Jim tenor, and Jesse baritone.

Jesse reflected on the sessions: "They had one mic for us to sing and play through, and then they had one extra mic for the bass. Back then there was no overdubbing. We knew our stuff pretty well, so we would do three or four cuts of each song, and when they got one they liked, they'd say, 'Well, go to the next song.' They'd listen in the control room, and we didn't get to hear any of it. So, actually, we never heard any of the material that we had recorded until it came out."[87]

Unfortunately, by the time they made these recordings, the *Kentucky Barn Dance* was winding down and the band had played out the Lexington area. They did their last program over WVLK on Friday, May 16, and made their last appearance at the *Barn Dance* on May 31.[88] After recording in Nashville, they returned to Lexington briefly, but times were lean and they soon disbanded. By the time "Are You Missing Me?," the first Capitol single, was released in September, Hoke Jenkins was back in North Carolina, Jim and Jesse had returned to Bristol, and Curly had received a fortuitous call to rejoin the Foggy Mountain Boys in Raleigh, North Carolina.

CHAPTER 5

Climbing the Ladder with Flatt and Scruggs

1952–1954

During Curly's absence from the band in 1951, the Foggy Mountain Boys recorded two more sessions for Columbia, producing such classics as "Earl's Breakdown," "Somehow Tonight," "Get in Line, Brother," "He Took Your Place," "Over the Hills to the Poorhouse," and "Don't Get Above Your Raising." Many of the sides from their great 1950 Mercury sessions were released that year, and they were receiving airplay and gaining visibility for the band. This increased attention enabled Flatt and Scruggs to begin to obtain bookings in some *Grand Ole Opry* package shows. On September 22 and 23, 1951, they performed on one such show presented by Connie B. Gay of WARL in Arlington, Virginia, at Griffith Stadium in Washington, DC. The lineup also included Lefty Frizzell, Ernest Tubb, Carl Smith, Moon Mullican, and the Duke of Paducah. According to *Billboard* the show drew fourteen thousand people, likely setting an attendance record for a "one-show appearance in the country field."[1]

After leaving Lexington, Kentucky, in December 1951 the Foggy Mountain Boys played a New Year's Eve package show at Memorial Auditorium in Spartanburg, South Carolina, along with Ernest Tubb, Grandpa Jones, and Jimmy and Leon Short and their Silver Saddle Boys.[2] From there they headed to WPTF in Raleigh, North Carolina, and on Wednesday, January 2, 1952, they began a weekday program from 1:30 to 2:00 P.M.[3] They also had a 6:00 to 6:30 A.M. (later 6:15 to 6:45 A.M.) program on Saturdays. The station had increased its power to 50,000 watts in 1941, greatly expanding its reach and making it the most powerful station in the Raleigh market. It became an NBC affiliate and added an FM signal in 1949, so the Foggy Mountain Boys' programs were being simulcast at 94.7 FM. On Wednesday, January 23, 1952, the band played on a *Grand Ole Opry* package show at Memorial Auditorium in Raleigh along with Lefty Frizzell, Cowboy Copas, Stringbean, Butterball Paige, the Tennessee Pioneers, and others.[4]

When they arrived in Raleigh, the Foggy Mountain Boys included Flatt, Scruggs, Everett Lilly, Jody Rainwater, and fiddler Art Wooten, who had replaced Chubby Wise while they were in Roanoke. Shortly afterward Wooten left and was replaced by twenty-three-year-old Benny Martin, who hailed from Lester Flatt's hometown of Sparta, Tennessee. Benny had already performed with Bill Monroe, Roy Acuff, and others, but he had been vying for a job with Flatt and Scruggs for several years, according to Jody Rainwater. He had ridden from Lexington, Kentucky, to Sparta with Lester one weekend in 1950. "He had to go home and see about some of the folks," Jody recalled, "and he had me to drive some. We got down there early Sunday morning, and Benny walked up there. He come in with a fiddle and says, 'I've learned some things since I saw you last.' But Flatt told him, 'Now, Ben, you're going to have to get better than that before I can hire you.'"[5] Benny was a quick study, and less than two years later he was a Foggy Mountain Boy.

Singer Mac Martin visited the band in Raleigh in early May 1952. Martin, who was from Pittsburgh, had developed a friendship with the Lilly Brothers while they were based at WWVA in Wheeling in 1948. He was a fan of Lester and Earl, having seen them when they were members of the Blue Grass Boys in 1947, but he had not yet seen the Foggy Mountain Boys. Everett Lilly invited him to visit them in Raleigh, so Mac and his wife Jean made it the final stop on their honeymoon. He recalled seeing the band perform at WPTF and then visiting the trailer park where they all lived.

"We were just there two or three days," he said. "We went to where they had the radio programs, almost like in an auditorium. They were on a stage, but there was no audience. It was set up that they could put folding chairs there [so we could] watch them. I remember Earl had his D-18 [guitar] there, and he had it clamped up, probably to play a gospel song. I picked it up to look at it, and they almost shot me, because once Earl had the capo on there you didn't dare move it. Then we went out to where they were living, to Everett's trailer. Benny, Earl, Lester, and Everett, their trailers were almost in a circle, with the backs [facing]. I could hear Benny Martin, back in his trailer, playing the fiddle, because he never stopped [playing]."[6]

Mac recalled that the Foggy Mountain Boys were doing tent shows, a practice they had begun while based in Roanoke. Everett invited Mac to attend one of the shows, but he declined, feeling a need to spend time with his new bride. Mac also thought there was some unrest among the sidemen. "It seemed to me they might have been planning to leave already. I guess in every band like that there was always the highlight of the music, how it was done so professionally, [but] the musicians wondering if they were getting a fair shake," he speculated.[7]

Jody Rainwater was the first of that group of sidemen to leave. After more than two years of working eighteen-hour days, doing the booking and promotions as well as performing, he was exhausted, and a doctor recommended that he find a less stressful job. Luckily, an opportunity presented itself. Jody was offered a job as a disc jockey at WSVS radio in Crewe, Virginia, near Richmond. He parted on good terms with Flatt and Scruggs. His last performance with them was in Keysville, Virginia, on the first weekend in June.

Banjo player Jim Mills, an avid Scruggs disciple, recalled hearing about that show from his father, who lived in Keysville at the time. "As a teenager, [my father] worked as a short-order cook at a little hamburger joint in downtown Keysville," Jim said. "There's a fork in the road, right before you get to the downtown area, and he said they set up a tent right there. A day before they were to play, Jody Rainwater came to town. He was kind of acting as their manager, and he would [recruit] people to help them get the tent set up, and he would put posters up around town. [Dad] said they came into town that morning and all of them came into the place where he worked. He served them hot dogs and hamburgers. That night he went to the show like everybody else in town. [He] said it was packed. Said they put on one unbelievable show. And Lester Flatt announced from the stage that that was Jody Rainwater's last night with them, that he was going to work at the radio station in Crewe."[8]

The next to leave the band was Everett Lilly. The Lilly Brothers had worked with fiddler Tex Logan at WWVA in Wheeling before Tex left to study at the Massachusetts Institute of Technology in Cambridge. In the summer of 1952 Tex was working with country music duo Jerry and Sky in Boston. The band's rhythm guitar player was drafted, and Tex contacted Everett to see if he knew of a good replacement. Everett was unable to suggest anyone, but Tex then asked whether Everett and Bea Lilly would consider coming to Boston to join him in a band. Everett called Bea, who said he would gladly go, and Bea called banjo player Don Stover, who without hesitation agreed to leave his job in a West Virginia coal mine. That settled it. Everett gave his notice to Flatt and Scruggs and told Bea, "I'll be through West Virginia the end of the week. You boys be ready and we'll head for Boston."[9]

Lester and Earl hired Charles Elza ("Kentucky Slim") to replace Jody Rainwater as comedian and bassist. They called Curly Seckler to replace Everett Lilly. When Everett left the Foggy Mountain Boys, they were preparing to move to WNOX in Knoxville. Their last program on WPTF was on Saturday, September 7.[10] Curly met them in Raleigh, and they headed to Knoxville to join the cast of WNOX's daily *Mid-Day Merry-Go-Round* and Saturday night *Tennessee Barn Dance*.

By this time the Foggy Mountain Boys had established themselves as one of the hottest new bands on the circuit. An article that appeared in the August 1952 issue of Nashville-based *Country Song Roundup* called them a "top-notch folk combination." It referred to Flatt and Scruggs as "veteran performers," and it noted that "Flatt-Scruggs and The Foggy Mountain Boys are sure of attracting capacity crowds wherever and whenever they appear because of their versatility and their load of natural musical talent. It is readily agreed by all critics of country music, that the Flatt-Scruggs outfit is going to hit the top of the ladder in the very near future."[11]

The move to WNOX was a step up that ladder. By 1950 Lowell Blanchard had firmly established the *Merry-Go-Round* and *Barn Dance* programs as the launch pads for country performers who had their sights set on the *Grand Ole Opry* in Nashville. Its 10,000-watt signal meant that WNOX had a tremendous audience, not only in East Tennessee but across the Southeast at night. Huge crowds would line the sidewalks, waiting to enter the WNOX auditorium at 110 South Gay Street for the live performances. Policemen were enlisted to handle the crowds and move them along, and sometimes the musicians barely had time to unload their instruments before being ordered to move their cars away from the front of the building.[12]

In addition to the Foggy Mountain Boys, the cast of the *Merry-Go-Round* and *Barn Dance* included Don Gibson, Carl Story, Archie Campbell, and comedy team Jamup and Honey, plus sidemen such as Junior Huskey, Benny Sims, and George "Speedy" Krise. Lance LeRoy, who later would become Lester Flatt's manager, was living in Asheville, North Carolina, in 1952. A huge Flatt and Scruggs fan, he would drive the 112 miles across the mountains to Knoxville to see them at the *Barn Dance*. Lance remembered that it was summertime when he first saw them there, so possibly the Foggy Mountain Boys appeared several times at the *Barn Dance* before they actually moved to Knoxville. Though Lance was unable to recall whether Everett Lilly or Curly Seckler played mandolin when he first saw them, he vividly remembered Benny Martin's fiddling. "He'd come out and play 'Katy Hill,'" Lance marveled. "And they'd pull the curtain back and say, 'Now, here's Lester Flatt, Earl Scruggs, and the Foggy Mountain Boys.' And, boy, here come Earl and Lester. They'd just about come running out there. Benny'd be about finishing up the first verse of 'Katy Hill' when you'd hear 'Do do doong' [Lester's G-note run on the guitar], and it was kind of dramatic they way they did it."[13]

One night Lance mustered his courage and followed Benny into the men's room. "I said, 'Benny, I just want to tell you I sure do like your fiddling. I've been playing a little bit on the fiddle.' He said, 'Oh, really? Come on backstage and I'll show you my fiddle.' So he went back with me and introduced me to Lester and Earl."[14]

From then on Lance followed the band, often driving hundreds of miles to see them at a school, theater, or courthouse. He recalled when he first became aware of Curly Seckler's presence in the band. "It was just unreal how good he was, [how] his voice blended with Lester's. Curly had that little 'yelp' in his voice, and they would just drag those notes out. The harmony was so good. They put so much punch in those duets. I put Lester Flatt and Curly Seckler, as a duet, right at the very top echelon. To me the top echelon is James and Martha Carson, Ira and Charlie Louvin, and Lester and Curly."[15]

The band followed a regular format in its live shows, Lance said. "They'd do a set—forty-five, fifty minutes, or maybe an hour. Then they'd take an intermission, and that's when they'd sell. They'd tell the audience, 'We'll be out there,' and the audience would just keep their seats. The band members would walk out through the auditorium [saying], 'Get it here, Flatt and

Scruggs records, songbooks.' Then they had the second part of the show, which was, like, thirty minutes. Curly would always start out emceeing that part. Earl would come out, but Lester wouldn't. He'd stay backstage. They'd feature Curly on one or two, maybe do an instrumental, and then Lester would come out just as they were finishing the last song. They'd do two hymns after Lester came out, and then they'd do one or two more secular songs and close it out after that."[16]

After the Foggy Mountain Boys arrived in Knoxville that fall, Howard Watts rejoined the band. Kentucky Slim was a fantastic comedian but a mediocre bass player, so Lester and Earl were happy to have Cedric Rainwater (Watts) back. Cedric's son Jarrett Watts explained that, after two years with Hank Williams, Cedric had become fed up with Hank's alcoholism. At a concert that fall in Virginia, Hank had been in such bad shape that Cedric decided to quit the band. "Hank was so drunk," Jarrett said, "that Daddy had to go out and do two hours of comedy while they [got] Hank sober enough to come out onto the stage. And when he did, they booed him off the stage. Daddy left a note [saying] 'I'm leaving. My little boy sick at home,' and he left. Lester and Earl and Daddy, they were good buddies, and I'm sure that when Daddy left Hank he probably made a phone call and said, 'Hey, can I come on?' That's when he went back with Lester and Earl for a while."[17]

With Cedric back, Lester and Earl wasted no time in getting back into the studio. On November 9, 1952, they recorded eight songs for Columbia at Castle Studio in Nashville. Included were one solo ("If I Should Wander Back Tonight"), one duet ("Why Did You Wander"), two trios ("Thinking About You" and "Dim Lights, Thick Smoke"), two banjo instrumentals ("Flint Hill Special" and "Dear Old Dixie"), and two gospel quartets ("Reunion in Heaven" and "Pray for the Boys") featuring Scruggs's guitar as the only lead instrument. The powerful Flatt-Seckler duet on "Why Did You Wander" shows that Curly was able to step easily back into his role, and he seemed to sing with even more authority than on previous recordings. Likewise, his mandolin break on "Thinking About You" rings with confidence. These were Benny Martin's first recordings with the band, and they showcase his blossoming talent. His aggressive approach, smooth noting and bow work, and frequent use of double stops brought a new excitement to the band's already dynamic sound. With Earl's precise, driving banjo playing and Curly's rock-solid rhythm chop to propel them, the band was turning heads. Musicians such as Sonny Osborne and Melvin Goins, who were just getting started in the business at that time, recalled the 1952–1953 Foggy Mountain Boys as a jaw-dropping aggregation.

Although things were going well for the group, the life of a hillbilly musician was still very challenging. They were traveling long distances on two-lane roads with five band members and instruments in a car. It was not unusual for them to leave Knoxville on Saturday night after the *Tennessee Barn Dance* and drive six hundred miles to one of the outdoor parks in Pennsylvania for a Sunday afternoon show. Curly recalled many occasions when he shaved using water in a cola bottle. On the rare nights when the band had time to sleep in motel rooms, there were often bedbugs to contend with. The band members received a weekly salary, as opposed to being paid by the job, but their wages were nonetheless modest.

Curly and his wife Mable were living in a small apartment near the railroad tracks, just north of downtown Knoxville. Sometime during the winter of 1952–1953 Mable developed a fever and a severe sore throat that became progressively worse. "Then she got so bad that I had to take her to the hospital," Curly said, "and they diagnosed it as being diphtheria. And that scared me to death, because my half-brother died with diphtheria." The doctors speculated that Mable had contracted the disease, which is a bacterial infection, from drinking water from unsanitary pipes where they were living. Curly then discovered that Mable had never been vaccinated against diphtheria, perhaps because she grew up in an extremely rural area. Curly had been vaccinated as a youngster in school, which explains why he didn't contract the disease.

While Mable was in Baptist Hospital her temperature spiked at 107 degrees, and the skin peeled off her ears and face. In order to visit her, Curly had to wear a protective gown and mask. During the several weeks she spent in the hospital Curly was on the road with the Foggy Mountain Boys but kept in touch with the hospital by phone. Finally, he related, "they called me on the road and said she had a fifty-fifty chance of living, but she had no chance at all unless she took what they called a 'kill or cure' shot. I said, 'Well, give it to her.'" The shot was likely either an antitoxin or a strong antibiotic, both of which can be used to treat diphtheria. It did indeed save her life, and Mable's physical health gradually improved enough that she was released from the hospital. But the extremely high fever had caused permanent brain damage, and she would never again lead a normal life.

Curly had been planning to retrieve his sons Ray and Monnie from the orphanage in North Carolina as soon as he and Mable were settled and his job seemed stable. All of that changed with her illness. Mable was now in somewhat of a childlike state herself, and Curly was in the position of having to take care of her. With medication she was able to function well enough that he could leave her at home while he was working, but her behavior, which was often erratic and unpredictable, was a source of constant concern for him.

While Mable was hospitalized, Curly received a bit of good news. Capitol Records released Jim and Jesse's recording of "I Will Always Be Waiting for You" backed by Curly's original "A Purple Heart." The record received a lukewarm review in *Billboard*: "Jim, Jesse, and Curley [*sic*] Seckler make up a trio for this weeper based on the current war situation in Korea. Such tunes haven't made too much of a dent in the past year or so—and this one doesn't figure to be the exception."[18] The song would stand the test of time, however, to become one of Curly's signature songs. It was recorded by a number of other artists and several times by Curly himself. He performed it with Flatt and Scruggs on WSM and on live shows.

About this time *Billboard* began rating the Country & Western records they reviewed. The ratings system was as follows: "90–100, Tops; 80–89, Excellent; 70–79, Good; 40–59, Satisfactory; 0–39, Poor." "Why Did You Wander," backed with "Thinking About You," was the first Flatt and Scruggs record to be rated. The review read:

> "Thinking About You": 72
> A pleasant side by singers Flatt, Scruggs, and Cruley [*sic*] Seckler, featuring good fiddle and guitar work by the Foggy Mountain Boys. Back country areas should like this side.
> "Why Did You Wander": 86
> Flatt and Seckler do the vocal work on this lively effort over hoedown backing. What they sing about is not very clear, but the string band lends good support. For rural areas.[19]

Although the review was generally positive and the ratings were high, the reviewer was clearly indicating that the Foggy Mountain Boys' appeal was to hill folk, not to a more sophisticated urban audience. But it would turn out to be a point in their favor. In May, Flatt and Scruggs played a show in

Livingston, Tennessee. Afterward, they were approached by Efford Burke, a salesman for Nashville-based Martha White Flour Mills. Burke, whose sales region included the Appalachian area of East Tennessee, was impressed with the Foggy Mountain Boys and felt they had the kind of appeal that would translate into sales if Martha White sponsored them. He picked up one of their show posters and a few days later took it to Martha White's president, Cohen T. Williams. The latter decided to drive to Knoxville to see the band for himself at WNOX. Lester and Earl invited him to ride with them to a show date the following evening in Harlan, Kentucky. Williams was impressed and invited them to come to his home in Nashville the following week to discuss a sponsorship and a slot on Martha White's early morning radio program on WSM.[20]

Curly recalled that Lester and Earl were not particularly interested in talking to Williams, though they did agree to visit him. They sat in Williams's back yard and he made the presentation, but Lester's mind was elsewhere. "Cohen told me that he was trying to talk business to Lester Flatt," Curly chuckled, "and there were squirrels and rabbits messing around up in the woods. That rabbit come out of there and Lester said, 'If I had my gun, I could get him in a minute.' He was more interested in killing that rabbit than he was doing business with Cohen Williams!"

The flour company president persisted, and they came to an agreement. According to Williams, "Flatt wanted to know what kind of contract I wanted, and what kind of a take they were going to have to kick in to me. I said, 'You aren't going to kick in anything to me, and the only kind of contract we will have is a handshake.' And that's the way it was for twenty years. We never had a contract."[21]

Williams made arrangements for Flatt and Scruggs to take over the Martha White radio program on WSM, and by the first week in June the band had relocated to Nashville. They moved their trailers to the Dickerson Road Trailer Park, where Lester and Gladys had lived while he was working with Bill Monroe in the forties. Curly and Mable rented an apartment a short distance away on Meridian Street.

Cedric Rainwater left the band prior to their move to Nashville. In his first stint with the Foggy Mountain Boys Cedric had been an equal partner, but when he returned in 1952 it was as a salaried employee, like the other band members. This arrangement was less appealing, and by the spring of 1953 he had decided to seek greener pastures. He returned to Nashville and worked with several country performers including Hank Snow and Ray Price. It is unclear who replaced Cedric in the Foggy Mountain Boys. Lonnie "Red" Murphy may have worked with them briefly. He was pictured with them in a photo of the cast of the WNOX *Mid-Day Merry-Go-Round* from about that time, and he was listed in a newspaper ad for their April 11 show at the Mosque Theater in Richmond, Virginia.[22] Junior Huskey, who was the staff bassist for the *Tennessee Barn Dance*, also filled in on a few shows.

According to Earl Scruggs, he and Flatt had wanted to hire Huskey when they received the Martha White sponsorship, but he had already taken a job in Nashville with Carl Smith.[23] Amateur recordings indicate that Huskey did play with the Foggy Mountain Boys on their first Martha White radio programs on WSM, likely because they did not yet have a regular bass player and Huskey was available in the mornings. Nashville studio musician Bob Moore also played bass on many of their early WSM programs. He was pictured with the band, standing behind a table filled with Martha White products, in the first songbook they published after arriving in Nashville. Neither Huskey nor Moore toured with the band on the road.

Jud Collins was the announcer for their first few WSM programs, but Grant Turner took over when he returned from vacation the following week. Flatt and Scruggs were seasoned pros by this time, and they easily stepped into their new roles as "flour peddlers." On a typical program they would sing the opening theme: "How many biscuits did you eat this morning? / How many biscuits can you eat this evening? / Always bake with Martha White. / Goodness gracious, it's good and light, / This morning, this evening, right now." Turner would welcome the listeners while Earl picked a banjo tune, then Benny Martin would whip out a short fiddle tune such as "Katy Hill" or "Back Up and Push." Turner would then deliver a commercial for Martha White flour or cornmeal. Lester would announce the next song, usually one of their recent recordings such as "Dim Lights, Thick Smoke" or "Why Did You Wander." Then he would mention their upcoming show dates, they would perform a gospel quartet, and Turner would be back with another pitch for Martha White. Occasionally Curly would get to sing a solo such as "A Purple Heart." Earl Scruggs would pick a banjo instrumental, and they would wrap up the program with the Martha White theme.

Lance LeRoy was an avid listener, and he attested, "It just couldn't be beat, what they were doing in the early morning shows. It was awesome. And they always seemed to have such a good time. There was always laughing going on. They had more inside jokes than the law allows! Lester'd comment on something, and you could hear all this laughter in the background, and then you'd laugh, too."[24]

One of the inside jokes that started about this time was Lester's referring to Curly as "The Old Trapper from China Grove." It started, Curly said, with a casual conversation in which he mentioned that he and his brothers used to set traps to catch rabbits in the early years. Lester enjoyed giving people nicknames, and he latched onto that story and never let it go. He would often introduce Curly that way on radio, amid hearty laughter from the band. Curly knew virtually nothing about trapping, but the nickname created interest among fans, who would inquire about it, much to the amusement of Curly's bandmates.

Martha White had been sponsoring the daily 5:45 to 6:00 radio program, which was called *Biscuit Time*, since the mid-forties. In 1948 it began sponsoring a regular fifteen-minute segment of the *Grand Ole Opry*.[25] Before the arrival of Flatt and Scruggs the group featured on *Biscuit Time* was Milton Estes and the Musical Millers. Estes was also appearing on the *Grand Ole Opry*. Cohen Williams wanted to put the Foggy Mountain Boys on the Martha White segment of the *Opry*, but he met with resistance. Bill Monroe had not been pleased when Lester and Earl had left his band to start a group of their own. Now they had made a successful return to Nashville and were perceived as his competition. Monroe was well established as a popular member of the *Opry* by this time, so *Opry* officials were leery of offending him by admitting them. Williams felt it best to avoid ruffling any feathers at that point, so he chose not to push the matter.

Flatt and Scruggs began booking show dates in central Tennessee, Kentucky, and northern Alabama. They continued to work some of their established venues in the Carolinas, Virginia, and eastern Tennessee, including the annual American Legion Carnival in Kingsport, where they headlined for six nights in June. They soon became regulars at the country music parks to the north, including New River Ranch in Rising Sun, Maryland, and Buck Lake Ranch in Angola, Indiana. By August the Foggy Mountain Boys were booked solid at schools, theaters, parks, courthouses, auditoriums, and legion halls from Philadelphia, Mississippi, to West Grove, Pennsylvania. Martha White arranged for their show posters and window cards to be printed by Hatch Show Print and assisted them in acquiring a stretch Cadillac limousine in which to travel.[26] The company also supplied them with coupons for discounts on flour and cornmeal, which they distributed at all of their performances.

On a typical workday, Curly said, the band members would arrive at the radio station between 5:00 and 5:30 A.M. Lester would have the program planned and they would go over the songs before going on the air. After the program, they would arrange a time to leave for the show date that night. The venues were generally within a two-hundred-mile radius of Nashville, since they had to be back for the 5:45 A.M. radio show the next morning. "And," Curly said, "sometimes we wouldn't hardly get back in time to lay down at the house, and it was time to go up there and do the show."

On August 29 and 30, 1953, the Foggy Mountain Boys went into the studio again. They were joined on these sessions by guitarist Louis Innis and bassist Bob Moore. Innis played a closed-chord "sock" rhythm, which provided a heavier beat and a more contemporary "Nashville" flavor, presumably to make the Flatt and Scruggs sound more palatable to a wider audience. These sessions produced one Flatt solo, one Scruggs banjo instrumental, one trio, two gospel songs, and three now-classic Flatt-Seckler duets: "I'll Go Stepping Too," "Your Love Is Like a Flower," and "That Old Book of Mine."

The latter was a Seckler original composed in the 1940s after the breakup of his first marriage. "We'd been singing it just a little bit, on WSM," Curly said. "We was in the studio, and Lester said, 'Seck, do you have a number that you'd like to do?' I said, 'Yeah, this one, here.' We run over it about two times, and then recorded it." Though Lester had taken half of the composing credit on several of Curly's songs, he let Curly maintain full ownership of "That Old Book of Mine" because of his wife's health problems. The song was not released until 1970, however, so Curly received no royalties for seventeen years after it was recorded. "Your Love Is Like a Flower," which was brought to Flatt by Everett Lilly, was not issued as a single, either, but it appeared on the band's first album, *Foggy Mountain Jamboree*, released in 1957.

"I'll Go Stepping Too," brought to Flatt and Scruggs by Troy Martin, became one of their trademark songs and is considered a bluegrass standard. Instrumentally speaking, Scruggs's banjo sparkles, and Benny Martin's fiddling is adventurous and authoritative. In vocal terms, Lester and Curly are hand in glove. By this time Curly had become an expert at matching his pronunciation, phrasing, and timing to those of whoever he was harmonizing with. This is a difficult skill to master, but Curly made it seem easy. "It just come natural singing with Lester Flatt," Curly said. "After he would do something once or twice, I would know how he was going to do it. Whatever he put on it, I'd do the same thing. The only thing Lester said to me, when I went to work with him in forty-nine, he said, 'Now, I lead pretty high. If I ever get them too high, you just tell me, and I'll lower them.' And we worked all these years together, and I never did say lower the first one."

On October 11, 1953, the Foggy Mountain Boys began a Sunday morning gospel program on WSM from 8:00 to 8:15. Sometime in 1954 they began a 5:45 to 6:00 Saturday afternoon program (just before the *Grand Ole Opry*) as well. Curly didn't remember being at WSM at that time of day on Saturdays, so most likely these shows were prerecorded to enable the band to travel to lucrative weekend show dates. According to Lester Flatt's biographer, Jake Lambert, by early 1954 Lester and Earl grew discouraged about being denied membership at the *Grand Ole Opry* and spoke to Cohen Williams about leaving Nashville to find another Saturday night venue. At that time, Saturday night barn dance shows such as the *Opry*, the *Wheeling Jamboree*, and the *Tennessee Barn Dance* were still very important to a hillbilly band's success. Williams agreed to let them leave and to continue sponsoring them if they would tape their radio programs and send them back to WSM to be aired.[27] So it is likely that, once they began to record their programs, Martha White decided to give them a Saturday afternoon slot as well.

In February 1954 Benny Martin left the band and was replaced by Paul Warren of Hickman County, Tennessee. He had been playing with Johnnie and Jack since he returned from service in World War II in 1946. His playing was more traditional than Benny Martin's, and he knew a large number of old-time fiddle tunes, many of which he had learned from Fiddlin' Arthur Smith. It was Lester's idea to feature some of these tunes on live shows, played by Paul and Earl on fiddle and banjo, with no other accompaniment. This pairing provided more variety in the program and lent a note of authenticity that appealed not only to the hill folk, but also to the more "high-brow" audience of the folk revival as it began to take hold a few years later.

In the spring of 1954, Flatt and Scruggs decided to return to WNOX in Knoxville, where they could perform regularly on the *Mid-Day Merry-Go-Round* and the *Tennessee Barn Dance*. A photo printed in one of the Flatt and Scruggs songbooks from the late 1950s shows Lester and Earl standing with Lowell Blanchard, Jamup and Honey, and Roy Acuff, with a caption reading: "This photo is a page from the past, taken when Lester and Earl appeared on the *Mid-Day Merry-Go-Round*, WNOX, Knoxville, in 1954."[28] Another photo of the cast of the *Merry-Go-Round* shows Lester, Earl, Curly, and Paul, along with Jamup and Honey, Don Gibson, Carl Story, and other cast members.[29]

It is not clear exactly when they arrived in Knoxville, but Hatch Show Print order files indicate that the Foggy Mountain Boys performed on multiple show dates in February and March with comedy duo Jamup and Honey, who were based at WNOX. From Monday, February 8, through Saturday, February 13, the two groups performed nightly in Virginia and North Carolina.[30] Several of the Virginia show dates were arranged by Jody Rainwater, who by this time was well established at WSVS in Crewe. The first week in March found the Foggy Mountain Boys back with Jamup and Honey in Hazelwood, North Carolina; Bakersville, North Carolina; Galax, Virginia; Wilkesboro, North Carolina; and Sandy Ridge, North Carolina. Two weeks later the two groups returned to the Carolinas for another weeklong tour.[31]

Flatt and Scruggs performed on an *Opry* package show on April 11 at the Mosque Theater in Richmond, Virginia, along with Webb Pierce, Marty Robbins, and the Duke of Paducah.[32] Exactly a year earlier they had shared headliner status at the Mosque with Lefty Frizzell on a "Hillbilly All-Star Roundup" show,[33] so they were becoming well known to Richmond audiences. An article about the Foggy Mountain Boys published on March 28, 1954, in the *Richmond Times-Dispatch* indicated that "Joe Stuart is comedian and bass fiddler."[34] Stuart was from Knoxville, so it seems likely that he joined the band upon their return to WNOX.

By May, bassist English P. "Jake" Tullock had replaced Stuart. Jake was originally from Etowah, a small town between Knoxville and Chattanooga. He had worked on radio in Knoxville with several bands, including Esco Hankins, the Bailey Brothers, and Don Gibson. Jake not only was an excellent bass player and comedian but he also had an extremely high voice that could soar even above Curly's piercing tenor. Lester and Earl took advantage of it in their next recording session, held on May 19, 1954, featuring Jake on high baritone harmony on "You're Not a Drop in the Bucket." That session also produced the Flatt-Seckler duet "Till the End of the World Rolls Around," the trio "Don't This Road Look Rough and Rocky," and the Scruggs banjo instrumental "Foggy Mountain Special," on which Chubby Wise was brought in to play fiddle. All of the band members were featured on this tune, including Jake. Curly also played a mandolin solo on "Don't This Road

Look Rough and Rocky," but it is barely audible in the mix. This would be the last Flatt and Scruggs recording to feature a Seckler mandolin break.

The Foggy Mountain Boys spent the summer of 1954 in Knoxville. Paul Warren's wife Eloise (who would later marry Curly) remembered that she and Paul and their six-year-old son Gary lived in a trailer park on the Clinton Highway, north of Knoxville. Their little trailer had no bathroom, and after Gary spent the day playing outside, Eloise would take him to the washhouse. "They had these big tubs, and I used to take Gary down there at the end of the day and put him in one of those tubs and give him a bath," she laughed.[35]

Jody Rainwater had kept in touch with Lester and Earl since leaving the band, and he had helped them find work in Virginia. He suggested that they relocate to Crewe and offered them a daily program on WSVS. Crewe is just sixty miles from Richmond, where 50,000-watt powerhouse WRVA was blasting out a weekly Saturday program called the *Old Dominion Barn Dance*. The *Barn Dance* had originated in September 1946 from the old Lyric Theater at the corner of Ninth and Broad Streets, just across from the WRVA studios. It was hosted by "Sunshine Sue" Workman, who had been a regular on WRVA since 1940. By 1954 the *Barn Dance* was well established and was featured once per month on the CBS network's *Saturday Night—Country Style* program, heard nationwide. On Saturday, July 10, 1954, the Foggy Mountain Boys played as guests on the *Barn Dance*.[36] This was likely an audition set up for them by Jody Rainwater. By the end of August they were accepted as cast members, and they were given star billing in the August 28 newspaper ad for the *Barn Dance*.[37]

They moved their families to Virginia, and everyone except Curly settled in a trailer park on the outskirts of Blackstone, just a few miles from Crewe. Curly and Mable and their pet cat stayed in a boarding house in downtown Blackstone. Eloise Warren (Seckler) remembered that, before they left Knoxville, Paul traded in their trailer for a newer model with a bathroom, and as part of the sales agreement the trailer company hauled it to Blackstone for them. She also recalled that Gary started school in Blackstone.

Earl Scruggs recalled, "We taped a daily program on WRVA in Richmond and did two daily shows at WSVS in nearby Crewe. We taped the Martha White shows in Crewe and sent them to Nashville, producing a total of four fifteen minute shows a day. We joined the cast on the WRVA Saturday night *Barn Dance* and continued to make personal appearances."[38]

At that time the band was still traveling in the white Cadillac limousine, and Curly remembered a hilarious prank that they pulled on Jake Tullock involving the herbal medicine that Lester took for his rheumatoid arthritis. "Lester always carried a little of that with him," Curly said, "because every now and then he'd get spells [of pain]. And it was the nastiest tasting stuff I ever tasted. So we was in this Cadillac, and Earl was driving, and [the driver] could lock the doors and windows. We got to talking about that stuff tasting pretty good, and built it up, and Jake said, 'Well, let me have a taste of it.' He took a big taste, and Earl locked the windows, and [Jake] was hollering, 'Whooh, ooh, ooh! Down, down, down, down!' And he had to swallow it. All of us just died laughing, because we knowed the taste of it."

Just a few weeks after Flatt and Scruggs arrived in Virginia, the cast of the *Old Dominion Barn Dance* went to New York City for a two-week run on Broadway. As the *Richmond Times-Dispatch* reported:

> Under the new title of "Hayride," the *Old Dominion Barn Dance* will open its New York engagement at the Forty-Eighth Street Theater on Monday night. Headed by Sunshine Sue, the company will take to Broadway the first hillbilly music revue of its kind ever to play there. In the past decade hillbilly music has come out of the hills to ramble around the big cities and kick up its heels on all musical best-seller lists. . . . The trend has become so big that a special act of Congress has designated May 26 as annual National Hillbilly Music Day.[39]

In addition to Sunshine Sue, the cast of *Hayride* included Flatt and Scruggs and the Foggy Mountain Boys—Paul Warren, Jake Tulloch [sic], and Curly Sechler (mentioned by name in the playbill)—Cousin Joe Maphis and Rose, the Coon Creek Girls, the Trail Blazers, Eddy "Texas" Smith, Quincy Snodgrass, Mary Klick, Zeb Robinson, Sonny Day, and Fiddlin' Irving. The show ran from September 13 to September 25, with performances at 8:00 P.M. each night, Monday through Saturday, and matinees on Wednesdays and Saturdays at 2:30 P.M.[40]

Curly remembered Lester's reaction on opening night, when the stage crew came around to apply makeup to the performers. "They was going to put makeup on him," Curly chuckled. "They said, 'Them bright lights'll kill you.' Well, Flatt said, 'You ain't putting that paint on me! I've hunted possums over in White County, Tennessee with brighter lights than that!' He just didn't want makeup on him, but then I think he finally went along and put it on."

Reviews were mixed. In general it seemed that the New York critics were unable to appreciate the show's "corn pone" humor and "down home" presentation. One critic stated that *Hayride* "is made up of people who don't sing so good and don't play so good but are plenty folksy in their hillbilly costumes. 'Hayride' merely aroused the damyankee in me. But, as a dutiful reporter, I must state that the audience sounded enthusiastic."[41] Indeed, Curly recalled, the two-week run was a success from the performers' standpoint. "That show really went over good up there," he said. "You'd encore on it, and we had a packed house every night." This was Curly's first trip to New York, and he brought his mother up to see the show. "And my brother [George] was living there, then. They all come over to the hotel where we was at. We had a ball."

Curly recalled that he, Lester, and Earl each received a check from Peer International as an advance on royalties for the performances of their songs on Broadway. The theater also wrote checks to the band members for their work, but because they were salaried employees, they were instructed to sign them over to Flatt and Scruggs.

If the Foggy Mountain Boys were not known outside the South before their stint on Broadway, by the time they left they had become a household name. An Associated Newspapers entertainment column published on September 20 noted: "Roy Rogers, the Duchess of Kent, Miss America, Marilyn Monroe, the Foggy Mountain Boys, and Gina Lollabrigida [*sic*], famous Italian movie star, are all in New York at the same time making it extra difficult to run into somebody who doesn't amount to much."[42]

The band returned to Richmond and spent the rest of 1954 as headliners for the *Old Dominion Barn Dance*. They shared the bill with Mac Wiseman, who had been a *Barn Dance* regular since 1953 but did not make the trip to New York because of other commitments. Flatt and Scruggs would take turns with Wiseman in playing a 7:00 to 7:30 P.M. program on WRVA before the *Barn Dance*. Then, following the *Barn Dance*, each group would perform a thirty-minute radio program.

Banjo player Ben Eldridge, who grew up in Richmond, had just turned sixteen in August 1954. He had received a banjo for his birthday, and was a fan of Earl Scruggs's playing. Ben had been listening to the *Barn Dance* on the radio, and occasionally attending in person, since its inception eight years earlier. He recalled that the Lyric Theater had about five to six hundred seats, with a balcony. "There was a control room over on one side, and they'd come out and tell us when to clap. It was just classic live music radio," he said. "The *Barn Dance* had a whole lot of different entertainers, and they would give Lester and Earl ten or fifteen minutes. They had two shows, at 7:30 and 9:30, and they would clear the audience [in between]. And then they would have this live show, in the studio, [with] Flatt and Scruggs and Mac [Wiseman]."[43]

Ben and a friend would sometimes go to watch Flatt and Scruggs do their late night radio show. "There were typically about ten, fifteen people that they let into the studio," he recalled. "It was just amazing to be in there with them. It was awesome. I remember Earl playing 'Dear Old Dixie.' I just wish I'd known more about the banjo at that time so I'd have understood what Earl was doing a little more. But I did get to watch him, up close and personal. And he was in his prime, back in those days."[44]

Ben remembered that Mac Wiseman's band at that time included Josh Graves on mandolin or bass, Curtis Lee on fiddle, and Donnie Bryant on banjo. "Donnie was just fresh out of high school," he said, "and during that three or four months that Flatt and Scruggs were in Richmond, he picked up a lot from Earl. It just really changed his whole approach."[45]

While they were at the *Old Dominion Barn Dance*, Flatt and Scruggs hired comic and dancer James "Chick" Stripling to work with them on occasion. Over the years Stripling had worked with a number of different bands including Ernest Tubb, the Stanley Brothers, and Jimmy Martin, and he had worked with Mac Wiseman in Richmond. "Lester and them brought him in to do some work, because he had worked some with Bill Monroe, and they liked what he done," Curly explained. "Boy, he was some entertainer. You couldn't keep him sober, but he was good. Lester was going to go squirrel hunting with him one morning," he laughed. "He went down there and couldn't get him up. [Chick] was drunk."

Curly remembered another adventure of Lester's in Crewe. "There was a service station there, where we used to get gas all the time," he said. "We went in there one morning and this fellow was selling chances on a double-barrel shotgun. So Flatt give him a dollar, and danged if he didn't win! We went back in there [later], and [the man] said, 'Flatt, you've won the shotgun.'"

Lester enjoyed winning, Curly noted, especially at poker, which was a favorite pastime while on the road. Jody Rainwater said that the band played poker while driving from Florida to Lexington in 1950. Jody's wife Emma stated that they played while they were in Blackstone as well. One night when Jody had gone to a show date with the band, they got into a poker game after the show. Emma recalled, "Louise called me, mad as fire! 'Have you heard from them scallywags?' I was sound asleep. I wouldn't wait up for [Jody]. And she waited up all that time, and she was mad, and she said, 'They're somewhere playing poker!'"[46]

Eloise Warren (Seckler) recalled that she, Louise Scruggs, and Gladys Flatt were close friends and would often get together while their husbands were on the road. Eloise had been pregnant when they moved to Blackstone, and that fall she suffered a miscarriage. "Paul and them were gone on a show," she said, "and Gladys and Louise went with me to the hospital, and Mable stayed with the kids. She was all right. She wasn't sick then.

"Randy [Scruggs] was just a little baby when Paul went to work with them," she continued. "I was at Louise's trailer one day, and he got a piece of a rattle caught in his throat, and she was just about to have hysterics. He was beginning to turn blue. I didn't know what to do, but I run my finger down his throat and got a hold of that and pulled it out. Louise still remembered that [years later]."[47]

The Foggy Mountain Boys continued taping their popular radio programs for WSM and headlining on the *Old Dominion Barn Dance* through the end of the year. Meanwhile, back in Nashville, Cohen Williams was working behind the scenes to convince the officials at WSM to allow Flatt and Scruggs to perform on the *Grand Ole Opry*. Television was becoming an increasingly powerful medium, and Williams had decided to use it to his advantage by purchasing time slots for Flatt and Scruggs on several stations. With the promise of Martha White sponsorship for their own television show, he convinced Lester and Earl to move back to Nashville. They began booking January show dates in Tennessee, and by December 22 they had resumed ordering window cards from Hatch Show Print.

The band members packed their families and moved to Nashville at Christmastime, returning for one last performance on the *Old Dominion Barn Dance* on January 1, 1955.[48] Curly bought a Chevrolet in Crewe in which to haul his and Mable's possessions. They found an upstairs apartment on Russell Street in east Nashville. The rest of the band moved back to the Dickerson Road Trailer Park. Their wandering days were finally over; Nashville would become their permanent home. Although success would not come overnight, 1955 was to be the year the stars aligned for Flatt and Scruggs and set them on the path to country music immortality.

CHAPTER 6

Goodness Gracious, It's Good

1955–1962

The Foggy Mountain Boys were back at Castle Studio in Nashville on January 23, 1955, to record four tracks: the gospel quartets "You Can Feel It in Your Soul" and "Old Fashioned Preacher" and the trios "Before I Met You" and "I'm Gonna Sleep with One Eye Open." On these recordings, the closed-chord "sock" rhythm guitar, played by Eddie Hill, was even more dominant than it had been on the previous session, totally obscuring Curly Seckler's mandolin chop. Clearly the producers at Columbia Records were looking for a more percussive beat to compete with the mainstream sounds that were emerging from Nashville.

There is a misconception that Flatt and Scruggs began appearing on WSM-TV in early 1955. According to television listings in *the Tennessean*, however, the first Flatt and Scruggs program on WSM-TV was not until Saturday, January 14, 1956.[1] Their first documented television show was at WSAZ-TV in Huntington, West Virginia, on Wednesday, February 2, 1955, from 6:00 to 6:30 P.M.[2] Then, on Tuesday, February 8, they began a weekly program on WATE-TV in Knoxville from 1:15 to 1:30 P.M.[3] After just four weeks on WATE, they moved to WJHL-TV in Johnson City on Tuesday, March 8, from 6:30 to 7:00 P.M. An ad in the local newspaper read: "Old-time

Country Music at its Best! 'THE FLATT and SCRUGGS SHOW.' From Bristol to Broadway, from Demopolis to Detroit, 'The Flatt and Scruggs Show' has set toes a-tapping and hands a-clapping."[4] On Friday, March 11, they began a weekly program at 7:00 to 7:30 P.M. on WDXI-TV in Jackson, Tennessee.[5]

With the band back in Nashville and the power of television on his side, Cohen Williams decided it was time to make his move with the *Grand Ole Opry*. According to Jake Lambert, Williams collected a huge bag of Flatt and Scruggs fan mail and took it to WSM general manager Jack DeWitt. He gave DeWitt an ultimatum: "Either they put Flatt and Scruggs on [Martha White's] half hour of the *Opry* or he would pull his company's advertising off the station."[6] In response, *Opry* management agreed to allow the band to perform occasionally as guests on the Martha White segment, but they would not be recognized as members of the *Opry*, nor would Lester Flatt be allowed to do any emcee work on the show.

The caption of a photo in a Flatt and Scruggs songbook published about that time reads: "The Flatt and Scruggs show has been a regular weekly feature on WDXI-TV Jackson, Tennessee; WJHL-TV in Johnson City, Tennessee; and WSAZ-TV in Huntington, West Virginia, for Martha White Foods."[7] The songbook also mentions their two-week stint on Broadway and their various WSM radio programs: Monday through Friday at 5:45 A.M., Saturday at 5:45 P.M., Sunday at 8:00 A.M., and on the *Grand Ole Opry* on Saturdays at 8:00 P.M.

Soon after that songbook was published, Jake Tullock decided to return to Knoxville because of some health problems. Following his departure the band went through a series of bass players including Benny Williams, Hoke Jenkins, and Joe Stuart. Finally, in May 1955, they called multi-talented entertainer Burkett "Josh" Graves.[8] Lester and Earl had first met Josh in Lexington in 1949, when he worked with Esco Hankins. They encountered him again in 1954, when he was playing mandolin, resonator guitar (Dobro)[9], and bass with Mac Wiseman's group at the *Old Dominion Barn Dance* in Richmond.

"I was with Mac when Earl called me," Josh said. "Earl asked me to come down and take two weeks and see if I liked them and see if we got along, with their music."[10] Josh arrived in Nashville on May 14. According to Curly, "Josh was scared to death" on the first show. "They hired him as a bass player and comic, and I was doing straight [man]. He was so scared that he wasn't going to be good enough. I told him, 'Don't worry about a thing.' And we got up there and pulled our stuff, and everything went off all right."

Although Josh was hired primarily to play bass, Lester and Earl would feature him on a Dobro tune on each show, and they soon found that audiences loved that new sound. After the two-week trial period, they met with Josh and asked him which instrument he would rather play. For Josh, the choice was easy: the Dobro. Lester responded, "Well, we was hoping you'd say that, because we want to try and get away from Monroe's sound."[11] They then brought Kentucky Slim back in to play bass and do comedy. For the next couple of years they used a succession of bass players on the road including Joe Stuart, Red Murphy, Benny Williams, Onie Wheeler, and Hylo Brown. In the studio they sometimes used session players including Howard Watts, Bob Moore, and Junior Huskey.

The addition of Dobro as a lead instrument gave the Foggy Mountain Boys' music a more contemporary feel. To further distance their sound from Bill Monroe's "high lonesome" bluegrass, Flatt and Scruggs stopped featuring the mandolin on their recordings. Except for a few tunes on which Curly had previously played lead, he was relegated to playing the rhythm chop. Curly had no problem with this change because he thought of himself as a singer, not an instrumentalist. "My mandolin picking wasn't fancy," he said, "but I got along with it all right until Josh come in. I had been taking breaks on the mandolin on [some songs], but when we went to record the next time, they asked me to go chop. So I run the action up on my mandolin. From that day on, I just more or less did chop on the mandolin, and they pushed the Dobro."

Earl Scruggs reflected, "I didn't like a lot of mandolin [solos], because we had gained popularity with Bill Monroe, and Bill played mandolin. So I was glad Curly didn't care about playing mandolin [solos]. I liked his mandolin playing. Curly played good rhythm."[12]

Scruggs told writer Neil Rosenberg, "Curly was a great asset to the group. I thought he had a good, full voice that blended in well. Lester had a lot of voice to me. Some bluegrass singers are kinda nasal type singers and I thought Lester sung down in his throat and so did Curly."[13]

Josh Graves recalled the power of Curly's voice. "Curly could get up at four o'clock in the morning and sing just as high as he could at twelve o'clock in the day. We used to tape these radio programs [at WSM's studio in the National Life Building]. They had the car sitting down on the street, and every hour I'd have to go down and plug the [parking] meters. I remember going down in front of WSM, feeding the meters, and coming back and getting on the elevator. I could hear Seckler's voice, singing with Lester.

You couldn't hear Lester, but you could hear [Curly's] tenor. I thought that was the funniest thing I ever heard, his voice cutting like that."[14]

Curly took Josh under his wing, and the two became fast friends. When Josh first joined the band, he was playing a lower-end resonator guitar.[15] About six months later he made contact with a man in Pennsylvania who had a better-quality Dobro for sale.[16] The man sent him a photo of the instrument and Josh wrote back, saying he would take it. "He wanted a hundred dollars to start out, and I got him down to seventy dollars," Josh said. "I got a notice from Greyhound [saying] he'd shipped it down in a crate, [COD]. My guitar was there, and I didn't have no money. Seckler heard me talking about it, and he said, 'Don't you worry about it. I'll let you have the money. Pay me back when you can.' And we built a friendship like that, and it still runs. I walk up, grab him, and hug him like he's one of my own brothers."[17]

This is just one example of Curly's generosity, and there are many more. He was always ready to help out a fellow musician, friend, or neighbor in need. He remembered being approached one night at the *Opry* by a banjo player from Chattanooga who worked with Bill Monroe. "He'd been on the road with Bill for a couple of weeks or better, and [Bill] only just give him money enough to eat on, and he wanted to borrow money from me to get home on. I told him, 'I won't loan it to you, but I'll give it to you.'"

Just weeks after Josh Graves joined the band, the Foggy Mountain Boys made their first advertised appearance on the *Grand Ole Opry*. On June 4, 1955, the *Tennessean*'s radio listings for WSM indicated that Flatt and Scruggs performed in the eight o'clock hour, in the segment that was normally filled by the Carter Family.[18] The following week the Carter Family was back, and they continued to occupy that slot for the rest of the summer, likely indicating that Flatt and Scruggs had appeared simply as featured guests. Still, it was a step in the right direction.

Flatt and Scruggs's stint on WJHL-TV in Johnson City only lasted three months, but by July they had a bi-weekly Tuesday slot on a major market station: WSB-TV in Atlanta, Georgia. Hatch Show Print order files indicate that on July 1 they ordered five hundred window cards that read: "Now on WSB TV—Channel 2 Alternate Tues. 5:45–6:15 P.M. . . . Stars of *Grand Ole Opry*."[19]

An *Opry* program indicated that Flatt and Scruggs appeared again on the Martha White segment on July 9, yet they were not listed in the WSM radio listings for that date. Based on radio listings in the *Nashville Banner*, it appears that Flatt and Scruggs officially became members of the *Grand Ole Opry* in September 1955. On September 10 they began making regular weekly appearances during Martha White's 8:00 to 8:30 time slot.[20]

At that time, Bill Monroe was appearing regularly in the seven o'clock hour of the *Opry*, and he did not take kindly to his former employees' moving into what he considered to be his territory. According to Jake Lambert, *Opry* manager Dee Kilpatrick, who replaced Jim Denny in 1956, observed that "Monroe remained withdrawn and refused to speak to either Flatt or Scruggs."[21]

Curly confirmed that while the Foggy Mountain Boys crossed paths often with Monroe backstage at the *Opry* he never acknowledged them, and he used his seniority to make things uncomfortable for them. "The Ryman [Auditorium] only had about three dressing rooms," he said. "Of course, Bill had [one]. Nine times out of ten we didn't get a dressing room. We tuned up in the hallway every time."

Still, things were going well for Flatt and Scruggs. They had television programs in three states, and their daily radio shows on WSM could be heard across much of the country. They were now full-fledged members of the *Grand Ole Opry*, with a powerful sponsor. Their records were receiving positive reviews in *Billboard* and were regularly featured in Columbia Records' full-page ads for best-selling folk records. Louise Scruggs had begun to handle the band's bookings and was keeping them busy on the road. It didn't hurt that the banjo had suddenly become a hot commodity.

A front-page article in *Billboard* in June 1955 read in part: RASH OF BANJO FEVER BREAKS OUT IN US. Record Hits Start Epidemic; TV Carries 'Bug'; Instrument Shortage a Problem." According to the article, the banjo buzz started in 1948 with Art Mooney's recording of "Four Leaf Clover." In addition, "folk music collectors have been attracted increasingly to the banjo stylings of Pete Seeger, whose albums sell well and who has prepared a banjo instruction course for the five-stringed instrument. Sales of new banjos in 1954 were up 27% over 1953. So far in 1955, sales are up 150% over the same 3-month period in 1954. Gibson is marketing a line of 6 new banjo models this year. Banjo is becoming increasingly popular on TV. Jackie Gleason has staged a production number utilizing 15 banjos."[22]

Just when it seemed that all the stars were aligned for Lester and Earl, tragedy struck. Earl's mother suffered a stroke, and on October 2, Earl, Louise, and their sons Gary and Randy set out for North Carolina to be by her bedside. They were on Highway 70 just east of Knoxville when a car pulled out in front of them, causing them to crash. The *Nashville Banner* reported that "Earl Scruggs, 31, hillbilly radio entertainer . . . had both hips broken. His wife, 27, sustained multiple cuts of the face, legs, and arms."[23] Gary and Randy, who were sleeping in the back seat, sustained minor injuries, but Earl and Louise were hospitalized for several weeks.

Earl underwent several surgeries and was unable to travel with the band for eight months. Eloise Warren (Seckler) recalled that, when her son Johnny was born on Wednesday, February 22, 1956, Louise Scruggs dropped her off at Baptist Hospital and then went across the street to Saint Thomas Hospital to visit Earl. During his time in recovery, the Foggy Mountain Boys never missed a show. Curtis McPeake and Donnie Bryant filled in for Earl on the road, and eighteen-year-old Haskel McCormick played on the *Opry* and some local show dates.

Just weeks before Earl's accident, the Foggy Mountain Boys had been back in the studio for their first session with Josh Graves in the band. On September 2 they cut the Scruggs instrumental "Randy Lynn Rag," the Flatt solo "On My Mind," and two classic Flatt-Seckler duets, "Blue Ridge Cabin Home" and "Some Old Day." At this session, Nashville studio musicians Jack Shook and Ernie Newton played sock rhythm guitar and bass, respectively. On September 3 they recorded four gospel songs, with Chet Atkins on rhythm guitar and Bob Moore on bass. No mandolin was used in this session, but Curly turned in some stellar vocal harmonies. The addition of Dobro as a lead instrument was seamless, and it was especially effective on the slower, bluesy numbers like "On My Mind" and "No Mother in This World."

By the summer of 1955 their regular appearances on WSAZ-TV in Huntington had made Flatt and Scruggs a household name in West Virginia. Frequently they would perform at a school or theater in a nearby town in the evening after doing their TV show on WSAZ. In June they began an association with C. D. Hagar, owner of a chain of drive-in theaters in West Virginia. Hagar furnished Flatt and Scruggs with a huge amount of work for the next several years, both in his own theaters and others that he rented. He was pictured beside his car in one of the Flatt and Scruggs songbooks. The car, which had a large speaker mounted on its roof, was plastered with Flatt and Scruggs posters.[24] Hager would drive through town on the day of a show barking out information about the show through the speaker, or "ballyhooing."

Melvin Goins remembered Hagar as an expert promoter. "He was a smart old man," Melvin said. "I learned a lot from him about ballyhooing. He would rent a theater, furnished his own movie, and give the boy that worked at the theater five dollars to run the film. Then Flatt and Scruggs would follow the film. Flatt and Scruggs, they had record-breaking crowds. It looked like a festival, almost, when you went to see them at a theater. [People would] line up an hour or two before, down the road, cars parked a mile long to get into the show. They had a little tent they put on top of the snack bar, and [the band] played, rain or shine. They carried their own sound, and tied it right in with the speakers [that mounted on the car windows]. People would blow their car horns for the applause. Boy, when them horns all got turned loose, it was something else!"[25]

Though Curly's wife Mable had functioned well enough while the Foggy Mountain Boys were based in Virginia, her mental illness became an issue once they moved back to Nashville. Her mother in West Virginia wanted to try to help Mable get better, so Curly took her to stay with her family in Huntington. He would visit her whenever the band went through Huntington for their appearances on WSAZ-TV. He was also looking into various hospitals as he traveled around West Virginia. Mable's aunt Martha had tried taking her to a general hospital in Huntington, but no one could help her there. Then her mother tried giving her natural remedies, to no avail. Aunt Martha then suggested that Curly investigate the Huntington State Hospital.

In late 1955 Curly went to visit the state hospital and spoke with a doctor there, who told him, "If she's still breathing, I believe I can help her." Curly decided to give it a try and went to Mable's mother's house to get her, but her mother refused to let him in. "She didn't want me to take [Mable] out of that house," Curly recalled, "because she thought I was going to kill her. She said, 'If you take her out of this house she'll die.' She threatened to have me put in jail. And she wouldn't open that screen door. Well, I took my fist and knocked that screen out and went in and got her. And it's the best thing I ever did for her.

"I signed papers for them to do whatever she needed [at the hospital]," he continued. "They give her what they called 'shock treatments,' and drugs with it. Anytime I'd get to the TV station in Huntington, when we was playing it, I would go over to see her. And she was in that state hospital six months and didn't even know she was there. Then one day I got a letter from her. She wanted to know why I'd left her in the hospital. She thought she'd been in there a couple of weeks."

By the fall of 1956 Mable had made enough progress that the doctors released her, and Curly brought her back to Nashville. That summer he had purchased a house trailer from Paul Warren after he and Eloise bought a house in Madison. Curly moved the trailer to spot number H-17 in Dickerson Road Trailer Park. Knowing that his wife was hospitalized, the kind manager of the trailer park allowed him to live rent-free until Mable was well enough to join him. Once Mable was settled in, Curly was finally able to bring his sons Ray and Monnie to live with them. The boys were enrolled in Shwab School, right next to the trailer park on Dickerson Road. At fourteen and twelve, they didn't need constant supervision, which was fortunate, since Curly was on the road with the Foggy Mountain Boys almost nonstop by this time.

In January 1956 the band began the Saturday evening television show on WSM-TV in Nashville. Their time slot on WSAZ-TV in Huntington was switched to Thursdays, and in February they began a Wednesday program on WBTW-TV in Florence, South Carolina. In March they added a Monday program on WRBL-TV in Columbus, Georgia. That show was short-lived, and on May 7 they switched to the newly opened WRGP-TV in Chattanooga. For the next several months the band worked a grueling six-days-per-week, twenty-five-hundred-mile circuit of live television, with theaters, schools, and courthouses at every stop along with way.

Earl rejoined the band in the spring. Even after surgeries and rehabilitation, the injuries he had sustained in the accident left him in constant pain and unable to tolerate long periods of time in a car, so in early 1956 Lester and Earl bought their first bus. They had the rear seats removed and replaced with bunk beds, so that the band members would have a place to rest on the long rides. This was a big improvement over riding in a car, but it was still primitive living compared to the tour buses of today. The bus had no air conditioning, no bathroom, and no refrigerator. Since their schedule left no time to stop for a sit-down meal, they would have to take food with them or be forced to survive on snacks they purchased at gas stations. Curly recalled, "Cohen Williams, who was head of Martha White, he'd go with us occasionally. The first time he went with us [on the bus] he couldn't understand what was going on. We'd go into a place and get some Nabs [Nabisco peanut butter crackers] and things, and he'd just sit there.

It didn't take him long until he caught on, he'd better get some Nabs, too. We went from Atlanta to Florence, South Carolina, and then Huntington, West Virginia. Well, our [show] date was cancelled. . . . Cohen Williams said, 'Thank God. Now we can go eat!' So he called a hotel down there and ordered everybody steaks."

Curly would often take a carton of hard-boiled eggs to eat on the road. Josh Graves was a bit more creative. "I was the cook," he said. "I bought me a Coleman stove, propane gas, bolted down, so it couldn't go nowhere. I cooked beans on there. We had big coolers. We'd buy our groceries and just keep going. We didn't have time to fool around. We had to make those dates."[26]

The first Flatt and Scruggs tour bus was painted a cream color, with red and black lettering and trim, and the band members referred to it as the Red Rider.[27] Made by the Flxible Company, it had an eight-cylinder Buick motor and ran on gasoline rather than diesel fuel. The motor mount was loose, and when the bus was moving, the motor would bounce, causing the spark plug wires to pop off, and the engine would catch on fire. Earl and Curly did most of the driving, while Josh and Paul would often ride "shotgun." Curly recalled a number of times when he would glance in the rear view mirror only to see that the engine was on fire. "You could always tell; when it would light up in the back, the thing was on fire. We had some sand in there [that] we'd pour on it." Josh remembered that he once volunteered to sit in the engine cage and hold the spark plugs on the engine so that the band could get to a show in time. Only after he had crawled in and the bus was on its way did it occur to him that he would not have been able to get out if the engine caught fire.

On one occasion, they were on the way to a show and Curly noticed they were almost out of gas. He told Lester he didn't think they had enough to make it to the show. "Lester said, 'Well, Seck, duck in there and get ten dollars' worth, at the first station you see.' So I pulled in there, stuck a ten dollar bill out the window, and [asked the attendant], 'Could you run in ten dollars [worth] right quick? We're in a hurry.' He went running back there, and directly he come back and said, 'Come back here and put the fire out first!'"

Another time, the engine caught fire when the band was at WSAZ-TV in Huntington. By this time the bus fires had become common occurrences. "We was in there, rehearsing our program," Curly said. "Somebody come

in and said, 'Your bus is on fire! Your bus is on fire!' We just kept on picking, and finally we got to the end of what we was rehearsing. We went out
there, and the fire trucks had done come and put it out. Earl looked over
at Lester and said, 'Wonder who called the fire department?'"

About this time, T. Tommy Cutrer became the announcer for the Flatt
and Scruggs television program on WSM-TV. Cutrer had arrived at WSM
radio in October of 1955.[28] He originally had been scheduled to begin working at the station in May 1952 but was seriously injured in an auto accident
on the way to Nashville from Shreveport, Louisiana, where he had worked
at KWKH. As a result of the injury his left leg was amputated, and he returned to Shreveport to recover. When he finally arrived at WSM he was
walking with a wooden prosthetic leg, and many people were unaware of
his handicap. Cutrer was a charming and charismatic emcee, and he soon
became an announcer for the *Grand Ole Opry*. Occasionally he would ride
along with Flatt and Scruggs to a show date.

Josh Graves recalled that T. Tommy was along when the band performed
in April 1956 at a benefit for tornado victims in Lexington, Tennessee. Onie
Wheeler was playing bass, and Kentucky Slim, whom Curly had dubbed
"Little Darlin'," was the comedian. It was a Friday night at the end of a long
week on the road, and after the show the band members were tired and
ready to crawl into their bunks. "Seck was driving," Josh said, "and I was
sitting up there with him. I happened to look in the rear mirror and I seen
that black smoke rolling, and the lights started dimming. I said, 'Seck, this
thing's on fire.' He pulled over to the side of the road and said, 'You get the
instruments. I'll wake up the guys.' I run back to the room where we kept
our instruments. I had instruments [stowed] all down the highway, and I
run back and tried to help him. Little Darlin' weighed 275 pounds, and we
had him a big couch back there that he slept on. I woke him."[29]

Curly picked up the story, saying, "We come back there and said, 'Fire!
Get everybody up!' Get Earl up, because he'd just had that hip operation.
They put pins in both of his hips. We said, 'Get Earl up, and T. Tommy's
back there, with just that one leg. Get him out of there.' Directly, T. Tommy
came hopping out of there with that artificial limb under his arm and said,
'Save yourselves, lads!'"

Curly recalled several accidents and near misses in that first tour bus as
well. He once knocked over a gas pump while backing the bus. Another time
he barely avoided disaster when the brakes failed as he was approaching a

stopped school bus. "I hit the brakes," he said, "and—no brakes. I couldn't stop the thing. And them kids, I just looked for one to come around that bus. If he had, I'd have run right over him. And Earl always told me, 'Don't dodge nothing, or you'll turn this thing over.' But if I'd have saw a kid, I guess I'd have tried to dodge it."

The outcome was not so fortunate on another occasion, when they were crossing the North Carolina mountains. "I quit driving in Chattanooga, and Earl got [behind] the wheel," Curly recalled. "We was going into North Carolina, on razorback roads. It had been raining and the road was wet, and a car come around the top of the hill, and it lost control and hit that bus, and it just sheared [the car] off. I think some of them got killed. I was in the bunk, asleep, and my knee hit the top, and I got a bruised knee. The insurance [company] wanted to know if I would settle for fifty dollars, and I said, 'yeah.'"

Lester and Earl had both bought houses on Donna Drive in Madison in early 1956, and they parked the bus at Earl's house. When it was time to board the bus for a road trip, Curly would pick up Josh, who had no car, and head to Earl's house. The band members would leave their cars there until the bus returned at the end of the trip. "I hit some bad luck, parking out there at Earl's," Curly chuckled. "I left my Chevrolet out there one time, and one of the [neighborhood] kids screwed the cap off of my gas tank and put sand down in it. Another time I [got back], somebody had took a baseball bat and knocked the windshield clear out of the same car!"

By the fall of 1956 Flatt and Scruggs had ceased doing television shows in Atlanta and Florence, and they had moved their weekly program in Jackson to Wednesdays. In April 1957 they finished their stint in Jackson but added a Tuesday program on WATE-TV in Knoxville. For a couple of months in the fall of 1957 they appeared on WTRF-TV in Wheeling, West Virginia, on Wednesdays. During this time they continued appearing on Mondays at WRGP-TV in Chattanooga, on Thursdays at WSAZ-TV in Huntington, and on Saturdays on WSM-TV in Nashville. They would return home to Nashville after the programs in Chattanooga and Knoxville and then would spend the night on the road between Wheeling and Huntington. The travel had become a bit easier by the summer of 1957, because they had hired bus driver Cordell "Toby" Sircy[30] and had replaced the fire-prone gas-powered bus with a diesel model. The new bus, which had blue trim, was dubbed the Blue Goose by the band members.[31]

While doing the television programs in Chattanooga, the band met a young high school student named Mike Longworth. Mike was a fan, and he would put up show posters around town for Flatt and Scruggs. He had taught himself to do pearl inlay and instrument repairs, and he noticed that Curly's F-2 mandolin was in need of some work. The curl at the bottom of the headstock was broken off, but Curly still had the piece, so Longworth offered to repair it. He also did some pearl inlay in the headstock and neck including the Gibson script, a "flowerpot," and an inscription reading "L-4." The "L" was for Longworth, and the "4" was to indicate that this was the fourth such inlay job that he had done. About this time Longworth also did inlay work on a Dobro for Josh Graves (numbered "L-3") and a D-28 Martin guitar for Lester Flatt (numbered "L-5").[32] While Longworth was working on his F-2, Curly played a Gibson F-4 mandolin that he borrowed from another musician. Curly later sent his F-2 to Gibson to have additional work done.

Curly can be seen playing the F-2 mandolin, prior to Longworth's repairs, on volume 7 of the *Flatt & Scruggs TV Show* DVDs released by Shanachie Entertainment and the Country Music Foundation in 2009. According to Jay Orr's liner notes, the film can for this show listed the airdate as July 30, 1956 (a Monday), but Curly thought it actually may have been done earlier. He believed it was one of the first television shows they did on WSM-TV after Josh Graves joined the band, since Josh was playing bass and also played the resonator guitar that he had when he first joined the band. Also, Jud Collins was the announcer, and, Curly recalled, Jud only appeared on a few shows before T. Tommy Cutrer took over. July 30, 1955, was a Saturday, but there was no TV listing for Flatt and Scruggs in the newspaper for that date (WSM-TV was airing Roy Rogers in the 6:00 to 6:30 P.M. time slot). As mentioned above, the first listing for Flatt and Scruggs on WSM-TV was in January 1956, although it is possible that they performed prior to that on a program of a different name. Television listings indicate that, from July 16 through October 1, 1955, WSM-TV was broadcasting a half-hour show at 8:00 P.M. on Saturdays called *Grand Ole Opry*,[33] so that program could have been the source of the early video footage of Flatt and Scruggs. With so much conflicting information, it is unlikely that we will ever know the exact broadcast date of that program, though it was certainly in 1955 or 1956.

If that show was, indeed, one of their earliest appearances on WSM-TV, it seems reasonable to assume that the Foggy Mountain Boys began singing the new Martha White theme song about the time they began appearing on television. Their performance of the theme on the show in question was particularly animated and more self-conscious than their later renditions, implying that it may have been fresh material. At the end of the program they performed an extended version of the theme, with the fiddle and banjo exchanging breaks, whereas in later television shows they would only perform a snippet of the theme following a commercial.

Curly confirmed that this new theme was written specifically for their television program. His recollection was that it was composed by Efford Burke, the salesman who first brought Flatt and Scruggs to the attention of Cohen Williams. The *Flatt and Scruggs Radio and TV Album and Songbook No. 2*, which was published in the spring of 1956, was the first songbook to include the "Martha White Flour Theme":

> Now you bake right—UH HUH—with MARTHA WHITE—yes Mam [*sic*],
> Goodness gracious good and light, MARTHA WHITE,
> Now you bake better biscuits, cakes and pies,
> Cause MARTHA WHITE self-rising flour, the one all-purpose flour,
> MARTHA WHITE self-rising flour has got HOT-RIZE.[34]

Chattanooga and Huntington proved to be the most successful television markets for Flatt and Scruggs outside Nashville. In January 1955 WSAZ-TV had doubled its power, and its signal reached large portions of West Virginia, Kentucky, and Ohio. Curly recalled that WSAZ was "one of the best stations there was. Huntington, West Virginia, man, it was on fire. Them people up there was crazy for bluegrass music." The area became a great market for Martha White as well, and in 1956 the company opened a new mill in Huntington to process cornmeal.

The symbiotic partnership between Flatt and Scruggs and Martha White was definitely enhanced by television. Audiences that had only heard their music on radio or records could now see this dynamic band in action. This, in turn, sold concert tickets. "When TV came along," Curly said, "that door was wide open for what we were doing. There wasn't fields big enough to get the people in. We always had to do two shows, everywhere we went." And Lester Flatt was the perfect "flour peddler," with his sincere and down-home delivery of the Martha White message. "I'll tell you," Curly stressed, "Flatt believed in what he was doing as much as any man that ever lived, and if he worked for Martha White, he worked for Martha White."

But Flatt's loyalty did not prevent him from voicing his opinion to Cohen Williams. About the time it began sponsoring Flatt and Scruggs, Martha White had added coffee to its line of products. Curly recalled a gaffe he made once on a show date when Cohen Williams just happened to be with them. It was Curly's job to talk about Martha White products and to announce that they would be giving out coupons at intermission. "And I announced the coffee," Curly chuckled, "[and said], 'And it's good to the last drop.' Well, that was [a slogan for] the wrong coffee. [Cohen Williams] said, 'Don't say that no more on stage!'" In any case, the coffee didn't last long, Curly noted. "Lester went to Cohen Williams and said, 'I hate to get up there and brag on something that I won't drink myself. That coffee's just no good.' So they just pulled it off [the program]. That was the end of Martha White coffee."

In the days of live television in Nashville, the commercials for Martha White products were done in a kitchen set on the opposite side of the studio from where the band was set up. Alice Jarman, Ann Abby, or another of Martha White's home economists would demonstrate how to put together the ingredients for a recipe, and then the finished product would be displayed while T. Tommy talked about how good it was. After the program, the band was welcome to eat the foods that had been prepared. However, Earl recalled, "sometimes you had to be careful of that, because she'd put stuff in there to make it [look better on TV]. Sometimes, if you dived into that, you'd get grease all over your face."[35]

"T. Tommy was always pulling something on Lester," Curly laughed. "I think they'd put shaving cream [on a dessert], that would show up better [on TV]. T. Tommy'd bring it over and say, 'Les, take a taste of this,' right on the show. And, of course, Lester would. He took a taste and he spit it out! I think he turned his back and got out of that all right, but they'd pull anything on him."

The shows at WSM-TV were shot with two cameras, enabling the producers to use a separate camera for the commercials and also to get two different angles on the band. Occasionally they would use mirrors to get an unusual camera angle, that of looking down from above. Three microphones were used: one for the vocalists, one for the instrumentalists, and one for the bass. Lester would plan the material for the television shows ahead of time and have the set list on a music stand, just as he would for the WSM morning radio shows. Jake Tullock's son Gary noted that Lester would save the cardboard squares that were packaged with new dress shirts and write the set lists on them.

The band members were adept at choreography, and since the format for the television shows was very similar to their stage shows, they needed very little direction. "When we first started," Curly said, "they had lines marked off for you, where to stand and so forth. It wasn't long before Lester thought we knowed how to do it without them telling us. Nine times out of ten, whatever he did, that's the way it was going to stay."

Josh Graves told of how a director at WBTW in Florence found this out the hard way. "This little guy made chalk marks around Lester's and Earl's feet," Josh recalled. "Flatt said, 'Scruggs, what the hell they doing with that chalk?' Earl said, 'I believe they're marking where they want you to stand.' Flatt took that guitar off his shoulder, and he went in the control room, and you talk about giving somebody a raking. He said, 'Don't you ever come in where I'm at and tell me where to stand! We'll do our show, and you tend to your own damn business!'"[36]

The material Lester chose for the programs followed a loose formula, usually including one or two fiddle tunes by Paul Warren, a banjo instrumental by Earl Scruggs, a comedy routine, a Flatt solo, one or two gospel quartets, and several duets and trios. Sometimes Curly would trade his mandolin for a guitar and render one of the solos he often sang at stage shows. He was still performing "Moonlight on My Cabin," "You Took My Sunshine," and "Hannah," as well as his own compositions "What's the Matter Now?" and "Who's Been Here?"

Many of the solos Curly sang had a decidedly bluesy feel to them. In fact, he counted Chuck Berry and B. B. King among his influences. Of King, he noted, "I used to really love to catch his programs. Boy, he could pick a guitar; get a better sound out of it than anybody I ever heard in my life!" Curly also enjoyed singing many of the popular country songs of the day. He would draw from the repertoires of Webb Pierce, Floyd Tillman, Hank Locklin, George Jones, and others with songs such as "I Don't Care," "Why, Baby, Why?" "Please Help Me, I'm Falling," "Sign on the Dotted Line," and "In the Jailhouse Now."

By the late 1950s rock and roll was sweeping the nation, and its effect on country music was devastating. Crowds at the *Grand Ole Opry* dwindled, show dates became sparse, and many *Opry* performers such as Bill Monroe and the Louvin Brothers could not afford to carry a full band on the road. But thanks to the power of television, Flatt and Scruggs's popularity never wavered, and they stayed busier than ever.

In the spring of 1957, Frank "Hylo" Brown joined the band, and he played bass on their July 11, 1957 recording session. Brown had first gained attention in 1954, when he recorded four songs for Capitol, including "Lost to a Stranger" and "Lovesick and Sorrow." He then spent two and a half years on the *WWVA Jamboree* in Wheeling before joining Flatt and Scruggs. In addition to playing bass, he was a featured vocalist, and he would switch to guitar to sing solos while Josh Graves took over the bass. The band could be seen in this configuration on a syndicated television program they made on October 15, 1957, for the U.S. Army called *Country Style USA*.[37]

Brown was well received as a singer, and Martha White decided to hire him to front his own group, the Timberliners, working on television stations in western Tennessee and Mississippi. According to Hatch Show Print order files, Brown began appearing that spring on WTWV in Tupelo, WJTV in Jackson, Mississippi, WDXI in Jackson, Tennessee, and WHBQ in Memphis.[38] But the Timberliners could not compete with the success of the Foggy Mountain Boys. After a little more than a year they disbanded, but not before they had backed Earl Scruggs at the Newport Folk Festival in the summer of 1959.

In early 1958 Jake Tullock rejoined the Foggy Mountain Boys, replacing Brown on bass. Kentucky Slim departed the band to tour with Brown and the Timberliners. Then just a few months later, Curly also left the Foggy Mountain Boys. According to Josh Graves, Curly and Lester had a falling out, after which Curly threatened to quit and Lester called his bluff. "Lester and Curly was jibbing at each other, and they got into it in Rocky Face, Georgia,"[39] Josh recalled. "He said something to Curly, and Curly said, 'Well, you can stop it in two weeks.' And [Lester] said, 'OK, just consider that.'"[40] Curly left Flatt and Scruggs a few weeks after their April 26 recording session, which produced four gospel tracks.

According to Josh, Curly's old friend and employer Carl Sauceman, who by then had relocated to Alabama, had made job offers to both Josh and Curly. "Sauceman wanted me and Curly to come down in Alabama and work for him," Josh said. "And Seck was ready to go. I finally said, 'John, I'm just not going to jump up and move for ten dollars a week difference. You just go ahead.'"[41] Curly joined Carl Sauceman at WRAG, a 1,000-watt station in Carrollton, Alabama, west of Tuscaloosa. Also in the band at that time were Joe Stuart, Jim Brock, Larry Richardson, and Jack Sauceman. Curly's stay was brief, however, and by summer he had returned to Nashville and was working some shows locally with the McCormick Brothers.

Curly had first met Haskel McCormick in 1955, when he was filling in for Earl Scruggs after Earl's auto accident. Though he was still in high school, Haskel was already an accomplished banjo player, having performed and recorded in a band with his brothers Lloyd, Kelly, and William. In 1947 Haskel had first heard Flatt and Scruggs on the *Opry* with Bill Monroe. Later he listened to the Foggy Mountain Boys over WVLK in Versailles, Kentucky. He became obsessed with music and with learning Scruggs's style and technique. In the early fifties, the McCormick Brothers began playing regularly over WHIN Radio in Gallatin. In 1954 they signed with Hickory Records, and they soon began receiving recognition in country music trade publications. Many of their most popular titles were instrumentals featuring Haskel's dynamic banjo playing. Lester Flatt took notice, and he used Haskel several times on the *Opry* and on WSM-TV while Earl was recuperating.

After returning from Alabama, Curly went to visit the McCormick Brothers. The youngest brother, Gerald, remembered, "He came up to our house and was wanting to work some with Haskel and Lloyd and all of them, because at that time they worked at [WHIN] every Saturday, and [were] doing some shows and playing dances every Saturday night."[42] The McCormicks welcomed Curly into the fold, and he began performing with them locally. "We played Thursday, Friday, and Saturday night square dances," Haskel said. "It was, like, Scottsville, Kentucky; Lafayette, Tennessee; Red Boiling Springs; and Gallatin, at the VFW building. And he worked pretty well all of them at that point in time."[43] Occasionally, Curly would travel with the McCormicks to such venues as the Brown County Jamboree in Bean Blossom, Indiana, and Ponderosa Park in Salem, Ohio. Curly also worked some square dances with a band that Lloyd McCormick put together for him that often included Charlie Smith on fiddle, Jim Smoak on banjo, Charlie Nixon on Dobro, Hayden Clark on bass, and various others.

Also, during this period, he did an album with Harold Morrison. As Curly recalled, "Mac Wiseman was on it, and Benny Martin was fiddling. Joe Zinkan was playing the bass, and Chester Atkins was playing on it. I sung two or three numbers in it. That was quite a deal to work with all those guys together, and Chet Atkins." The album was originally released in 1959 as *Blue Ridge Square Dance* in a *Reader's Digest* collection. It was reissued several times, most recently in 1984 by Old Homestead Records, with the title *Bluegrass Classics*.

Curly returned to work with Flatt and Scruggs in May 1959. The entry in Paul Warren's date book for Monday, May 4, said, "Seck Came Back."

During the year that Curly was gone, Everett Lilly had returned to the band for about seven months. He maintained that the main reason he left his brother Bea in Boston and rejoined Flatt and Scruggs was that he "wanted to check out the *Opry* and see if it was some place [he'd] like to be."[44] Apparently he decided it was not, and he returned to Boston at the end of the year. Lester and Earl then hired Curley Lambert, who had played previously with the Stanley Brothers, Bill Clifton, and Bill and Mary Reid. He sang tenor on the Foggy Mountain Boys' next two recording sessions, held on January 23 and April 5, 1959. These sessions produced Flatt and Scruggs's second and third chart hits, "Cabin on the Hill" (brought to the band by Hylo Brown) and "Crying My Heart Out Over You." But Lambert was never really comfortable as a tenor singer, having sung mostly baritone with other groups, and he parted amicably with Lester and Earl soon after the April session. According to Hatch Show Print files, Hylo Brown toured with the Foggy Mountain Boys in March and April, but by fall he was again playing some show dates with his own band.[45]

While Curly Seckler was away, there were frequent changes in the band's television schedule, and for a time they traded with Hylo Brown and were playing the western circuit of Tupelo and Jackson, Mississippi, and Jackson, Tennessee. By the time Curly returned, the television schedule was WRGP in Chattanooga on Monday, WATE in Knoxville on Tuesday, WHIS in Bluefield, West Virginia, on Wednesday, both WSAZ in Huntington and WBOY in Clarksburg, West Virginia, on Thursday, and WSM in Nashville on Saturday. In April 1959 Flatt and Scruggs had begun taping television shows in Huntington. Doing so allowed them to record a show there earlier in the day and then do a live show in Clarksburg that evening. By September they had ceased doing live television in Bluefield and Clarksburg and had begun taping four shows at a time in Huntington.[46]

Several other companies shared sponsorship with Martha White on the Foggy Mountain Boys' television circuit during 1958 and 1959. Bryan Brothers, a meat packing and processing firm, sponsored them in Mississippi, while Colonial Coffee promoted them in western Tennessee. In West Virginia they were advertising peanut butter for the Sessions Peanut Company from Enterprise, Alabama.

In September 1959 the Flatt and Scruggs program in Chattanooga was moved from WRGP-TV to WTVC-TV, the new ABC affiliate, with transmitter and studios on Signal Mountain. It was there that Curly lost his prized

Gibson guitar. He had bought the Southern Jumbo model guitar in the mid-fifties for $35 from a musician who worked with Wilma Lee and Stoney Cooper. Curly carried it on the road to use when he sang solos, and Earl also used it when he played gospel songs.[47] "He liked the sound of that Gibson," Curly explained. "We recorded with it some. It was a really good guitar. He liked to use that Gibson, because when he put a capo on it, regardless of where he put [the capo], he didn't have to retune it."

"We was doing the Martha White show in Chattanooga, and I come out before the rest of them," Curly recalled. "We had those bins underneath the bus where we kept our instruments, but I didn't have a key. So I just set the guitar down and carried my mandolin on inside [the bus]. When [the others] came out, they forgot to put my guitar [in the bin]. Sircy was driving at that time, and he backed right across it. Busted it all to pieces. And I just kicked it down the hill and left it over there. I never did open the case."

Toby Sircy may have been a capable bus driver, but he didn't fit in well with the group. According to Jake Lambert, "There was some bickering between some of the Foggy Mountain Boys and Sircy."[48] Perhaps the last straw was when he reported Flatt and Scruggs to the musicians' union for not compensating the band members for working on the *Grand Ole Opry*. "I don't know why he did that," Curly said. "He wasn't even in the musicians' union. He was in a truck [drivers'] union. We agreed to work for a certain [weekly] salary. Sircy just got it in his head that we wasn't getting the money that we deserved, comparing [the musicians'] union to his union. None of us went along with it, but we all had to go before George [Cooper]. He was the president of the [musicians'] union then. George Cooper told him pretty quick he needed to keep his mouth out of it."

According to Jake Lambert, soon after Sircy was let go in early 1962, Lester and Earl sold the bus and briefly went back to traveling in a station wagon before purchasing their third bus. The entry in Paul Warren's date book for Saturday, March 31, 1962, indicates that they played the *Opry* and then says, "Left for Iowa in a station wagon." By this time Earl was often flying to long-distance show dates. In 1958 he had decided to get a pilot's license, and he subsequently bought a small four-seated airplane. In addition to flying to concert appearances, Earl told Curly, he would sometimes make blood deliveries for the Red Cross to various parts of Tennessee.

In the summer of 1961 Earl offered to take Curly up for a ride. Curly had never flown, and at first he was resistant. Earl persisted, saying, "We'll fly close to the highway and if something happens, we'll just go down on the highway." Curly agreed, and they had an uneventful flight around central Tennessee. At the band's next television taping, Lester said, "Neighbors, we've got a new member here in the group today, 'Sky King.' [Earl] took Curly up, and before he got him down [Curly] ate two rolls of Rolaids."[49] Curly chuckled, "But that's some of Flatt's tales, you know. He got to calling me 'Sky King' there for a while."[50] After that, Curly flew several other times with Earl, including a trip to Memphis with Earl and Murray Nash when the Foggy Mountain Boys played a package show at an auditorium there.

In February 1960 the band began taping their television programs at WSM-TV. Initially they would tape the show on Saturday for airing that night, but by spring they were taping several shows at once, on whatever day they were free. This enabled them to play package shows on weekends when they were not performing on the *Opry*. Flatt and Scruggs were still taping their daily radio programs as well. Paul Warren's date books indicated that they typically would record seven radio shows in a day, although on occasion they taped as many as fourteen.

In August 1960 Martha White announced a new co-sponsorship agreement with Pet Milk for the weekly Flatt and Scruggs shows originating at WSM-TV. The taped programs were sent out for broadcast in seven additional cities, including WSAZ-TV in Huntington, WSLS-TV in Roanoke, and WCYB-TV in Bristol.[51] They continued to perform on live television in Chattanooga and Knoxville, and from October 1960 through January 1961 they resumed a live Wednesday program over WDXI-TV in Jackson. The last live program they played was on Tuesday, February 7, 1961 at WATE-TV in Knoxville.[52]

With the ability to tape their television programs, Flatt and Scruggs were able to travel to new areas to perform and could be out on the road for longer tours. In June 1960 they spent several days in New York rehearsing and then performing on the CBS network special *Spring Festival of Music: Folk Sound, USA*. The following week they headed north again for a show on Long Island and an appearance at the Newport Folk Festival, with tour dates each night along the way. In November they embarked on a ten-day package tour with Johnny Cash, Johnny Western, and Gordon Terry that took them to Ottumwa, Iowa, Hammond, Indiana, Detroit (a layover), Hitchner and Peterborough, Ontario, Washington, DC, Richmond, Virginia, and Baltimore.[53]

When he was away from home for days or weeks at a time, Curly was afraid to leave his wife Mable unattended because of her reoccurring psychological problems. Sometimes he would make arrangements for her to stay with someone who could monitor her behavior. On one such occasion in the winter of 1959, he took her to stay with her younger brother Charles in Huntington. Charles was a music fan, and he and Curly got along well.

Linda Sowards Kuhn, Charles's wife at the time, recalled the circumstances. "They came to our house and he asked us if we could keep Mable until he came back. She would have paranoid symptoms, and she would be almost catatonic. She was there with us about two weeks, and her condition kept getting worse, and then we had to put her in the hospital. She was in the hospital maybe, four, six weeks. They gave her electrical shock therapy and medicine. The shock treatments would get her out of her worst stages, but they made the patients forget things. We would go visit her at least once a week, and she would be very vacant and distant, due to the shock treatment." But, Linda hastened to add, "Even at her worst, she was so sweet and kind to my children. She was really a good-hearted, sweet person. She was beautiful. [Curly] cared a lot about her. And he was just a super nice guy."[54]

Ray Seckler confirmed that, when he and Monnie first came to live with Curly and Mable in 1956, "She was real good to [them]." Curly gave Ray a guitar for Christmas that year, and Mable sat down with Ray and helped him learn to play it. But he also remembered that she could be obsessive and paranoid. Once, when Ray changed the station on her radio, "She threw a hot iron at me, she got so mad," he recalled. "When she'd get low on that medicine, she was hell on wheels sometimes. Dad was somewhere recording one day, and somebody called up and said, 'You better get home. Mable's out there with a bucket on her head and a shotgun.'"[55]

Mable's erratic behavior took its toll on Curly. Earl Scruggs said, "Looking back, I don't know how he could put up with stuff like that. But he handled it. Boy, he must have loved her, because she got dangerous. She just didn't know what she was doing."[56] According to Lance LeRoy, "Curly was difficult to work with along in that period, because he was moody. Lester always told me he thought Curly was so moody because of his problems with Mable. So he had a lot of sympathy for Curly, but things got so bad they finally had to let him go."[57]

In late March 1962, upon returning from a show date, Curly got the news. "We pulled up at [Earl's] drive, where we usually parked the bus," he recalled. "I parked it there. Everybody's getting off, and he said, 'Curly, you stick around. I want to talk to you.' Lester'd done gone toward his house. I didn't have no idea of getting fired. [Earl] said, 'We're going to reduce the band some, and we're going to have to let you go.' And I thought, 'Good Lord a-mercy, what am I going to do?' Me with four hungry mouths to feed and not even a job."

Josh Graves was waiting in the car for Curly to take him home. "It was pouring down rain," he recalled, "and in a little bit, here come Curly. He was always saying, 'Somebody's going to get the ax,' because of some problems we'd had. He jumped in, as wet as he could be, and I said, 'Well, John, who got the ax?' and he said, 'I did.'"[58]

Uncle Jim Sechler (*left*) and Calvin Sechler (*right*) pulling out stumps with the family mules on the farm in China Grove, North Carolina, circa 1925. Photo courtesy of Curly Sechler.

The Sechler brothers in front of the old family home, China Grove, North Carolina, circa 1935. *Left to right*: Marvin, George, Curly, Duard ("Lucky"). Photo courtesy of Curly Sechler.

Poster from a Yodeling Rangers show on November 12, 1938,
near Landis, North Carolina. Photo courtesy of Curly Seckler.

Charlie Monroe and his Kentucky Partners, 1939. *Front row, left to right:* Curly, Dale Cole, Tommy Edwards; *back row, left to right:* Charlie Monroe, Tommy Scott. Photo courtesy of Katona Productions, Inc.

Curly Seckler, circa 1940.
Photo courtesy of Curly Seckler.

Tommy Scott with his ventriloquist's doll Luke McLuke in the 1940s. Photo courtesy of Curly Seckler.

Curly Seckler and
Leonard Stokes (right)
in front of the WNOX
studios in Knoxville
in the fall of 1942.
Photo courtesy of
Curly Seckler.

Curly's sons Monnie
(*left*) and Ray at the old
family home in China
Grove, late 1940s.
Photo courtesy of
Curly Seckler.

Charlie Monroe and his Kentucky Partners at their first recording session in Atlanta, Georgia, September 30, 1946. *Left to right:* Larry "Tex" Isley, Curly, Charlie Monroe (seated), Paul Prince, Robert "Pickles" Lambert. Photo courtesy of Curly Seckler.

Publicity photo of Curly Seckler and the Country Boys while based at WROL in Knoxville in 1948. *Left to right:* Duard "Lucky" Sechler, Curly (seated), Ralph Mayo, Bob Oaks. Photo courtesy of Jim Mills.

Poster from a Smoky Mountaineers show on February 4, 1949, in Estill, South Carolina. Photo courtesy of Curly Seckler.

The Foggy Mountain Boys in front of the General Shelby Hotel in Bristol on March 26, 1949, just after Curly joined the band and before they left for Knoxville. *Left to right:* Art Wooten, Howard Watts, Curly, Earl Scruggs, Lester Flatt. Photo courtesy of Tim White and the Appalachian Cultural Music Association.

Lester Flatt, Curly, and Earl Scruggs in Knoxville in 1949. Curly and Earl had just gone with Lester to purchase a new suit. Photo courtesy of Curly Seckler.

The Foggy Mountain
Boys burning Curly's
hat before leaving
Knoxville, late 1949 or
early 1950. *Left to right:*
Howard Watts, Curly,
Earl Scruggs, Benny
Sims. Photo courtesy
of Curly Seckler.

The Foggy Mountain Boys at the *Kentucky Mountain Barn Dance* in Lexington,
Kentucky, in 1950. *Left to right:* Jody Rainwater, Earl Scruggs, Lester Flatt,
Benny Sims, Curly. Photo courtesy of Les Leverett.

Curly and Mable at their wedding in Huntington, West Virginia, on December 29, 1950. Photo courtesy of Curly Seckler.

The Sauceman Brothers band relaxing, probably at Lou Smith's boarding house in Bristol, in the fall of 1951. *Left to right:* Clarence "Tater" Tate, Larry Richardson, Carl Sauceman, J. P. Sauceman, Curly. Photo courtesy of Jim Sauceman.

The McReynolds Brothers and the Cumberland Mountain Boys in the spring of 1952. Front: Jesse McReynolds, Jim McReynolds; rear: Curly, Hoke Jenkins. Note that Curly is wearing the same tie that he wore in the 1949 photo with Flatt and Scruggs. Photo courtesy of Curly Seckler.

WVLK's *Kentucky Barn Dance* Beauty Contest at Woodland Auditorium in Lexington on March 1, 1952. Curly is fifth from the left, in a white shirt and shorts. Jesse and Jim McReynolds are third and fourth from the left, respectively. Photo by Jewel Russell.

The Foggy Mountain Boys in Knoxville, late 1952. *Left to right:* Charles Elza ("Kentucky Slim"), Benny Martin, Lester Flatt, Earl Scruggs, Curly. Photo courtesy of Curly Seckler.

The cast of the WNOX *Mid-Day Merry-Go-Round*, early 1953 in Knoxville. *Left to right:* host Lowell Blanchard, Speedy Krise, Fred E. Smith, Benny Sims, Earl Scruggs, Harry "Jamup" Levan, Benny Martin, Curly, Bessie Lou Murphy, Lee Davis "Honey" Wilds, Lester Flatt, Red Murphy (kneeling), Jim Barber, Sonny Burnette, Don Gibson, Junior Huskey. Photo courtesy of Chris Huskey.

The Foggy Mountain Boys performing "Don't This Road Look Rough and Rocky" at the *Old Dominion Barn Dance* in Richmond, Virginia, on December 11, 1954. *Left to right:* Paul Warren, Curly, Earl Scruggs, Lester Flatt. Photo by Lorraine Sisson Smith, courtesy of Walt Saunders.

The Foggy Mountain Boys in early 1955, at WSAZ-TV in Huntington, West Virginia.
Left to right: Earl Scruggs, Jake Tullock, Paul Warren, Curly, Lester Flatt.
Photo courtesy of Curly Seckler.

The Foggy Mountain Boys perform on Martha White's segment of the *Grand Ole Opry*
in August 1956. *Left to right:* Little Jimmy Dickens, Curly (with his Gibson guitar),
Jimmie Selph (partly obscured), unknown, Josh Graves, Paul Warren, Earl Scruggs,
Lester Flatt, Kenny Hill, George McCormick (partly obscured), Grant Turner.
Gordon Gillingham photograph © Grand Ole Opry, LLC.

A song written by Curly while staying at the Hotel Huntington with the Foggy Mountain Boys in the late 1950s. Photo courtesy of Curly Seckler.

The Foggy Mountain Boys at G Bar B Ranch in Collamer, Indiana, on June 16, 1957.
Left to right: Paul Warren, Earl Scruggs, Curly, Josh Graves (kneeling), Lester Flatt,
Kentucky Slim (kneeling), Hylo Brown. Photo courtesy of Jim Mills.

The Foggy Mountain Boys taping their Martha White radio shows at the WSM studio in October 1960. *Left to right:* Josh Graves, Paul Warren (partly obscured), Earl Scruggs, Jake Tullock, Curly, Lester Flatt, T. Tommy Cutrer. Photo by Les Leverett.

The Foggy Mountain Boys taping their television program at WSM-TV on October 28, 1960. *Left to right:* Josh Graves, Earl Scruggs, Curly, Jake Tullock, Lester Flatt, Paul Warren. Photo by Les Leverett.

The Foggy Mountain Boys boarding their second bus, the Blue Goose, in October 1960. *Left to right:* Jake Tullock, Josh Graves, Paul Warren, Lester Flatt, Curly (looking out the window), Earl Scruggs, Cordell "Toby" Sircy (partly hidden inside the bus). Photo by Les Leverett.

Curly singing with Bill Monroe at Carlton Haney's Camp Springs Festival, September 6, 1970. *Left to right:* Bill Monroe, Curly, Vernon Brown, Jimmy Arnold. Photo by Tony Williamson.

At Paul Gerry's studio in Ferndale, New York, recording the album *Curly Seckler Sings Again*, May 1971. *Left to right:* Herschel Sizemore, John Palmer, Billy Edwards, Curly, Tater Tate. Photo courtesy of County Records, Charlottesville, VA.

Curly with his wife Mable in
the 1970s. Photo courtesy of
Curly Seckler.

The Nashville Grass in 1973. *Left to right:* (kneeling) Charlie Nixon, Marty Stuart,
Paul Warren; (standing) Johnny Johnson, manager Lance LeRoy, Lester Flatt,
Haskel McCormick, Curly. Photo courtesy of Curly Seckler.

The Nashville Grass in the summer of 1975, possibly in Oklahoma. *Left to right:* Kenny Ingram, Paul Warren (partly obscured), Curly, Jack Hicks, Marty Stuart. Photo courtesy of Marty Stuart Archives.

The Nashville Grass performing at Opryland in Nashville on September 1, 1977.
Left to right: Charlie Nixon, Tater Tate, Marty Stuart, Kenny Ingram, Pete Corum
(partly obscured), Lester Flatt, Curly. Photo by Les Leverett.

The Nashville Grass on November 3, 1978, just weeks before Lester suffered a cerebral aneurism. *Left to right:* manager Lance LeRoy, Curly, Pete Corum, Tater Tate, Marty Stuart, Blake Williams, Charlie Nixon, Lester Flatt. Photo by Les Leverett.

Lester Flatt's funeral at Cole and Garrett Funeral Home in Hendersonville, Tennessee, May 13, 1979. *Left to right:* Grandpa Jones, Bobby Osborne, Chuck Webster, Roland White, Marty Stuart, Billy Smith (behind Marty), Mike Cupit (behind Billy), Glen Varble (Hunter Funeral Home), Mark Jones, Joe Stallings (Cole and Garrett Funeral Home), Charlie Nixon, Tater Tate, Curly, Roy Acuff, Bill Carlisle, Ernest Tubb. Photo courtesy of Marty Stuart Archives.

The Nashville Grass circa 1985. *Left to right:* Johnny Warren, Bob Rodgers, Kenny Ingram, Willis Spears, Curly. Photo courtesy of Curly Seckler.

Curly with his old bandmates Benny Martin (*left*) and Josh Graves (*right*) circa 1992. Photo courtesy of Curly Seckler.

In the studio to record 60 *Years of Bluegrass with My Friends* in 1994. *Left to right:* Jesse McReynolds, Curly, Jim McReynolds. Photo courtesy of Curly Seckler.

A recording session at Flat5 Studio in Salem, Virginia, on June 14, 2004. *Left to right:* (seated) Curly, Gary Reid of Copper Creek Records; (standing) Larry Perkins, Herschel Sizemore, Kevin Sluder, George Buckner, Penny Parsons, Dudley Connell, Tater Tate. Photo by Richard Boyd, courtesy of Gary Reid, Copper Creek Records.

Eddie Stubbs (*right*) introducing Curly as the newest member of the IBMA Hall of Fame on October 7, 2004, at the Kentucky Center in Louisville. Photo by Dan Loftin.

Curly celebrating his IBMA Hall of Fame induction after the awards show on October 7, 2004, in Louisville. *Left to right:* Cleo Scott Cheek (Tommy's sister), Curly, Tommy Scott, Eloise Warren Seckler. Photo by Penny Parsons.

Curly performing with Larry Sparks at the IBMA FanFest on October 8, 2004, in Louisville. Photo by Penny Parsons.

David Grisman (*left*) with Curly and the restored Gibson F-2 mandolin at the Hardly Strictly Bluegrass Festival in San Francisco on October 7, 2007. Photo by Jay Blakesberg.

In Kenbridge, Virginia, on October 25, 2008, with the Steep Canyon Rangers. *Left to right:* Nicky Sanders, Woody Platt, Curly, Mike Guggino, Charles Humphrey, Graham Sharp. Photo by Penny Parsons.

Curly joining Marty Stuart to tape the *Marty Stuart Show* for RFD-TV on January 24. 2011. Photo by Bill Thorup, courtesy of Marty Stuart Archives.

Curly's induction into the Bill Monroe Bluegrass Hall of Fame in Bean Blossom, Indiana, on September 24, 2011. Photo by Penny Parsons.

Flatt and Scruggs tribute band The Earls of Leicester with Curly, his family, and a few Foggy Mountain friends, after a private concert in Hendersonville, Tennessee, on November 24, 2014. *Left to right:* (front row) Bryan Graves, Evelyn Graves, Jerry Douglas; *(back row)* Eddie Stubbs, Tim O'Brien, Shawn Camp, Gary Warren, Curly, Gary Tullock, Eloise Warren Seckler, Johnny Warren, Charlie Cushman, Barry Bales. Photo by Penny Parsons.

CHAPTER 7

Traveling Down This Lonesome Road

1962–1972

His dismissal from the Foggy Mountain Boys was a shock to Curly, but he later came to see it as a blessing in disguise. Flatt and Scruggs were working six and sometimes seven days per week. They kept their employees on a salary, so the pay was better than that of sidemen who were paid by the job, but it was still challenging to make ends meet. Although the band no longer had to drive the weekly television route, it was traveling longer distances for show dates and was away from home as much as ever.

The band's music was changing as well. After the success of "Cabin on the Hill," which featured five-part vocal harmony, Lester and Earl were recording more often with multiple harmony parts. By the time Curly had rejoined them in 1959 following his year away, they had ceased recording duets.[1] With the exception of the six gospel quartets recorded in their October 1959 session, Jake Tullock's soaring high baritone vocal was now more dominant in their sound, obscuring Curly's distinctive tenor. Once drums were added to the mix in 1960, Curly's percussive mandolin chop was also eclipsed.

Louise Scruggs was taking an ever-expanding role in management of the band. Based on Earl's success at the Newport Folk Festival in 1959, she had begun to book Flatt and Scruggs at colleges and folk music venues and encouraged them to adapt their material to new audiences. Beginning with their April 1960 recording session (their first with drums) some very different material was starting to creep into their repertoire. The bouncy rumba beat of "The Great Historical Bum" and the drum-heavy rhythm of "Polka on the Banjo" were big departures from the straight-ahead traditional gospel sounds of their two previous sessions. When they recorded Earl's *Foggy Mountain Banjo* album in August and September 1960 (with drums), Curly was not invited to participate.

In November 1961 the Foggy Mountain Boys made their first trip to California. According to Paul Warren's date book, they left home on Tuesday, November 7, at 9:00 A.M., and arrived in San Diego fifty hours later, on the morning of Thursday, November 9. They performed a three-night stand at the Circle Arts Theater in San Diego on November 10–12, then drove to Los Angeles on the thirteenth. On Tuesday, the fourteenth they drove to Berkeley to perform at the University of California. Then, on the fifteenth,, they returned to Hollywood for twelve nights at the Ash Grove, a well-known folk nightclub, at which they played two or three shows each night. Among those in the audience at the band's Ash Grove performances was television producer Paul Henning. Favorably impressed, he would later contact Lester and Earl about performing the theme for *The Beverly Hillbillies*, which made its debut in the fall of 1962. Their participation in the show would elevate them to a whole new level of fame.

The band gave twenty-eight performances in twelve days at the Ash Grove. In addition, on November 22, it entertained at a reception for a Soviet ballet company in conjunction with the U.S. State Department's Cultural Exchange Office. On November 24 and 26, the Foggy Mountain Boys participated in recording sessions for an instrumental square dance album by fiddler Gordon Terry. Once again Curly was not included, so he spent those days with his cousin Mary, who lived nearby. Curly had never met her, but he called her when he arrived in California. When they made plans to meet, Mary wondered how they would recognize each other. Curly replied, "Well, if you've got a Sechler nose, I'll know you when I see you!" He recalled, "We'd get together and go over and spend a whole day in Disneyland, ride the rides. I enjoyed it very much."

The Foggy Mountain Boys arrived back in Nashville at about 10:00 P.M. on November 28, and less than twenty-four hours later they were headed to Virginia. This trip also included show dates in Boston, New York, and the Washington, DC, area. The band's schedule finally slowed down a bit in December, and the members actually had two weeks of vacation over the Christmas holiday. Curly took the opportunity to take Mable back to West Virginia to visit her brother Charles and his family.

In early 1962 Hylo Brown began accompanying the Foggy Mountain Boys as a guest on some show dates, and by February he was appearing on their television programs as well. He would usually sing two solos on the television shows, which meant that Curly was no longer being featured as a soloist. As Curly understood it, Lester and Earl decided they would replace him with Hylo.

Curly's last recording sessions with the Foggy Mountain Boys were on March 18 and 21, 1962. These sessions produced the album *Folk Songs of Our Land*, which was released in August. "Nine Pound Hammer," which Lester and Curly normally performed as a duet on live shows, radio, and television, was recorded as a Flatt solo. Perhaps this was because Lester and Earl had already decided to let Curly go. The exact date of his last show with the band is not known, but it was likely at the end of March, right before they went to Iowa in a station wagon. Curly was present when they recorded television programs at WSM-TV on March 22 and 23, but he had left the band by the time they embarked on a week-long tour of North Carolina and Virginia on April 6.

Although Earl was the one who delivered the news, Josh Graves maintained that it was Lester's decision to fire Curly. "He thought all the time it was Earl that didn't want him in the group," Josh said. "That was wrong. It was Lester, because I was there. Lester jumped off the bus and ran. He didn't want anything to do with it. He was the one that had it done, but all them years Curly thought it was Earl. Because Earl done the hiring and firing, you know. Flatt just didn't want to do nothing but handle the show."[2] Lance LeRoy confirmed this account. "Lester wasn't that much on firing somebody. I had to do all the firing when I took over [as Lester's manager]. He just wouldn't do it. Lester'd tell me, 'Fire so and so. When I get gone, you fire him.'"[3]

Always resourceful, Curly wasted no time in finding a new career for himself, using his experience as a bus driver to land a job driving a truck. Actually, he had already been supplementing his income by occasionally riding along with a neighbor who worked for a mobile home company. "Once in a while, when we weren't working or they would let me go [in 1958–1959]," Curly said, "I'd go with him in his truck and we'd go to Indiana and pick up a new trailer and bring it to Wiley Trailer Sales on Dickerson Road. I'd make as much on one of them trips as I'd make with Lester and them in a week, almost."

After leaving the Foggy Mountain Boys in 1962, Curly went to Elkhart, Indiana, to meet with Rachel Watson at Morgan Driveaway, a company that specialized in pulling mobile homes. She agreed to hire him as soon as he bought a truck. Until that time Curly had always paid cash for anything he needed, but he realized he would need to take out a loan in order to purchase a truck. He decided to go to the bank where Lester Flatt had an account. But when he met with the manager he was told that, since he was no longer working with Flatt and Scruggs, he was not eligible for a loan. According to Josh Graves, this was because, unbeknownst to Curly, "Lester went to the bank and tried to harm him, [so that he couldn't] borrow money to get him a truck. I know that. He did me that way when I left," Josh added.[4]

Having been turned down by Lester's bank, Curly then called his friend Lloyd McCormick, who was well respected in the community, and explained his dilemma. In order to qualify for a loan and to obtain credit, he would need a co-signer. Without hesitation Lloyd replied, "All right, you meet me at the bank in Gallatin in the morning, at nine o'clock." The following morning Lloyd told the banker, "He's a good friend of mine. You give him whatever he wants, and I'll sign the note. And if he ever misses a payment, don't call him, you call me."

"That's the first credit I ever had," said Curly, "and I got it through Lloyd McCormick. I took that truck, and it wasn't no time until I had a pretty good business built up. I jumped from a hundred and thirty some dollars a week, [working] seven days a week with [Flatt and Scruggs] into a job paying five hundred a week, driving that truck. I had my refrigerator full of T-bone steaks, anything I wanted to eat. My whole life just turned clear around."

Hauling trailers was now Curly's primary occupation, but he never gave up his music. He went back to working some shows around Gallatin with the McCormick Brothers, Jimmy Maynard, and other local musicians, and he played a few dates with Carl Sauceman in Alabama. A photo from the collection of Jim Sauceman dated August 1962 showed Carl's band performing at a political rally in front of the Carrollton Hotel with Curly standing next to Carl, playing the mandolin. Curly also remembered doing a benefit show in Asheville, North Carolina, with Clyde Moody and Red Rector. On the way, they stopped in Knoxville and performed live on the *Cas Walker Show* on WATE-TV.

During the 1960s Curly was contacted by several different musicians who were interested in teaming with him. One was Ira Louvin, whose wife saw Curly in a restaurant and told him Ira wanted to get in touch with him. Another was Earl Taylor, who played mandolin and harmonica with Flatt and Scruggs for about a year in 1965–1966. "He was in Cincinnati," Curly said. "About every two weeks, he'd write and say, 'You need to come up here, and we can work these clubs and make all kinds of money.' I never did answer his letters." Yet another was his old nemesis, Hylo Brown. "He come over to my trailer, and there was snow on the ground," Curly recalled. "He parked over at Pico's Truck Stop and walked across that holler, up to my trailer. He wanted me to quit my trucking business, and me and him team up, and we'd really do good. I said, 'Hylo, I just ain't interested, in no way, shape, form, or fashion.' I guess I kind of hurt his feelings, but I meant what I said."

Curly also received several offers from Lester Flatt to come back to the Foggy Mountain Boys. "He called me one night and told me to come down to the *Opry*. We went over at Linebaugh's [Restaurant] and he bought me a big steak." Over dinner, Lester admitted that he and Earl were having problems and tried to convince Curly to return to the band. But Curly was adamant, saying, "If you gave me your gross every night I wouldn't come back. I promised the Good Lord that I'd never work with you two again if the Lord would just give me a job to where I could make a living and feed my family."

With his truck, he was able to do just that and more. Morgan Driveaway had terminals all over the United States, and as soon as he reached one destination, there would be another job waiting for him. He sometimes stayed on the road for two weeks at a time. Eventually, Curly had enough money saved to buy a piece of property on Edwin Street. He then established his own small mobile home court, with three rental units in addition to his own trailer.

In 1969 Flatt and Scruggs decided to end their partnership and go in separate musical directions. Earl was interested in exploring new ideas and playing in different types of venues. His teenaged sons were developing as musicians, and he was enthusiastic about performing with them.

Lester wanted to stick with the tried-and-true traditional sounds that had brought him and Earl so much success in the past. He had become increasingly unhappy as material from modern songwriters such as Bob Dylan, Ian Tyson, Donovan, and Buffy Sainte-Marie had become more and more prominent on their recordings. He told Curly, "You can't give it away. People won't buy it."

Lester and Earl made their last appearance together on the *Grand Ole Opry* on February 22, 1969. The notation in Paul Warren's date book for Saturday, March 1, said, "Earl Bust Up" and indicated that the band played the *Opry* that night without Earl. A couple of weeks later Flatt and Scruggs officially announced the split. After some legal wrangling, they agreed that neither of them would use the Foggy Mountain Boys name. Lester retained the Martha White sponsorship along with the weekly syndicated television program. Flatt and Scruggs had ceased performing on the early morning *Biscuit Time* radio show in 1964, but Flatt reclaimed the program within weeks of the breakup and continued it for the next eight years. Band members Paul Warren, Josh Graves, and Jake Tullock remained with Lester, and he hired Vic Jordan and Roland White, who had both been working with Bill Monroe, to play banjo and mandolin, respectively.

Paul Warren's date book indicated that the band did not work from March 2 through March 16, while Lester was "in process of forming a new band." On March 17 the new band rehearsed, and on March 18 and 19 it taped radio and television shows. During the rest of March and April, Lester and the band continued to tape the Martha White programs but gave no live performances except on the *Opry*. On April 9 Lester and Gladys moved from Sparta to a house that they bought from Roy Acuff on Old Hickory Lake in Hendersonville.[5]

Lester hired Lance LeRoy to be his booking agent and manager, and in May the new band hit the road, with dates that month in New Jersey, Ohio, Massachusetts, Ontario, Connecticut, New York, West Virginia, Virginia, and Pennsylvania. At the end of the year, Lester's new band still did not have a name, and fellow *Opry* member Porter Wagoner had the idea of holding a naming contest. From thousands of fan entries, Martha White Mills picked "The Nashville Grass."

By this time, bluegrass festivals were becoming another source of work for bands. In 1965 music promoter Carlton Haney had presented the first weekend-long bluegrass festival, in Fincastle, Virginia. Other entrepreneurs who were bluegrass fans jumped on the bandwagon, and within a few years, festivals were springing up all around the Southeast. Those promoters remembered Curly from his days as a Foggy Mountain Boy, and they began to contact him. They would hire him to act as emcee for the festivals, and he would also make guest appearances with various artists, including Lester Flatt and Jimmy Martin. Curly would arrange with the trucking dispatcher to schedule a delivery job for him near the festival site, so he could work both angles. "I still worked my show business on the side," he explained. "When the festivals got right, I'd work five or six of them in a year's time. I'd get me a run close to where the festival was, then I'd go in and emcee it, and play with Lester or whoever else was there."

In the late 1960s Curly was contacted by fiddler Joe Greene about pulling his trailer to Nashville from his hometown of High Point, North Carolina. Greene had first gained attention in bluegrass circles when he recorded a twin fiddle album with Kenny Baker for County Records in 1968. In 1969 Greene recorded an acclaimed solo album for County, backed by Chubby Wise on guitar, J. D. Crowe on banjo, Roland White on mandolin, and Benny Williams on bass. After moving to Nashville, he worked on the *Grand Ole Opry* with several groups, including those headed by Roy Acuff and Little Jimmy Dickens.

Curly hauled Joe Greene's trailer to the trailer park on Dickerson Road and parked it one row over from his own. When they would see each other in passing, Joe would ask Curly about performing together. At first Curly was not interested, but he finally agreed to book some shows for the fall of 1970. Joe put together a band that included Jimmy Arnold on banjo, Vernon Lee Brown on guitar and lead vocals, and Roger Dalton on bass. They called themselves the Greene Men. One of their first appearances together was at Carlton Haney's sixth annual Labor Day weekend festival at Camp Springs, North Carolina. By this time a regular feature of Haney's festivals was his presentation of "The Blue Grass Story," featuring Bill Monroe, on Sunday afternoon. For this day, he would book many of Monroe's former sidemen and would bring them on stage with Bill one by one to perform material from their tenure as Blue Grass Boys. Among those present in 1970 were Don Reno, Mac Wiseman, Clyde Moody, Jim Eanes, Chubby Wise, Del McCoury, Sonny Osborne, and Tex Logan.

Although Curly had never worked with Bill Monroe, Haney decided he wanted Curly to sing with Bill during the Blue Grass Story. Perhaps he was looking for a way to include a connection to Flatt and Scruggs in the presentation, since there was no chance that either of them would appear with Monroe at that time. Curly and Joe Greene were on their bus when Carlton came and asked Curly if he would sing with Bill. Curly agreed, and he and Joe and the Greene Men joined Bill for four numbers. First Joe played twin fiddles with Kenny Baker on the Monroe instrumental "Wheel Hoss." Then guitar player Vernon Brown stepped up to sing lead on "Little Cabin Home on the Hill," while Monroe sang tenor and Curly sang baritone, in the key of B. Next up, Greene and Baker were featured once again on the instrumental "Roanoke." Finally, Monroe suggested that he and Curly could sing "I'm Sitting on Top of the World," a song that Bill often performed.[6]

Curly recalled that there was some discussion away from the microphone. "[Bill] said, 'You lead it.' I said, 'No, I'm going to tenor it today.' And Joe Stuart was playing with Bill then. He slipped over to me and said, 'You're gonna be sorry for that.' [Bill] put it up two frets above where he'd ever sung it!" Then Carlton Haney introduced the song: "Here's one of the few times you're going to hear anybody sing tenor with Bill Monroe. Because Curly Seckler has sung and made so many great records singing tenor with Lester and Earl, he's going to sing tenor with Bill Monroe on this song. Bill will do lead, in D, fellows. 'Sitting on Top of the World.' All right, Curly, get ready."[7]

Before Carlton finished speaking, Baker and Greene kicked off the song with their dynamic twin fiddle harmonies. Monroe sang the first verse, which was in an impressively high range, even for him, and Curly stepped up to the mic to join him on the chorus. "And I went across them treetops like a jet!" Curly declared. "Back then I didn't care how high they got it. And I sung tenor to Bill Monroe, leading that song."

Herschel Sizemore was there that day, playing mandolin with the Shenandoah Cutups. He noted that Monroe would often challenge his fellow musicians and "liked to make somebody else look weaker than him." But in this case, Herschel said, "[Curly] busted it wide open."[8] Tony Williamson, who was sixteen at the time, was in the audience with his tape recorder. He said "Basically, Monroe was challenging Curly. Curly hit it square on. I mean, he nailed it, just nailed it, that first verse! If Curly had missed it, Bill would have looked at him, but he looked straight ahead. And it was strong!"[9]

Tony's recording of the performance is proof that neither Curly, at age fifty, nor Bill, at nearly fifty-nine, had lost any of the vocal power and range that elevated them to legendary status. "It was another stroke of genius of Carlton Haney, to get these two giants of tenor singing together," Tony said. "Everybody there knew the songs, knew the stories, and they knew who these people were. It was absolutely an electric moment. They were two mighty men of the tenor, going up toe to toe, and it was pretty amazing."[10]

Tony pointed out that Curly and Bill Monroe had similar styles of singing, which might be why they sang so well together. "Curly Seckler is what I consider a broad-voiced tenor," Tony explained, "which is different from a pinpoint tenor, like Bobby Osborne. When Bobby sings his tenor note, it's just pure note, and there's no overtones. When Curly sings it, there's a lot of air, and there's a wide variety of overtones. It's a different style. To me it's more inviting. It's like coming into a living room and sitting down and wrapping yourself in a warm blanket, as opposed to standing out on top of a mountain and shooting your laser voice off it. And Monroe was like that also."[11]

About this time Curly and Joe Greene played at a festival somewhere in Virginia, and they were scheduled to perform a Sunday morning gospel set. Singer Red Smiley, who had ceased touring because of health issues and no longer had a regular band, was also in the line-up. Red came to Curly to ask if Curly would sing tenor with him on his set. Curly responded, "Red, I've been wanting to do that all my life." Curly proposed that they combine their bands and their time slots and perform together for the time allotted. It would be the first and last time Curly ever sang with Red because Smiley passed away at age forty-seven in January 1972.

On Thanksgiving weekend in 1970, Curly and Joe performed at the second annual South Carolina State Bluegrass Festival at the Convention Center in Myrtle Beach. This festival was presented by Roy Martin, who also started the Georgia State Bluegrass Festival in Lavonia and a number of other events. Curly often worked on Martin's shows during the 1970s and 1980s. Joe and Curly were at the 1970 Myrtle Beach festival all three days: November 27, 28, and 29. Bill Monroe was also there each day, and was featured in reunion performances with Clyde Moody, Don Reno, Ralph Stanley, Carl Story, Mac Wiseman, and Chubby Wise. Lester Flatt and the Nashville Grass were there on Saturday and Sunday, and a Sunday "reunion concert" featured Lester, Curly, Mac Wiseman, and Chubby Wise.

In December Seckler and Greene played a house concert in Montvale, New Jersey, at the home of Loy Beaver. For a couple of years, Beaver and

Dave Freeman put on a series of monthly house concerts with various bluegrass artists including Bill Monroe, Ralph Stanley, and the Lewis Family.
Freeman, who owned County Records, had recently released Joe Greene's
fiddle album, so they decided to book him. This would turn out to be a
fortuitous occasion for Curly.

Joe agreed to bring along a band to play with him. Dave recalled, "It
turned out he brought Cliff Waldron and Curly Seckler. I remember we
were surprised. We didn't know exactly who he was going to come up with.
It was a good show, and they did a lot of the old Flatt and Scruggs stuff,
because they all knew it. Joe loved to do the Benny Martin–type fiddle
breaks. Anyway, we got to talking to Curly, and I asked him if he would be
interested in doing an album."[12]

Dave later came to Nashville to meet with Curly. They discussed the
album project and agreed on the Shenandoah Cutups as the band to back
Curly on the recording. This group, formed in the spring of 1969, was originally composed of three former members of Red Smiley's Bluegrass Cutups:
fiddler-guitarist Tater Tate, banjoist Billy Edwards, and bass player John
Palmer. Smiley had decided to retire from touring after his television show
at WDBJ-TV in Roanoke was taken off the air. John Palmer then called
mandolinist Herschel Sizemore, who had just finished a two-year stint in
Jimmy Martin's band, and singer Jim Eanes. Sizemore relocated to Roanoke
from Alabama. "I came to Roanoke the fifteenth of April, 1969," he said,
"and we bought Red's bus and all of his equipment. Mac Wiseman had a
booking agency in Wheeling, West Virginia, and we started working the
Wheeling Jamboree, and he was booking us."[13]

They initially took the name Shenandoah Valley Cutups, which was an
amalgam of Jim Eanes's band's name, the Shenandoah Valley Boys, and the
Bluegrass Cutups. Eanes departed the band after a year, and they shortened
the name to Shenandoah Cutups. Just before Eanes left, they recorded their
first album for County Records, called *Shenandoah Valley Quartet, with Jim
Eanes.*

Decades later, no one seemed to remember exactly whose idea it was to
put the Cutups together with Curly. It is likely that disc jockey and writer
Bill Vernon was involved. Like Freeman and his associates Charles Faurot
and Loy Beaver, Bill was a part of the close-knit New York bluegrass scene
of the 1960s and early 1970s. Though his father, a corporate tax attorney,
had had high hopes that Bill would make it on Wall Street, his life had taken

a different turn. When he was about thirteen, Bill first heard Lester Flatt and Curly Seckler singing "We Can't Be Darlings Anymore" on the radio, and from then on he knew he wanted to be involved with bluegrass music. After briefly attending Brown University he did spend twelve years working in finance, but his passion for music eventually took precedence. In 1964 Bill started a weekly radio program of his own at WBAI-FM in New York. Then, in 1970, he left his job on Wall Street and began working full-time in radio. He also became the record review editor for Carlton Haney's *Muleskinner News*, one of the leading bluegrass publications of that time.

Vernon had avidly followed Flatt and Scruggs during the 1950s and 1960s when they performed in the New York area and had struck up a friendship with Curly. Bill was also a fan of the Shenandoah Cutups, and he wrote the liner notes to their 1970 album on the County label.[14] He may have encouraged Dave Freeman to enlist them to record with Curly. In any case, Dave said, "It seemed to be a good match, because they knew the stuff, and they had the same kind of feel for the music. They had cut the gospel album for us, and we were on pretty friendly terms with them, and we might have just suggested [to Curly], 'Hey, here's a band that's all ready to go and could back you up fine.'"[15]

Another associate of Dave's in the New York scene was Paul Gerry, who had recently opened a recording studio in Ferndale, New York. Freeman had enlisted his services as an engineer for several County releases, and Gerry also had been recording the house concerts at Loy Beaver's home. Dave arranged for Curly to record at Gerry's studio on May 12 and 13, and Gerry arranged some bookings in the area for Curly with the Shenandoah Cutups to help pay their travel expenses. Curly drove to Roanoke to meet the Cutups and then rode with them on their bus to New York.

The list of songs Curly had picked out to record included his originals "No Mother or Dad," "That Old Book of Mine," and "What's the Matter Now?," as well as Tommy Scott's "You Took My Sunshine." The former two he had recorded with Flatt and Scruggs, and the latter two he had sung often on their live shows. Other favorites from his Foggy Mountain days included "Old Salty Dog Blues," "Some Old Day," "Thinking About You," and "Don't This Road Look Rough and Rocky." "Worries on My Mind" was a good example of the type of bluesy solo he always enjoyed singing, and, of course he had to include his trademark song, "Moonlight on My Cabin." The gospel quartet "Remember the Cross," written by Curly's old bandmate Howard

Watts, and Hank Williams's "Sing, Sing, Sing" (which Curly probably learned from Charlie Monroe) rounded out the collection.

"That's the numbers that I was singing back then," Curly explained. "I had some good help. Just very well educated when it comes to knowing what to do in bluegrass music was Tater Tate. Billy Edwards was not only a good guy, but a good entertainer. And he knowed how to play a banjo [right]. John Palmer, you couldn't beat him, when it come to playing a bass. And Herschel Sizemore was as good a mandolin picker as any man would ever want on an album. We didn't get to rehearse, very little, on it. We just run over a number or two and then recorded it."

Dave Freeman remembered that the session went very smoothly. "Curly was a real pleasure to work with," he said. "It was a nice atmosphere, no big problems. Somebody like Curly, whatever he wanted to do was fine. In those days we pretty much did it with two or three mics, and let it go."[16] Herschel Sizemore recalled that "we just went in and started cutting, just like we worked together all the time. Because the feel of what Curly wanted to do was just pretty much what we was doing all the time. The rhythms, the timing, and all, was the same as what Flatt and them had done. It was a lot of fun for me, because I got to go back and play the breaks that Curly played on the original stuff. In other words, just do some of the stuff he had done [with Flatt and Scruggs].[17]

The night before the recording session, Curly was having throat problems and was afraid he might not be able to sing the next day. Bill Vernon came to his rescue. "I was so hoarse, it was pitiful," Curly said. "I couldn't even sing that night on our show. And Bill Vernon says, 'I know something that'll straighten you up and you'll be singing like a bird in the morning.' So we went and got some Nyquil. He said, 'You take a big swig of that [when] you go to bed tonight, and in the morning you'll be singing.' And sure enough, it worked. I went in that studio the next day and sung that album. You'd never know I was hoarse the day before."

After the album was recorded, Curly and the Cutups began to appear together often at festivals. They performed at Roy Martin's Third Annual Georgia State Bluegrass Festival in Lavonia on the weekend of July 30 to-August 1. On the last day Lester Flatt and the Nashville Grass performed, and Curly made a guest appearance with them, along with Mac Wiseman and Chubby Wise. Dave Freeman was there, and he arranged for photographer Alan Whitman to take the photo that would appear on the County album cover. Curly posed holding Lester Flatt's guitar (perhaps because it was a Martin, and at that time Curly was playing a Yamaha), but at Whitman's suggestion he turned the guitar strap over so that Lester's name was not visible.

In November 1971 Curly once again performed at Roy Martin's Myrtle Beach festival and made a guest appearance with Lester Flatt. They sang "Roll in My Sweet Baby's Arms" and "Salty Dog Blues." Soon afterward the County album, titled *Curly Seckler Sings Again*, was released. Bill Vernon gave it a glowing review in the January 1972 issue of *Muleskinner News*. Walt Saunders gave it a five-star review in *Bluegrass Unlimited* magazine, calling it "a thoroughly enjoyable set by one of the all-time greats of bluegrass." Saunders noted, "Curly, who established himself long ago as one of the best tenor-singing sidemen in bluegrass, emerges here as a formidable soloist as well."[18]

The 1972 festival season was Curly's busiest yet. His bookings included the Montgomery County Bluegrass Festival in Troy, North Carolina; Rual Yarbrough's First Annual Alabama Bluegrass Festival in Tuscumbia, Alabama; Bill Monroe's Third Annual Kentucky Bluegrass Festival in Jackson, Kentucky; and the Blue Grass Special at Country Music Park in Lawtey, Florida. In early July 1972 Curly took Roland White's place with the Nashville Grass for a week, while Roland was in California for his father's funeral.

On the last weekend in July, Curly was back at Roy Martin's festival in Lavonia, Georgia, along with the Shenandoah Cutups. The lineup included Lester Flatt, Bill Monroe, Jimmy Martin, and others. Curly was acting as emcee, and when he introduced Jimmy Martin, Jimmy asked Curly to sing a song with him. They sang "Mother's Not Dead, She's Only Sleeping," a song that Curly had recorded with Charlie Monroe in 1946. Bill Monroe, who was listening, apparently saw an opportunity to challenge Curly again. Before Jimmy's second set, Monroe called Jimmy aside and told him, "This time, when you call him out, you slip it up another key or two on him. I'd just like to see him where he couldn't do it." So when Jimmy introduced Curly, he said, "We're gonna sing 'Mother's Not Dead.' Let's shoot it way up yonder." Curly laughed, "I forget where he put that thing, but I still sung it, and when it was over, [Jimmy] jumped up and kissed me, right on the stage!"

Curly worked several of Roy Martin's indoor shows that fall, including concerts at auditoriums in Charlotte and Atlanta, and at the annual Myrtle Beach festival. Lester Flatt was also booked at most of the events Curly worked, and Curly would make his usual guest appearance on Lester's set. The two often stayed in the same motel, and occasionally even shared a room. They were rooming together once in Myrtle Beach when Curly had to get up early on Sunday morning to perform a gospel program with the Shenandoah Cutups. He left Lester asleep and went over to the convention center, only to realize that he had forgotten to bring his guitar. Curly returned to the motel and had to beat on the door to wake Lester. "[Lester] said, 'You're a great entertainer, going off to work without your guitar!'" Curly chuckled.

"But anywhere that we were at, why he was always after me about coming back [to the band]. I said, 'Flatt, I'm doing too good with my truck.' And so one day he said, 'I want you to name your price.' I don't remember how much it was, but I put him a pretty good figure. He said, 'You've got a job.' But I said, 'Now, one thing that I didn't get years ago, if we do anything on the side, I get my money plus my salary.' He said, 'Anything you ask for, you shall receive.' Then he said, 'I want you to promise me one thing. I want you to shake my hand, and the longest day we both live, we're going to be together.' And I did just that."

CHAPTER 8

The Nashville Grass

1973–1994

Curly's decision to return to working full time with Lester Flatt was based in part on the influence of a young man who had begun touring with the Nashville Grass in September 1972. Marty Stuart was only thirteen years old when he joined the Nashville Grass and realized his dream of becoming a full-time professional musician. Marty grew up in Philadelphia, Mississippi, listening to country music and watching the *Flatt & Scruggs TV Show* every Saturday evening. He began to play guitar, fiddle, and mandolin at an early age, and his parents frequently took him to live music events. In 1971 he went to Bill Monroe's Bean Blossom festival and saw Lester Flatt perform live for the first time.

Many years later, Marty still remembered being in awe as he watched Flatt walk down the dusty road from the tour bus to the stage. "I wanted to go up and get his autograph, and I choked up and couldn't," he recalled. "I followed him all the way to the stage. What really touched me was how, when he walked through a crowd, it was like people just kind of parted. Hippies and farmers, old people and young people, they all just wanted to touch him."[1]

Although he was too intimidated to speak to Flatt, Marty did strike up a conversation with Nashville Grass mandolin player Roland White. "And he was really kind to me, let me play his mandolin, took time to show me some things," Marty said.[2] The following summer Marty toured with the Sullivan Family Band, a gospel group from Alabama. When they played at festivals where the Nashville Grass was also booked, Marty would spend time with his new friend Roland. "As the summer closed, I was having to think about going home and going to school," Marty recalled. "[Roland] gave me his phone number and [said], 'If you ever want to come up, hang out, ride the bus, let me know. I'll ask Lester, and you ask your mom and dad.' So right after I got back to school, I hated it, because I'd been out on the circuit and seen the world. I discovered applause and girls and wonderful people and creative spirits, and got paid on top of that, so to go back to the mundane world of ninth grade didn't work out. I got dismissed from school one day, and I went home and called Roland. He invited me up, Labor Day weekend, 1972. We went to Delaware."[3]

Feeling like a seasoned veteran after his eye-opening summer on the road, Marty was no longer afraid to approach Flatt. As soon as the bus was under way, Marty made up for lost time. "I spun his head around for twelve miles, and just never let up on fact after fact of what I liked about him, Earl, and the Foggy Mountain Boys, and the Nashville Grass," Marty laughed. "And when I finally shut up, he said, 'Where in the hell did you come from?' I said, 'Mississippi.' He said, 'Well, put 'er here,' and he stuck his hand out, and we were buddies from there on."[4]

"Lester was really enamored with this little boy," Roland White recalled. "You talked to Marty, it was like talking to an adult. He was a really sharp little kid."[5] As they rode along, Lester heard Marty and Roland jamming in the back of the bus, and he decided to have Marty perform with the band that weekend. The audiences loved Marty, and at the end of the trip, Flatt offered him a job. Marty's parents agreed to let him move in with Lester and Gladys, and Lester promised that he would make sure Marty continued his education while on the road.

By this time Josh Graves, Jake Tullock, and Vic Jordan had all left the Nashville Grass. Jordan left in March 1971 and was replaced by Haskel McCormick. Tullock had suffered a heart attack in May 1970, and by the summer of 1971 he had decided to retire from the road. Johnny Johnson, who had been playing rhythm guitar with the band, took over as bass player. Graves left the band in early 1972 after a dispute with Flatt. His replacement, Jack Martin, was with the band when Marty Stuart joined them, but left a few weeks later and was replaced by Charlie Nixon.

In early 1973 Roland White received a call from his brother Clarence, who had just finished a stint with folk-rock band the Byrds and was interested in putting together a bluegrass band to tour in Europe. Roland (mandolin), Clarence (guitar), and their brother Eric (bass) grew up playing music together and, after their family moved from Maine to California, they formed a band called the Country Boys. After changing their name to the Kentucky Colonels, they spent several years touring on the folk-bluegrass circuit before disbanding. Roland then joined Bill Monroe's band (playing guitar), and Clarence took up the electric guitar. Clarence worked with various groups and did session work for several years before joining the Byrds in 1968.

Roland agreed to reunite with Clarence and Eric for the European tour and turned in his notice to Lester Flatt. It was then that Lester met with Curly Seckler and was finally able to convince him to join the Nashville Grass. Marty Stuart, who was living with Lester at the time, recalled that "Curly came out [to the house], and him and Lester had a long talk, just the two of them, in the living room. I knew better than to go in there. It was business between those two guys."[6]

Marty was thrilled to hear that Curly was coming back as Lester's singing partner. "Curly came in, and it was like a train came back in the band," he said. "There was just this oak-tree–like presence that Curly brought back to that band. It would have been kind of like had Babe Ruth come back to the Yankees and could really do it again. When Curly came back, it brought a piece of [Lester's] architectural kind of sound, and put it back in focus. 'Seck' brought that traditional Foggy Mountain Boys spark, the original fire, and it was a welcome thing. Lester took a lot of pride in having Curly back, and I think Curly was glad to be back. And, boy, he hadn't lost an inch of ground musically. He just sounded rested and revived and charged up, ready to go. They fell right back into their old brotherly routine."[7]

Marty had first met Curly shortly after arriving in Nashville. "Me and Roland White were headed somewhere, and there was a Morgan truck," Marty recalled. "Curly was driving for Morgan Trucks, and something had happened to his truck, and he was off to the side of the road, waiting for somebody to help him. We pulled over, and I met Curly. And I thought, 'Wow, Curly Seckler!' He didn't have on a hat and tie, [but] he was still Curly Seckler."[8]

Curly didn't recall that chance meeting, but he had a vivid recollection of an encounter they had about a month later at a festival in Lawtey, Florida.

Curly had made a mobile home delivery near the festival site, and when he arrived at the festival in his truck, he saw the Nashville Grass tour bus. "Soon as I parked that truck," Curly laughed, "directly that door popped open on the bus, and here come Marty with that little bitty hat on, running with a piece of paper, wanting my autograph. He was so little he couldn't get up in the truck. I ain't never forgot, that's the first time I met him." The experience was unforgettable for Marty, as well. "He was playing that Yamaha guitar, and he was wearing that brown suit he [wore] on the cover of *Curly Seckler Sings Again*, and we backed him up. He also came over and sang a song—or, as he said—'a number or two' with Lester."[9]

After that, every time they were booked on the same event, Marty would spend time with Curly. He initially had been resistant to Lester's invitations to come back, and it was Marty's enthusiasm that finally swayed him. "He was just a super little guy," Curly said, "and he always said I needed to come back and get in there. He just kept kind of hammering around about this and that. So we finally worked out a deal and I turned my truck over to my son."

Curly's arrival was the exclamation point at the end of the sentence declaring that Lester Flatt had reclaimed the torch for traditional bluegrass. Although he immediately had returned to a more traditional sound in his stage shows after the split with Scruggs, it had taken longer to get there in the studio. Flatt's initial recordings with the Nashville Grass were elaborate productions supervised by Columbia's Bob Johnston, who had taken over producing Flatt and Scruggs in 1967 when Don Law retired. Johnston had pushed Flatt and Scruggs to embrace the contemporary material that, in the end, was to contribute to Flatt's dissatisfaction. The material on Flatt's first sessions was a bit more traditional than were the final Flatt and Scruggs recordings, but the instrumentation still included heavy drums, electric bass, twelve-string guitar, piano, and harmonica. When Flatt moved to RCA Victor in 1970, he began to recapture the style that had brought him so much success in earlier years. The drums and piano were still there but were much less dominant, and Flatt sounded more comfortable with the lyrics. Along with new songs written by Flatt, Josh Graves, Bob Leftridge, and others, and instrumentals by Vic Jordan, Flatt rerecorded some of his earlier classics such as "Little Cabin Home on the Hill" and "Head Over Heels in Love."

In late 1970, after performing together at Roy Martin's festival in Myrtle Beach, Lester Flatt and Mac Wiseman came up with the idea of recording together. Flatt had invited Wiseman to join him on stage to sing "We'll Meet Again, Sweetheart," a song they originally recorded together in 1948. "He called me out, and the audience just erupted," Wiseman recalled. "He turned to me and said, 'Hey, we might be on to something here!'"[10] This would turn out to be an auspicious move for both of them. In March 1971 they were in the studio to record the first of what would be three highly successful albums. These duets with Wiseman harkened back to the earliest days of Flatt and Scruggs, and they were the first duets that Flatt had recorded in more than a decade. Both the band and the singers sounded relaxed and comfortable, and producers Bob Ferguson and Jack Clement obviously knew when to step back and let the music flow naturally. By 1972 Flatt and Wiseman not only were performing together at festivals but also were booking some show dates as a package, backed by the Nashville Grass.

Marty Stuart first recorded with the Nashville Grass on October 18, 1972, just six weeks after he joined the band, and a couple of weeks after his fourteenth birthday. At this session, Marty played some nice twin fiddles with Paul Warren and sang the high baritone vocal part, which had been missing from the band's sound since Jake Tullock's departure. In January 1973 Roland White made his last recordings with the Nashville Grass. Once Roland left the band, Marty Stuart stepped ably into the mandolin slot, and Curly Seckler came aboard as the second rhythm guitarist. Curly's first weekend out with the band included three days in Missouri, March 15–17.

Lester Flatt and Mac Wiseman made their final recordings together for RCA on July 5, 1973. Curly did not participate. He first recorded with the Nashville Grass in August and September 1973. Those sessions produced two Flatt solos, one gospel quartet, one duet, three trios, and Haskel McCormick's instrumental "McCormick String Picnic." Curly easily stepped back into the mix, although he discovered that Flatt was now singing in a lower register than he had been earlier.

About this time, Curly acquired the Martin D-35 guitar that he continued to play for the rest of his career. When Marty Stuart first saw Curly playing a Yamaha guitar in Florida, he had thought, "He needs a Martin."[11] After Curly joined the Nashville Grass, Marty came across the D-35 and arranged for Curly to buy it. Curly then sold his Yamaha to Lester, who wanted it for his granddaughter to play.

Within weeks of the September recording session, Haskel McCormick departed the band and was replaced by twenty-one-year-old Kenny Ingram. Kenny had begun his career with James Monroe and the Midnight Ramblers and then worked about a year and a half with Jimmy Martin before joining the Nashville Grass. A dedicated Scruggs disciple, he brought the band even closer to the classic Flatt and Scruggs sound.

It had been eleven years since Curly had toured with Flatt and Scruggs, and significant changes in venues had occurred during those years. The folk boom of the 1960s had opened doors for bluegrass in arts theaters and concert halls. Flatt and Scruggs had played at Carnegie Hall just months after Curly left the band and, in the years that followed, they had played a number of urban nightclubs such as the Ash Grove in California. By 1973 bluegrass festivals were cropping up all across the country, providing a good source of work during the summer months. Many well-known bluegrass performers, including Bill Monroe and Mac Wiseman, had started their own festivals or lent their names to such events. In June 1973 Lester Flatt launched a festival in Mount Airy, North Carolina. The following year it was moved to a campground that Flatt purchased near Pilot Mountain. Lester Flatt's Mount Pilot Bluegrass Festival quickly became one of the most popular festivals in the Southeast.

The glory days of filling several drive-in theaters in one night were over, but there was good work at state fairs and amusement parks. Curly recalled one such carnival somewhere in the Northeast at which he and Lester were relaxing on the bus between shows while several of the band members explored the midway. At one point they happened to look out the window and spotted Marty Stuart with Lester's guitar, perched on the back of an elephant. Lester did not appreciate it, and when Marty returned to the bus, he was soundly reprimanded. "I'll never forget," Curly laughed, "Lester said, 'Don't you never get up on an elephant with my guitar again!'"

There were new opportunities in Nashville as well. The parent company of WSM, the National Life and Accident Insurance Company, had built the Opryland theme park in 1972 as a precursor and companion to the new Grand Ole Opry House, which would debut in 1974. In addition to rides and concessions, Opryland presented music of all kinds on a regular basis, and the Nashville Grass played there several times in 1973. Although Martha White had ceased to sponsor Flatt on his own weekly television show in 1970, there were other opportunities for television appearances. Soon after Curly joined the band, the Nashville Grass appeared on the *Porter Wagoner Show*, which was broadcast on WSM-TV and a number of affiliates on Saturdays at 5:00 P.M. Central time. Then, on October 2, they taped the popular rural-themed *Hee Haw* program, which aired nationally on CBS.

Perhaps the most significant development was the amount of work now available for bluegrass musicians at colleges and universities. Flatt and Scruggs had played their first college show in April 1962 at the University of North Carolina, just days after Curly's departure. From then on, colleges became a lucrative source of bookings, and Flatt's agent and manager, Lance LeRoy, continued to capitalize on those opportunities. In the first couple of months after Curly joined the Nashville Grass, they played at Nicholls State University in Louisiana, Western Carolina University, the University of Georgia, Morehead State University in Kentucky, and Michigan State University. They went on to play more than twenty-five different colleges that year.[12]

They were usually successful events, but this was during the 1970s, and college audiences were not at all like the country folk who had flocked to Flatt and Scruggs shows in the 1950s. Curly recalled, "Lester and us went into many a [college], and whoever was in charge of the program would come in [the dressing room] and want to know what kind of dope or whiskey we wanted! Lester said, 'We just want some six-packs of Coke, that's it.' They said, 'Well, so-and-so was here and had it in their contract that we had to have such-and-such a bottle of whiskey and so much dope for them.' And you could go in some of those auditoriums, and I swear that stuff [marijuana smoke] was so strong it'd almost make you drunk."

He remembered one particular outdoor concert at a university where things got so out of hand that the band ended the show and left. "They had kegs set up out there for them kids to drink beer. And they just got drunk, drunk, drunk. Them boys was taking those ladies and just pouring beer down their tops. Just silly as a bunch of ants. They got so bad, some of them got on the stage with us, and you couldn't do nothing. We just had to close the show and forget it."

Not all of their college experiences were like that. On Monday, March 18, 1974, Lester Flatt and the Nashville Grass were joined by Bill Monroe and the Blue Grass Boys for a concert at Vanderbilt University in Nashville. The show was recorded by RCA for the album *Lester Flatt Live! Bluegrass Festival*. Flatt and Monroe had famously ended their long-running feud in 1971, when Flatt performed at Monroe's festival at Bean Blossom. By the time of this recording, they had renewed their friendship and would appear on stage together occasionally when they were booked at the same events. They enjoyed performing the classic songs on which they had originally collaborated, including "Little Cabin Home on the Hill" and "Will You Be Loving Another Man?"

Both bands were at the top of their game for this concert, and the audience greeted them with wild enthusiasm. Flatt and Monroe each chose to perform some of their most traditional material, including a number of instrumentals. Lester and Curly reprised several classic duets from the old days, including "Lost All My Money" ("Long Journey Home"), "Nine Pound Hammer," and "Dig a Hole in the Meadow."

The *Bluegrass Festival* album was Flatt's last release for a Nashville-based major label. By the mid-1970s Nashville was remaking its image and seeking to appeal to a broader, more sophisticated audience. This meant that hillbilly music was no longer welcome as the major labels shunned fiddles and banjos in favor of violin orchestras and brass. In response, a number of independent folk record labels were springing up.

Although he had been dropped by RCA, Flatt recorded one last session in RCA's Studio B. It was his first and only all-gospel album with the Nashville Grass, released in 1975 on Canaan Records. Like the live Vanderbilt recording, *Flatt Gospel* included several popular titles from the Flatt and Scruggs repertoire: "Let the Church Roll On," "Brother, I'm Getting Ready to Go," "God Loves His Children," and "You Can Feel It in Your Soul." There were several traditional gospel favorites, as well as some newer material, including the Flatt-Seckler duet "He Didn't Stop at Calvary," written by Flatt and Ruby Moody. Flatt sounds relaxed and the band seems completely comfortable on these recordings. By this time, sixteen-year-old Marty Stuart had matured into a fine musician, proficient on both mandolin and lead guitar. Kenny Ingram had taken command of the banjo slot, Charlie Nixon and Paul Warren contributed dependably as always, and newcomer Jack Hicks had easily assumed the bass duties. Curly and Lester were back to their hand-in-glove harmonies, and Curly's voice was as strong as ever.

Soon after *Flatt Gospel* was released, the band recorded the *Lester Raymond Flatt* album for Chicago's Flying Fish Records. This project was presented as a retrospective, with liner notes by Lance LeRoy that detailed Flatt's musical career and remarks by Lester interspersed with the songs. Nearly all of the material came from the Flatt and Scruggs repertoire, including Curly's original "That Old Book of Mine," on which Curly took a rare mandolin break. The one exception, Alton Delmore's "When It's Time for the Whippoorwill to Sing," turned out to be a perfect vehicle for a brotherly Flatt and Seckler duet.

Next, Flatt signed with California based CMH Records, which was founded in 1975 by Martin Haerle and North Carolina guitarist Arthur

Smith. This label was to become the home for many traditional bluegrass artists of the day, including Jim and Jesse, Mac Wiseman, Carl Story, Josh Graves, Benny Martin, Don Reno, and the Osborne Brothers. Arthur Smith, who had achieved great success with his hit "Guitar Boogie" and his popular television show on WBTV in Charlotte, had opened the first recording studio in the Carolinas in 1957. Once he partnered with Haerle, many of the CMH recordings were made at Smith's Charlotte studio, a convenient stopover on the southeastern bluegrass circuit.

The first Lester Flatt recording for CMH was *Living Legend*, a two-LP set released in early 1976.[13] Like the *Lester Raymond Flatt* recording, most of the material was reworked from the Flatt and Scruggs repository. Lester and Curly turned in more laid-back versions of such classic duets as "I Don't Care Anymore," "We Can't Be Darlings Anymore," and "Why Don't You Tell Me So?" Curly added his tenor or high baritone harmony for the first time to several songs that Flatt and Scruggs had recorded after his departure, including "Bummin' an Old Freight Train," "Please Don't Wake Me," and "Good Times Are Past and Gone."

Flatt's next release was titled *Heaven's Bluegrass Band* after a song of the same name written by producer Arthur Smith. By this time, Jack Hicks had left the band, and North Carolinian Jervis "Pete" Corum was playing bass. Marty Stuart was now a confident, multi-talented eighteen-year-old. While the other band members were pictured on the album cover wearing conservative brown suits, yellow shirts, brown sash ties, and plain straw hats, Marty stood apart, with long hair, bellbottom blue jeans, an open-necked shirt with a bandana around his neck, a stylish black jacket, and a wide and colorful feather band on his hat. Flatt was still singing well, though he sang in a noticeably lower register than he had in earlier years. Curly's vocals were generally low in the mix compared to the Flatt and Scruggs recordings, but he did shine on the one duet, "Ten Years of Heartaches," written by Flatt, Jake Lambert, and Josh Graves.

Soon after the release of *Heaven's Bluegrass Band*, on October 16, 1976, Lester Flatt and the Nashville Grass performed at South Rowan High School in China Grove. This was a special day for Curly, as the town had declared it "John Sechler Day," and hundreds of Sechler relatives from several states had gathered at Mount Zion Church for a family reunion. It was Curly's first public performance in his hometown in more than thirty-five years. After a covered-dish meal at Mount Zion the band gave two performances in the high school gym. Emcee Harold Mitchell of WBOB radio in Galax,

Virginia, presented Curly with an award from the local Lions Club in recognition of his outstanding contribution to the development and promotion of country music.

Lester Flatt remained with CMH for the rest of his career, but *Heaven's Bluegrass Band* was one of the last studio albums he made. Things had been going well for him professionally, but in the summer of 1974 Flatt's private life had begun to crumble. In the fall he filed for divorce, ending forty-two years of marriage to Gladys. During this time, when the band was on the road, "a lot of mornings you could come up out of your bunk and Lester'd be sitting up there in the seat, crying," Curly recalled. "And I'd say, 'Flatt, is there anything on God's earth I could say or do that would help you in any way?' He said, 'Seck, you know what we always said on this bus: if you've got a problem at home, leave it there.' So that was as far as it would go. He never would talk about their problems."

Lester's health began to deteriorate, and in July 1975 he underwent heart bypass surgery. In March 1976 he had gallbladder surgery. According to Jake Lambert, Flatt suffered from diabetes and hepatitis as well.[14] After recovering from his bypass surgery, Lester moved into an apartment in Hendersonville with Joyce Goodwin and her teenaged son Danny. Flatt had originally met Joyce when she was working at the Sparta hospital where he was treated after his first heart attack in 1967. According to Jake Lambert, Joyce was not a registered nurse, but she had nursing skills, and as Flatt's health declined she became his constant companion, both at home and on the road.

Curly recalled that Lester spoke with the band about it before he started bringing Joyce along. "Lester said, 'I always told all of you that we'd never carry no women on our bus, and we didn't. But I've got to the shape where I've got to do it.' And he said, 'If you don't like it, and you don't like it'—he pointed to every one of us—'get out now, because she's coming on that bus.' Well, most of them snarled their nose up about it, but it didn't hurt me. Because I knowed Lester Flatt was getting to the point where, if he didn't have some help, we'd have to haul him to a hospital every night on the road somewhere. But there she was, and she took care of it. If it hadn't been for her, I'd have had to done it, or somebody else. That's why I thought the world of her, because who on God's earth would have did the things she did for that man?"

Lester was not the only one with health issues. Fiddler Paul Warren's health began to go downhill not long after Flatt had heart surgery. Paul was in and out of the hospital with liver problems, was taking pain medication, and was also having issues with cramping in his fingers. By January 1977 Paul had become too ill too travel, and he left the band. He passed away on January 12, 1978. Initially, Paul was replaced by Benny Martin; it was an ironic twist of fate, since Paul had replaced Benny in the Foggy Mountain Boys almost exactly twenty-three years earlier. Martin only stayed for a few months, then Marty Stuart briefly held down the fiddle slot until Curly's old friend Tater Tate came on board. Tate arrived just in time to participate on the band's next album, *Lester Flatt's Bluegrass Festival*, a live two-LP set recorded over the weekend of June 22–25, 1977, at Lester's Mount Pilot Festival.

Longtime WSM announcer Eddie Stubbs, who was born in 1961 in Gaithersburg, Maryland, grew up listening to recordings by Flatt and Scruggs over WAMU radio in Washington, DC. While learning to play fiddle he became a big Paul Warren fan, but he was never able to meet his hero. Paul had already left the band when Eddie went to his first Nashville Grass concert, which was at Baird Auditorium in Washington, on February 27, 1977. It was an unforgettable evening for Eddie, who was already obsessed with the music he had heard on radio and recordings. Eddie had a copy of Flatt's *Living Legend* album and he had memorized every nuance of that album cover. "I had studied the way these guys combed their hair, the way they knotted their ties, the suits they had on," he recalled. "[That night] Curly was wearing that black suit that he wore on the album [cover]."[15]

The next time Eddie saw the band was in early June at a festival at Indian Springs, Maryland. "That was the very first festival that I'd ever been to," Eddie said. "I went there with one intention, and that was to see Lester Flatt and the Nashville Grass. I got my picture made with Curly at that event. Charlie Nixon invited me onto the bus, and Lester was sitting up there in that big chair in the front. I was, like, in heaven, to go to their inner sanctum! They're getting ready to go on stage, and Curly comes up to the front of the bus. In the wheel well, those Silver Eagle buses had a mirror that was about six inches wide and ten inches in height. Curly had one of those sash ties that they wore, and he stood there and tied that tie. I asked him how he did that, and he taught me how to tie that tie that day. And I remember how he wanted every hair in place, and put that hat just right, and he looked himself over. It was pure show business, pure theater. It just really impressed me, Curly and Lester, how much pride they took in the way they looked. I never forgot that."[16]

Eddie also remembered that during their set Lester walked off the stage at one point, leaving Curly to take over as emcee until Lester returned to close out the show. That was not unusual—he had been doing this since the Flatt and Scruggs days—but over the course of the next year, as Lester's health continued to decline, Curly was forced to assume an even greater leadership role. In the winter of 1977, Flatt spent three weeks in the hospital with pneumonia. By the spring of 1978, he was too weak to stand on stage, and would perform sitting on a stool. Joyce would walk alongside him from the bus to the stage as he leaned on her for support. Lester was suffering from congestive heart failure, and it was gradually robbing him of his ability to perform. By August 1978, when Flatt was scheduled to make another live recording at Martha White's Bluegrass Caravan Festival in Church Hill, Tennessee, he was struggling to sing. Only three of his vocals, one of which was a recitation, made it onto the album. The rest of the two-LP set was comprised of performances by the Nashville Grass, the Bluegrass Cardinals, Buddy Spicher and the Nashville Superpickers, and others.

"[Lester] was just skin and bones," Curly recalled. "He got to where, if we got up to sing 'Salty Dog Blues,' he'd lose his time on it. He'd say, 'Seck, what's wrong with us?' Well, I couldn't say, 'Flatt, you just ain't got it no more.' Then I got him talked into not trying to do no more singing. Sometimes he'd come in and introduce us and then he'd leave [the stage]. It got to where he wasn't able to even come in the schoolhouse or wherever we was playing, so I wouldn't mention about him being there. He'd say, 'Don't mention that I'm on the bus. Just go do the show.' But he still liked to ride that bus."

Marty Stuart noted, "The older Lester got, and the sicker he became, he really relied on Curly. And Lester, when he couldn't sing, he'd turn up the charm. He'd sit on that stool and introduce us and build us up. The statement that brought it all home to me, Lester said [to the audience] one night, when it was Curly's time, 'I want to introduce you to my brother now.' And I know Lester Flatt. He didn't throw words around. If he didn't mean it, he wouldn't have said it."[17]

The beginning of the end came on November 21, 1978, when Flatt was admitted to Baptist Hospital in Nashville after suffering a cerebral aneurism. At this point, the reality set in that he would never be well enough to travel with the band again. Flatt met with Lance LeRoy and asked him to inform the band members that he would no longer be able to keep them on the payroll. If Flatt was able to work again, or if the band fulfilled any remaining obligations, they would be paid by the job, but their salary had to stop. Marty Stuart realized he would need to start looking for other work.

On December 2, while Lester was still in the hospital, Bob Dylan played at Nashville's Municipal Auditorium. After the show, Marty went backstage to talk with him. Dylan asked about Lester and Earl, and Marty replied, "Well, Lester's dying, and they don't speak much anymore. They're always talking about getting together, but it never seems to happen." Dylan responded, "That's really sad. Abbott and Costello were going to do that, but they never got around to it."

Marty later recalled, "When he said that, it was like a bag of rocks fell on me. I left Bob's dressing room, went to a pay phone, got Earl's number, called Earl, introduced myself. I said, 'Can I come out and speak to you?' He said, 'Well, sure.' And I sat there with him and Louise, and I stated my case: 'Lester's dying, and I know that he don't want to die without saying goodbye to you, because he loves you.' I wrote the [hospital] room number down, and the phone number. He said, 'I'll think about it,' and he left it at that. And the Nashville Grass had to go out and play a couple of concerts. When we came back, Lance met us where we parked the bus, and he had tears in his eyes, and he said, 'Earl went and saw Lester.' And when he said that, it was like a green light went off in my heart. I knew I [could] move on. But Curly, beyond anybody else, stuck it out to the bitter end. Lester kind of bequeathed it all to him."[18]

Lester was upbeat when he told Curly about his visit with Earl. "He said that they had quite a little talk," Curly recalled. "And he mentioned that they said they might do another thing together. But he didn't live to make it." Although Lester recovered enough to go home for Christmas, he was extremely weak. He did not work at all through the winter, but by March he was feeling well enough to return to the *Grand Ole Opry*. He told an AP reporter, "I feel a little better all the time. The doctor told me the last time he saw me that I was in the best shape in a long time."[19] But Curly had been watching his friend's decline, and he knew that Flatt's days were numbered. He felt that the time had come for Lester to get his spiritual life in order.

Curly had attended Mount Zion Church in his youth, but he had never been deeply religious until he began to spend time with Marty Stuart and his family in the mid-1970s. It started when Curly was driving the bus for the Nashville Grass, and Marty would sit up with him and ride shotgun

They would pass the hours talking, and on a road trip in 1977, Marty told Curly of a religious conversion he had recently experienced. "In the dark of the night, going through the middle of nowhere, I said, 'Curly, I've had a change in my life, and it feels real good.' And the more I told him about it, the more he listened and the quieter he got," Marty said. "And I carried him to my preacher, and I saw Curly make that change. And more than anybody else [that] I've ever walked down to that altar, Curly grabbed a hold of it and has never wavered."[20]

Curly began to attend church with the Stuart family and was baptized at First Baptist Church in Smyrna, Tennessee, on September 17, 1978. Marty laughed when he recalled that, even in church, Curly kept his playful sense of humor. "When Curly came up out of the water, he stuck a hand out and said, 'Thank you, neighbor,' to the preacher."[21] Curly had invited several musical friends, including Flatt, to join him at the event, and he chuckled when he remembered Lester's reaction. "When I went under the water, he tapped whoever was sitting beside of him on the knee and said, 'He dunked a good one!'"

In early 1979 Curly began to talk with Lester about his spiritual life and urged him, "Why don't you try to do something for the Lord before it's too late?" Flatt had also been talking with his pastor friend Olan Bassham, who agreed to make arrangements for his baptism. On March 7, 1979, Curly drove the bus with Lester, Joyce, and several band members and friends to Main Street Church of Christ in Manchester, Tennessee. There Lester was baptized by Bassham, with assistance by pastor Leamon Flatt.[22]

Curly had been watching a faith healer on television, and he felt that this man might be able to help Lester. The week after he was baptized, Flatt was scheduled to appear on Friday night at the *Grand Ole Opry*, but Curly called him and asked him to consider attending one of this evangelist's services instead. Curly told him, "In my opinion you've did all you'll ever be able to do for the *Opry*, and they can't do nothing more for you. Let's get into some revivals." Lester thought it over, called Curly back and said, "Well, I've cancelled the *Opry*. What's next?" Curly responded, "We need to get in your bus and take off to Fort Lauderdale, Florida."

Curly, Lester, Joyce, and her son Danny set off for Fort Lauderdale, where the evangelist was conducting a tent revival. Once there, they met with the evangelist, and he arranged a place for Lester to sit on the stage. "They sat Lester Flatt down in that chair, and there was just hundreds of people, all of them praying for Lester," Curly said. "Big teardrops coming out of his eyes, and him hollering, 'Amen!' And from that day on I kept him in them revivals."

After spending the weekend of March 16–17 in Fort Lauderdale, Lester made his return to the *Grand Ole Opry* for Old Timer's Night on Friday, March 23. It was his first *Opry* appearance since he had been hospitalized in November, and he was warmly welcomed. A photo from that night in Jake Lambert's book showed Lester to be frail and emaciated but smiling broadly.[23]

During the next several weeks Curly took Lester to revival meetings in Alabama and Texas. Curly's intentions were good, but Lance LeRoy believed that the evangelist's were not. "Oh, he was purely a crook," Lance maintained. "He was trying to hit Lester up for big money. And right before Lester died he told me he realized the guy was [just] after his money."[24] LeRoy may well have been correct, because the evangelist later was convicted and served time in prison for tax evasion. Curly maintained that he never saw Lester hand over any money, other than a nominal contribution to the collection plate.

Lester returned for what would be his final performance on the *Opry* on Friday, April 6. The following week, after they attended a revival in Louisiana, Lester asked Curly to go with him to the back of the bus so that they could talk privately. He then told Curly, "Seck, if I get back on that *Opry*, after we do the Martha White theme song, I'm going to call you up to the microphone and introduce you as my partner. Then, when I'm not able to play the *Opry*, they can't keep you out. You can go down there and handle the Martha White show just as good as I do."

Unfortunately, Flatt was unable to carry out his plan. On April 23 he was admitted to Baptist Hospital in Nashville for a "re-evaluation" of his heart condition.[25] According to Lance LeRoy, by this time Lester had advanced congestive heart failure. One of his doctors told Lance, "He's got a very weak heart. The walls of his arteries are real thin. One of them could break any time."[26] Flatt's condition continued to deteriorate, and on Friday, May 11, 1979, he succumbed to heart failure. Although it was no secret that his health had been fragile for some time, the bluegrass world was shocked by the news. Bluegrass music had been in existence for only thirty-three years, and one of its most well-loved originators and leaders was now gone, at the relatively young age of sixty-four.

On Sunday, May 13, a memorial service was held at Cole and Garrett Funeral Home in Hendersonville, and on May 14, Flatt's funeral and burial took place in his hometown of Sparta. Olan Bassham presided over both services. Many of Flatt's friends and associates from the *Opry* attended the service in Hendersonville. Several hundred friends, family members, and fans filled the funeral home in Sparta on Monday to say their goodbyes.[27] Curly, Marty Stuart, and other band members were pallbearers. Also present at both services were Gladys Flatt and Joyce Goodwin, who by that time claimed to be Flatt's common-law wife.

Joyce came to Curly after Flatt's death and asked for his help in obtaining a share of Flatt's estate. According to Jake Lambert, the estate was divided between Flatt's daughter Brenda (who was actually his niece but was raised as his daughter) and her two children.[28] No provision was made in Flatt's will for Joyce or for Gladys, and no provision was made for the Nashville Grass, even though Lester had specifically asked Curly to keep the group together. Curly did help Joyce, and she was awarded some modest compensation, but Curly was left to fend for himself.

Before Flatt died, Curly recalled, "he wanted me to shake hands with him and tell him that I would take the group and carry on, and [keep] the music down to earth, like he had it. And he said, 'One of these days they're going to accept you, without [me].' And they did, but it was several years before they decided to. I lost quite a bit of money, holding things together, because there was nothing for me to work with. Lester didn't leave me nothing. He was aiming to, [but] he didn't put it in his will. He wanted to hand it to me, [but] he didn't live long enough to do that."

Flatt still had some bookings for the 1979 festival season, and Curly intended to honor them. When Flatt died, some promoters cancelled the band's appearances, others cut the band's fee, and a few, such as Roy Martin, honored the original agreement. At that time, the Nashville Grass included Curly on guitar, Tater Tate on fiddle, Charlie Nixon on Dobro, Blake Williams (who had replaced Kenny Ingram in June 1978) on banjo, and Pete Corum on bass. Marty Stuart had found work with Vassar Clements's band but still played an occasional show with the Nashville Grass. "The agreement was, as long as all of them stayed with me, they got an equal split," Curly explained. "The first couple of years it was really rough, because we had six men, and we had to rent a motor home to travel in. This one dropped out, and that one dropped out, and it wasn't long until it was just me and

Charlie [as partners]. And the first couple of years we went in the hole about $20,000. Then Charlie got sick and had to leave the road. Then it was all up to me, and I made back what I'd lost, and then I made the best money I ever made in the music business."

Curly was featured in a cover story in the November 1979 issue of *Blue-grass Unlimited*. The interview was conducted in late 1978, and the article was scheduled in anticipation of the release of what was to be Curly's second solo album, *No Doubt About It*. Accompanied by the Nashville Grass, Curly had made the recordings in late November 1978, while Lester Flatt was recovering from his stroke. At the same time the band had backed Tater Tate on his instrumental album, *The Fiddler and His Lady*. Both recordings were made for Paul Gerry's Revonah Records. Gerry had started the label about the same time Curly had recorded the County album in Gerry's studio. His roster of artists included the Shenandoah Cutups, Del McCoury, Mac Martin, Red Rector, and a number of lesser-known regional bands. Though *No Doubt About It* was originally intended to be a solo album, it was ultimately released in the summer of 1979 as the first recording by Curly Seckler and the Nashville Grass. The cover photo of Curly holding his guitar and standing in front of Lester Flatt's tour bus made a clear statement: Curly Seckler is ready to carry Lester Flatt's music forward. Bill Vernon's liner notes state, "The day before he died, Lester Flatt asked Curly Seckler to, in his words, 'carry on.' And that's exactly what Curly and the band have been doing, with great success. So, in a very real sense, this album is not an end, it's a beginning."[29]

For the album, Curly chose a nice mix of Foggy Mountain Boys material ("No Doubt About It," "What's Good for You," "Bouquet in Heaven"), solos he had sung through the years ("Who's Been Here?," "No Time for Tears," "Hannah"), and old favorites ("Swing Low, Sweet Chariot," "In the Jailhouse Now," "Valley of Peace"). He also brought Paul Warren's son Johnny in to play the fiddle tune "Lime Rock." Charlie Nixon became ill during the sessions, so Curly called Gene Wooten, an avid disciple of Josh Graves, to play Dobro on several songs. Marty Stuart sang lead on all of the duets, trios, and quartets. But this was clearly Curly's show, and he came across as comfortable, confident, relaxed, and as evidenced in his lively, hilarious performance of "Hannah," a consummate showman.

Once Curly took over leadership of the Nashville Grass, he decided he would like to have a mandolin again. Josh Graves had convinced Curly to sell his Gibson F-2 soon after he left Flatt and Scruggs, and Curly had been content to play guitar in the ensuing years. With Marty Stuart now working elsewhere, Curly felt it was time to find another mandolin. Lance LeRoy was at a festival when he came across a good-sounding instrument that had been built in 1978 by Pennsylvania luthier Frederick Snyder. Lance checked with Curly, and then purchased it for him. It was a copy of a Gibson F-5 with the moniker "The Sound" inlaid on the headstock. Curly kept the instrument and used it often for the rest of his career.

During the summer of 1979, Curly and the Nashville Grass fulfilled Lester Flatt's remaining festival commitments. Charlie Nixon took over management of the band, and he and Curly began booking shows. They hired Billy Smith to sing lead and play mandolin or guitar. Mike Cupit, a young left-handed guitar and fiddle player from Mississippi, filled in before Smith joined the band. Cupit, like Marty Stuart, had started as a teenager with the Sullivan Family and had made guest appearances with the Nashville Grass while Flatt was alive. Curly would continue to call on him whenever the band was short-handed.

After Flatt died, singer Red Allen called Curly, wanting to partner with him. Curly declined his offer but agreed to make an album with him. Red had filled in for Lester Flatt after his heart attack in 1967, and Red enjoyed singing the Foggy Mountain Boys material. He asked Curly and members of the Nashville Grass to join him on a Lester Flatt tribute album for Folkways Records.[30] In October 1979 they went to the Scruggs Sound Studio, which was in Earl Scruggs's basement. Earl's son Steve was the engineer. Just as they were starting the sessions, Blake Williams left the Nashville Grass and was replaced by Kenny Ingram, who had been touring with Jimmy Martin. North Carolinian Gene Wooten, who had worked on the *Opry* with Wilma Lee Cooper, was the Dobro player for these sessions. Red had brought his son, Harley Allen Jr., along, and he played rhythm guitar and sang high baritone on "I'm Waiting to Hear You Call Me Darling." About halfway through the sessions, Red's voice gave out, so Harley sang lead on five of the twelve songs as well.

Curly enjoyed singing with both Allens. "Harley was a good singer," Curly stated. "He phrased his singing a lot like his daddy. Red had some good ways of singing songs like 'Over the Hills to the Poorhouse.' I liked the way he [phrased] it better than the way Lester did. It was altogether different from the way Lester sung it, but after he went over it one time, then I knowed exactly where he was going with his voice, and we matched up, to a T."

Just weeks later, on November 10–12, Curly and Marty Stuart took the Nashville Grass to Hilltop Studios in Madison, Tennessee, to make their first new recording without Lester. Martin Haerle of CMH Records had called soon after Flatt died to ask whether Curly wanted to continue the relationship. Haerle then came to Nashville to meet with Curly and Charlie Nixon, and they signed a two-album contract. Haerle asked Marty Stuart to produce the recordings. By this time Marty was well established in the Nashville music community and had befriended many of its performers, including Johnny Cash, for whom he eventually would work. Curly suggested that Marty invite Cash to make a guest appearance on the first recording, since Cash had always enjoyed Lester Flatt's music. Cash accepted and sang two songs, including "Mother Maybelle," written by Joe and Rose Lee Maphis about Cash's mother-in-law Maybelle Carter, who had died just a year earlier. It was to become one of Curly's favorite songs. He recorded it several times over the years and continued to sing it often on stage through the rest of his career. For this album Curly also revisited the old favorite from his Foggy Mountain repertoire, "Sign Upon the Dotted Line," which was originally recorded by country singer Floyd Tillman in 1946. The album, titled *Take a Little Time,* was released in 1980.

At about that time, Curly joined his old friend Tommy Scott on an album for Folkways called *Now & Then*. They were accompanied by Tater Tate on fiddle, Marty Stuart on guitar and mandolin, and several members of Tommy Scott's band. Curly and Tommy reprised some of their old-timey duet singing, and the music was an eclectic mix. Also in 1980, Old Homestead Records released an LP titled *Rambling Tommy Scott and Curley Seckler: Early Radio, 1941.* It was compiled from transcriptions that Tommy had saved from when he and Curly worked at WRDW in Augusta, Georgia. The LP, which provided a glimpse of what live radio was like in the early forties, included gospel and secular songs, commercials for Vim Herb tonic, and a comedy routine by Tommy with his ventriloquist's doll.

The Nashville Grass returned to Hilltop Studios in 1980 to record one last album for CMH. This time the special guest was gospel singer Betty Jean Robinson. She had first come to Nashville as a songwriter, and had been named Female Country Songwriter of the Year in 1968 by *Billboard*. She then entered the gospel field and had a successful career as a singer and inspirational television personality. The material for this all-gospel recording, *There's Gonna Be a Singing,* included originals from Robinson, traditional hymns, and gospel favorites. Charlie Nixon was in declining health and was unable to participate in the sessions, so Curly enlisted the dependable Gene Wooten to play Dobro. By this time Tater Tate had left the Nashville Grass, and Johnny Warren had stepped in to play fiddle. Johnny had learned from his father Paul Warren, and his playing brought an infusion of the vintage Foggy Mountain Boys sound to the band.

In the spring of 1981 Johnny helped bring back even more of that classic feel to the Nashville Grass by introducing Curly to an unknown singer who would give him a new lease on life and music. Johnny was a regular participant in picking sessions at the home of Bruce Weathers, a banjo player who lived in Madison, just north of Nashville. Bruce had repeatedly told Johnny, "There's this guy you've got to meet. He sings just like Lester." He was referring to forty-two-year-old Willis Spears, who lived in Summertown, about seventy miles south of Nashville. After Billy Smith left the band, Johnny mentioned Willis to Curly as a possible replacement. One day Bruce called Johnny and said, "Willis is coming up. Do you think you can get hold of Curly?" Johnny called Curly, and they met at Bruce's house. "And they got over there, and they sang some stuff," Johnny recalled. "It was just like, that was it, from then on."[31]

"We got together, and I bet we sung for an hour before we ever stopped," Curly said. "He could sing anything, and he sung just like Lester did; used a thumbpick just like Lester, and he sung just as high as Lester did in his early fifties." Curly offered Willis a job and, after taking a week to think it over, Willis accepted. For Curly, this was a dream come true. He noted, "After Lester left, it just wasn't working right. But when I got Willis, then everything just fit like a glove. We went to work and got to doing some of them old numbers, and people really accepted us."

Eddie Stubbs remembered watching Willis and Curly perform together at the Delaware Bluegrass Festival on Labor Day weekend and being amazed at how much they sounded like Lester and Curly had in the 1950s. "Sonny Osborne and myself were standing there," Eddie recalled. "And I said, 'This is really spooky, isn't it?' Sonny said, 'Yeah, it is. I'll tell you what's even spookier; the fact that I saw it the first time around.' And we were standing there in the hot sun, sweating, comparing the chill bumps on our arms."[32]

Bass player Pete Corum had been in and out of the band while he performed in the musical *Cotton Patch Gospel* in New York. He finally left for good in 1981 and was replaced by Bob Rodgers. By this time, Charlie Nixon had also left the band for health reasons. Once Willis joined the group, Curly went back to playing mandolin on live shows and recordings, as he had done in his days with the Foggy Mountain Boys.

The band had been traveling in rented motor homes, but after Nixon left Curly found a yellow Ford station wagon with low mileage and a motor powerful enough to pull a trailer. The car was much less expensive to operate than a motor home, and the band members could store their clothes, instruments, and recordings in the trailer. When they were on the road, the driver and shotgun rider could sit in the front, and the back seat could be folded down so that the other three could sleep in the rear of the vehicle. Curly laughed as he recalled that Kenny Ingram nicknamed the car the Yellow Banana.

Willis had many fond memories of traveling in the Yellow Banana. He recalled, "The first trip I went out on, we went up to Smith Mountain [Virginia], and then went from there to Columbus [Ohio]. On the way up that night we got to harmonizing, just every number we could sing, me and Johnny and Kenny and Curly, leaning up in the Banana. I remember Curly saying he had the band that he'd always wanted. That made me feel good, because I felt like he liked singing with me."[33]

This particular group stayed together for the next five and a half years and made two albums. The first, *China Grove, My Hometown*, produced by Kenny Ingram and Red Allen, was released in 1983 on Folkways Records. The title track was composed by Curly and Nashville songwriter Randall Hylton, who was one of the more prolific bluegrass songwriters of the decade. By this time, Dobro player Gene Wooten had become a fixture on Nashville Grass recordings, and J. T. Gray was brought in to play bass.

In September 1983 promoter John Maness, who had restored Carlton Haney's old Blue Grass Park festival site at Camp Springs, organized a Foggy Mountain Boys reunion as the Saturday night feature of his Labor Day weekend event. The two-hour performance was special not only for the audience but also for the musicians, who had never all been assembled in one place before. Among those present in addition to Curly were Josh Graves, Jake Tullock, Jim Shumate, Jody Rainwater, Jim Eanes, and Hylo Brown. The Nashville Grass served as the core band, with Willis Spears capably playing the role of Lester Flatt. Kenny Ingram provided the Scruggs-style banjo and guitar picking, and Johnny Warren represented his father Paul.

Johnny noted that it was the first time he'd ever played with Jake Tullock. Willis recalled that he and Johnny both heard Jake tell someone backstage that he hadn't played a bass in two years. Later, during the show, John Maness announced that he'd like Jake to come out and play bass on the next song, which, according to the set list, was to be the full-throttle "Roll in My Sweet Baby's Arms." Willis and Johnny looked at each other anxiously. But as soon as Maness announced the song, Willis recalled, "Kenny took off on that thing, and old Jake just hit it right on top of the beat, and [kept] going just like that all the way through!"[34]

For the band's next recording, Curly signed with the pioneering independent label Rich-R-Tone. Originally based in Johnson City, Tennessee, the label was founded in 1946 by Jim Stanton. Its early roster included the Stanley Brothers, the Bailey Brothers, Wilma Lee & Stoney Cooper, and the Sauceman Brothers, among others. Eventually Stanton moved the label to Nashville and opened his own studio on Church Street. Stanton basically ran a one-man business. He produced and engineered the sessions, designed the covers, and wrote the liner notes, all on a modest budget.

Despite poor sound quality, the material on this recording, titled *What a Change One Day Can Make*, was an interesting and enjoyable mix. Curly recorded his own "A Purple Heart" for the first time since making the original in 1952 with Jim and Jesse. Johnny Warren was featured on two fiddle tunes, the traditional "Long Bow John" and his own "Little Paul" (named for his new son), and he sang a rare lead vocal on "Hot Corn, Cold Corn." Marty Stuart joined the band in a surprising but effective performance of Gram Parsons's "Sin City."

In late 1986 Johnny Warren and Kenny Ingram had growing families, and both decided to leave the band. By this time Curly was completely comfortable singing with Willis Spears, and on January 1, 1987, he offered Willis a partnership in the Nashville Grass. They immediately went to work on their next Rich-R-Tone album, an all-gospel release. Since the band was in transition, they brought in Tater Tate to play fiddle and bass, Josh Graves to play Dobro, and eighteen-year-old Ron Stewart to play banjo and guitar. Stewart had made his recording debut at the age of nine, playing fiddle with Flatt and the Nashville Grass on the *Tennessee Mountain Bluegrass Festival* album, and he had since become a skilled multi-instrumentalist. Perhaps in order to save money or to expedite the album's release, only six of the thirteen songs included on the aptly (if unimaginatively) titled *Bluegrass Gospel* album were new recordings. The rest were borrowed from Curly's earlier County and Revonah releases and from a recording he made with banjo player Cranford Nix.[35]

In early January 1987, fiddler Harold Jones and banjo player Larry Perkins joined the band. Larry was from Kannapolis, North Carolina, just a few miles from China Grove, and he had crossed paths with Curly several times at festivals. On one of those occasions he had told Curly, "If Kenny ever leaves, I'd like to have that job." So, when it was time to play the annual New Year's weekend festival at Jekyll Island, Georgia, Curly got in touch with him. "Jekyll Island was the first time he worked with me," Curly said, " and he worked with me up until I retired. He's a good man in the studio, because he could play the banjo or the guitar, in the style that I liked, and we did an awful lot of picking together."

Later that year, Curly received an invitation from David Grisman to take part in his album *Home Is Where the Heart Is*. Grisman, who had started out playing bluegrass but by this time had ventured into acoustic jazz, wanted to record a collection of traditional songs with some of his favorite artists. Guests for the two-LP set, released in 1988, included Doc Watson, Del McCoury, Tony Rice, J. D. Crowe, Ricky Skaggs, Red Allen, and many others. Curly sang three songs: "My Long Journey Home" with Grisman and Doc Watson, "Little Cabin Home on the Hill" with Grisman, Tony Rice, J. D. Crowe, Jim Buchanan, and Roy Huskey Jr., and "Salty Dawg Blues"[36] with Grisman, Rice, Crowe, Sam Bush, and Huskey. Curly enjoyed recording with such a talented group of musicians, and noted, "Dave [Grisman] is one of the hottest mandolin pickers that's ever been on this earth."

On Saturday, June 25, 1988, Earl Scruggs and Marty Stuart joined Curly and the Nashville Grass on stage for a historic reunion at the Frontier Ranch festival near Columbus, Ohio. It was the first time Earl and Curly had performed together since 1962, and it was Earl's first public performance in seven years. Fans came from as far away as California, Japan, and Austria for the event.[37] Earl was still battling chronic hip and back pain related to his 1955 car accident. His right hand had recently been injured in a fall, and he was clearly struggling to play, but the audience welcomed him enthusiastically. Curly directed the show as they re-created the old magic on many Flatt and Scruggs favorites, including "The Ballad of Jed Clampett," "Down the Road," "Foggy Mountain Breakdown," "Salty Dog Blues," and the Martha White theme. Curly recalled, "We took two encores, and [Earl] said, 'We ain't going to take another one. Leave them wanting more.' And we didn't go back on the stage."

Unbeknown to fans, there was actually a discussion of making a series of repeat performances, but nothing ever came of it. By this time Curly's wife

Mable had become so unstable that he had taken her to Park View Hospital's psychiatric unit. It was an expensive private facility, and psychiatric care was not covered by Curly's insurance. "My bill at one time ran over a hundred thousand dollars," Curly said. "Earl heard about some of my bills, so he came over to my trailer. He said, 'I always wanted to do something for you. We'll just take this band that you've got, and work these big schoolhouses, and I'll go along as special guest.' Well, I got Willis and we went out to Earl's and talked that thing over." Curly and Willis were ready to book some shows, but that was the last they heard about the idea. Curly later speculated that Earl had made the proposal without first discussing it with Louise. She was known for running his business affairs with an iron hand and perhaps she felt that Earl teaming with Curly would be a poor business decision.

In September 1988 Curly, Willis, and the Nashville Grass performed at the annual International Bluegrass Music Association (IBMA) FanFest in Owensboro, Kentucky. The IBMA was founded in 1985 by a group of bluegrass businesspeople. Curly was an early supporter of the organization, and once it began to sponsor an annual festival, he was a frequent performer. Artists donated their time, and proceeds from the event went toward the newly established Bluegrass Trust Fund to help artists and their families in time of crisis.

In June 1989 Curly and Willis were back in the studio to record their final album, *Tribute to Lester Flatt*, which was released on cassette in 1990 on Dave Freeman's Rebel Records. Ron Stewart once again was enlisted to play fiddle, and Larry Perkins provided the Scruggs-style banjo and lead guitar. Willis's son-in-law, Philip Staff, was the bass player. Producer Bill Vernon was clearly attempting to re-create the sound and feel of Curly's earliest days with the Foggy Mountain Boys. The material included classics such as "Roll in My Sweet Baby's Arms," "Cabin in Caroline," and "No Mother or Dad," as well as lesser-known gems like "Little Pal," "Give Me the Roses Now," and "God Sent My Little Girl." Curly reprised his trademark mandolin chop and even played breaks on "Why Don't You Tell Me So?" and "I'm Waiting to Hear You Call Me Darling," just as he had on the original recordings forty years earlier.

By this time Curly had started to reduce his touring schedule and was only playing selected show dates. Sometimes he took a band and at other times he worked with a band provided by the promoter. In order to stay closer to home, he performed often at nursing homes in the Nashville area with whatever group of musicians he could put together for the occasion. In January 1992 Larry Perkins organized a reunion of several former Foggy Mountain Boys at the Jekyll Island festival. On hand were Curly, Josh Graves, Chubby Wise, Benny Martin, and Jody Rainwater. That June, Curly and his old friend Benny Sims performed together again at a festival in Summersville, West Virginia.

Now in his seventies, Curly was having some health issues, fueled in large part by the challenges of trying to manage his life at home. About the time Curly took over the Nashville Grass, Mable's condition had begun to deteriorate. "She got to where she wouldn't take her medicine like she was supposed to," he said. "She got in real bad shape." Mable had been a beautiful woman, and she was very particular about her appearance. She spent hours watching home shopping channels and would order everything from wigs to jewelry to exercise equipment, creating thousands of dollars in debt for Curly. "I would wake up at two of a morning, and she'd be on the phone, talking to somebody in Chicago, ordering some junk," Curly recalled. "I had a utility trailer [filled] to the roof with junk that she bought. I let her do what she wanted; that was my fault."

As she became more disoriented, Mable began to wander around the trailer park, sometimes in the middle of the night, so Curly had to put an inside lock on the door. She became increasingly paranoid and was convinced that Curly was trying to kill her. She would stuff quilts under the door of her bedroom to prevent him from pumping any poisonous gas into her room. She hid food under her bed and in drawers and refused to eat anything from a container that had already been opened. She sometimes threw things at Curly, and once tried to attack him with a hammer. One day she hit him and pushed him down onto a coffee table, then grabbed a heavy glass ashtray. "And she had that thing up over my head by the time I come to," Curly said. "If she'd have hit me on the head with that, she'd have killed me. I just happened to look up in time to catch it before it hit my head. I took an awful chance of her killing me. The only thing I could do [to stop her] would be to just wrestle her down to the floor; then she'd give out."

Marty Stuart recalled that he first realized the gravity of the situation when he went with Curly to perform at his church in the mid-1980s. "Mable came to church with Curly, and when she walked in I thought, man, she's really in trouble now," Marty said. "And right in the middle of the service, here she comes down the aisle and she was pulling on the preacher's pant leg. And Curly just as lovingly got up and put his arm around her and kind of scooped her up. But I remember thinking, 'Man, Seck's really got his hands full right now.'"[38]

Finally Curly was forced to have Mable committed to Central State Hospital on Murfreesboro Road. "I had to get two doctors to certify that she was in the condition that she had to go in," he said. "Then I had to get the police to come and pick her up." Once she had been committed, Curly was able to bring her home occasionally on leave, but he had to manage her medications and watch over her constantly. If she became violent before her leave was over, he would have to take her back. "I took her back several times a little early, because she was getting out of hand," he said. "But I felt so sorry for her, being out in that place."

Everyone in Curly's inner circle attested to Curly's love for and loyalty to Mable. His son Ray noted that Curly felt so bad about sending Mable back to the hospital that sometimes "he would just keep her when she should have been in there, locked up."[39] Curly's sister Mary and her husband Walter Freeze added, "He really took care of her while she was in there. He took her [her favorite] White Castle hamburgers every blessed day. Anything that she wanted, she got."[40] Lance LeRoy recalled that every Thursday Curly would bring Mable a set of clean clothes and take her dirty clothes home to wash them. Lance added, "She definitely was insane. She used to call me, usually late at night, and she was always telling me that Curly wanted her dead. She said, 'They're fixing to send me up on the fourth floor. They're butchering them up there, and Curly told them to send me up there.'"[41]

But Mable did have occasional lucid moments. Once, when Mary and Walter went with Curly to visit her at the hospital, she asked Walter if he would like to hear her sing. Walter replied that he certainly would. "She lit in and sung some of those old Hank Williams songs, word for word," he marveled. "And she was on the right pitch and everything. And I told her how much I appreciated it, and it done her so much good."[42]

Eventually, Mable began to resist being returned to the hospital at the end of her leave times, and she told Mary several times that she would kill herself before she would go back. And so, when the phone rang on November 26, 1992, Mary had a premonition that the worst had happened. "I was sitting at my sewing machine, and I said, 'Something's happened,'" she recalled. "It wasn't but a little bit until the phone rang, and he said that Mable had killed herself. I said, 'We'll be there just as quick as we can get there.'"[43]

Curly had brought Mable home for the Thanksgiving holiday, and that morning he had gone out to pick up some groceries and their dinner. "Boy, it was cold that morning," he recalled. "She had made a list [and] she wanted me to go to the Kroger's and pick up some stuff. Shoney's was next to Kroger's, and she said, 'Then go down there and get us a couple of turkey dinners for Thanksgiving. Put on your heavy coat, because it's cold out there.' So I went to Kroger's and then to Shoney's. When I come back, the door was hooked [with a chain]. I couldn't get in. I hollered and I couldn't get no answer. I took a clothes hanger and unhooked [the chain]. Then I went in and she was laying between the couch and the coffee table. I said, 'What's wrong with you?' And then I saw the bullet cartridge, and I said, 'Good Lord, she's shot herself.'"

Curly had a small pistol that he kept well hidden in a box in the closet, but while he was gone Mable had found it. Mary felt that Mable was lucid that day and understood what she was doing. Ray Seckler recalled, "I was the last person to talk to her. I called to wish them a happy Thanksgiving. We talked ten or fifteen minutes, and everything seemed normal. She said, 'Dad's gone to get us some Thanksgiving dinner.' She was just as nice and happy as she could be, seemed like."[44]

After finding Mable, Curly immediately called 911. When the police arrived, they ordered him out of the trailer and began questioning him. They made him wait on the porch while they investigated, then they took him with them to the hospital. Curly had known Mable was dead when he had found her, but the doctors still tried to revive her. "They had a thing crammed down her throat," Curly recalled. "They made me go in there and identify her. It was awful." The police initially had wanted to detain Curly, but they dropped their suspicions as soon as they discovered Mable's medical history.

Mable's funeral was on Monday, November 30, at Forest Lawn Funeral Home. Mary and Walter Freeze had arrived on Friday, and after the funeral they helped Curly clean out Mable's clothes, shoes, and other items, all of which he donated to Central State Hospital. Mary and Walter then took Curly back to China Grove to stay with them for several weeks. In the interim, Curly's son Monnie and his wife replaced all of the carpet, curtains, and furniture in Curly's trailer.

After forty years of trying to cope with Mable's problems, and then going through the trauma of her death, Curly was exhausted. "He had been through literal hell," Ray Seckler said. "He took more than I believe any man could have took. He was run down, and he looked so bad it scared me to death."[45] Curly began having episodes of illness due to gallstones, and on April 1, 1994, he had surgery to have his gallbladder removed. Soon afterward, he decided it was time to retire from traveling. Curly and Willis Spears played their last official show as partners on November 26, 1994, at the Myrtle Beach festival. They were accompanied onstage by the Del Mc-Coury Band. It was intended to be the final performance of an illustrious sixty-year career.

But it was not to be the end of the road for Curly Seckler. In music and in life, some of his best days were yet to come.

CHAPTER 9

The Old Man Has (Not) Retired

1995–2014

In early 1994 Nashville producer-songwriter Billy Henson approached Curly about making a recording to commemorate his sixtieth anniversary in music. Enthusiastic about the project, Curly began calling a number of his musical associates to invite them to participate. The result was *60 Years of Bluegrass with My Friends*, released in 1995 on Henson's Vine Street Records. Artists from early in Curly's career who took part included Mac Wiseman, Jim and Jesse McReynolds, Benny Sims, Ralph Stanley, Benny Martin, Josh Graves, Tater Tate, and Grant Turner. Jimmy Martin, Doyle Lawson, and Alan O'Bryant had never worked with Curly, but he chose to include them because he admired their singing. A couple of tracks were borrowed from other labels in order to include artists who were unable to be at the sessions. "Shine on Me," with the Sauceman Brothers and Joe Stuart, was taken from a collection of radio transcriptions from the early 1950s that had been released by Copper Creek Records. Revonah Records contributed "Swing Low, Sweet Chariot," featuring Marty Stuart and the Nashville Grass, from 1978.

Curly had some specific ideas in mind when matching the material to the singers and players. For instance, he chose to sing "We'll Meet Again,

Sweetheart" with Mac Wiseman since Mac had originally recorded it with Flatt and Scruggs before Curly replaced him in the group. He enlisted Benny Sims to sing "Salty Dog Blues" because Benny had sung lead on the original recording in 1950. Benny Martin had played some amazing fiddle parts on the 1953 recording of Curly's "That Old Book of Mine," so Curly brought him back for a repeat performance. The original plan was to reprise "A Purple Heart" with Jim and Jesse, but Curly decided he'd rather include another song from his years with the McReynolds Brothers. He chose "Somebody Loves You, Darling," composed by his old friends Wiley and Zeke Morris. Curly's early days with Charlie Monroe were represented by "Moonlight on My Cabin," which he learned while based at WWVA with Charlie, and by his duet with Jimmy Martin on Charlie's "I'm Coming Back, But I Don't Know When." Representing Curly's most recent years, Willis Spears joined him for a fine rendition of the classic "I'll Go Stepping Too," and Curly sang his newly written song "While in This World," with the guitar accompaniment that he so enjoyed from Larry Perkins.

Curly had just begun to record these sessions in late March 1994 when he became ill and had to undergo emergency gallbladder surgery. After spending nine days in the hospital and a couple of months convalescing, he resumed work on the album in June. "And I was weak as a broom straw when I went back in the studio to complete it," he said. Photos taken during the sessions showed him to be puffy and pale. About one snapshot he quipped, "It looks like death eating a cookie!"

Determined to get his health back on track, Curly took to heart the advice of his surgeon: "You need to get out and walk!" Curly discovered that RiverGate Mall in Goodlettsville, just north of Nashville, was a popular haunt for fitness enthusiasts who wanted to walk in climate-controlled conditions. He soon developed a routine of driving to RiverGate each morning at nine to join the regular group of dedicated walkers. In the beginning it was a challenge, but eventually he worked his way up to walking two to three circuits around the mall. Not only did he lose weight and improve his overall health, but he also had an unexpected encounter that was to change his life in ways he never imagined.

One morning in 1995, Curly was strolling past the food court when he spotted some friends and stopped to say hello. One of them was Eloise Warren, Paul Warren's widow, who had begun walking with a group of friends at RiverGate after she retired and moved to Hendersonville. Eloise recalled, "We stopped to get a drink after we'd walked a round or two, and was sitting around a big table, and Curly come by and stopped to talk. He saw me sitting there, and he said, 'Oh, Lordy, I'm not going to shake hands with this one,' and he come around the table and give me a big hug. Then I got started walking with him after that. From there it became going to lunch together [at] Morrison's Cafeteria in the mall." Before long, Eloise began cooking lunch for Curly at her home in Hendersonville. She laughed as she later said, "He told me one day, 'You know that old saying, don't you, that how to get to a man's heart is through his stomach?' I said, 'What do you think I'm doing all this cooking for?'"[1]

Eloise had been a widow for seventeen years when she and Curly had their chance meeting at the mall, and a romance with Curly Seckler was the last thing she had expected. Ironically, the seed originally had been planted several years earlier by Eloise's friend Myrtle LeRoy (Lance's wife), after Curly's wife passed away. "Myrtle was always kidding me," Eloise said. "She could see an old man that couldn't hardly walk going down the road, and she'd say, 'There's one for you, Eloise.' But Myrtle and I went to the funeral home, and when we come out, she says, 'Now, there's one for you, right there: Curly.' I said, 'Myrtle, you're crazier than a bedbug! Curly and I have been friends for years, but I've never thought of him that way.'

"So you never know what's going to happen," she reflected. "I think it kind of surprised everybody. We just went from friendship until we both saw things about the other one we liked, and we had the same type of background, and it just seemed like a natural thing to do."[2]

Curly and Eloise continued to spend time together for the next three years. He took her to meet his family in China Grove, and she took him with her to church. Although Curly had retired from touring, he had continued to make appearances at music events, including the IBMA FanFest. After receiving an IBMA Distinguished Achievement Award in 1996, he returned in 1998, accompanied by his grandson Robbie, to perform at the IBMA FanFest in Louisville, Kentucky. On the drive home to Nashville, Curly told Robbie that he had decided to ask Eloise to marry him.

Curly and Eloise laughed when they looked back on how matter-of-fact his proposal was. They were sitting in her living room one day in October when Curly said, "Gal, how would you like to get married, about the day after Christmas?" Eloise recalled, "I think I just sat there and looked at him for a little bit, before I said anything. It took me by surprise. I said, 'Well, I kind of like the idea.'"[3]

Friends were also surprised by this "Foggy Mountain romance," but they soon grew to embrace the idea. Marty Stuart remembered when he heard the news. "I asked Johnny Warren to come out and play the *Grand Ole Opry* with me one night. He said, 'Did you hear about Seck and Mama? They ran into each other walking at the mall, and they've been dating, and they're going to get married!' It struck me strange at first, but the more I thought about it, I thought, man, if they're happy, let it rock!"[4]

With only two months to plan the wedding, Curly and Eloise issued their invitations informally, by phone rather than mail. Marty received the call from Curly: "Little 'un, I'm a-getting married. Reckon you want to come?"[5] The couple was married by Leamon Flatt in a small ceremony on December 26, 1998, the day after Curly's seventy-ninth birthday. In addition to their families, guests included Earl and Louise Scruggs, Tater and Lois Tate, Connie Smith and Marty Stuart, Eddie Stubbs, and a few other friends. Marty and Eddie both remembered that Curly was smartly dressed, as always. Marty noted, "Seck wore his two-tone [shoes]. Me and John Hartford used to say, 'There ain't nothing like a Foggy Mountain man in a pair of two-tones!'"[6] Eddie recalled that he remarked to Earl Scruggs about how sharp Curly looked, and Earl replied, "You know, nobody could wear a white shirt like Curly."[7]

Curly and Eloise spent their "honeymoon" cleaning out his trailer and moving him into her condominium. He was seventy-nine and she was seventy-three when they married, but they were both in good health and they kept up an active social life. They took frequent trips to visit his family in China Grove, her family in West Virginia, and friends such as Tommy Scott. Curly regularly worked at his singing and songwriting around the house and made appearances at musical events several times a year, accompanied by his new wife and best friend. Those events included the annual convention of the Society for the Preservation of Bluegrass Music in America (SPBGMA) in Nashville, a guest appearance at the Ryman Auditorium with Marty Stuart, and a performance at the opening of a Sauceman Brothers exhibit at the Mountain Music Museum in Bristol, Virginia, in April 2003.

After his retirement Curly had frequently been asked, and had graciously agreed, to appear as a guest on projects by other artists, including Larry

Perkins, the Flint River Boys, Marshall Stephenson, and the Jones Brothers. Stephenson was a bandleader and festival promoter from North Carolina who had presented events in the Raleigh area since the early 1970s. After Curly recorded with him in October 2002, he booked Curly to appear at an event called "Legends of Bluegrass" in Smithfield, North Carolina, on March 12 and 13, 2004. Also appearing were Josh Graves, Kenny Baker, Tater Tate, Les Sandy, Allen Shelton, Herschel Sizemore, and John Shuffler—all sidemen who had made significant contributions to bluegrass.

At about this time, Curly began making plans for one last recording project of his own. He had a stash of original songs that he had written over the years, and he figured that this was his last chance to get them on record. He also wanted to make an album that was different from anything he had done in the past. Curly was fond of the stripped-down, old-timey sound of just vocals and guitars, which harkened back to his earliest days of picking on the front porch. Though he loved the classic Flatt and Scruggs material, he wanted to get away from recording everything with a full bluegrass band.

I first visited Curly in 2003 to interview him for an article for *Bluegrass Unlimited* that was ultimately published in June 2004.[8] I was amazed at his vitality and mental sharpness at age eighty-three. When he told me of his hope to record again, I contacted Larry Perkins, who enthusiastically agreed to help me produce the project. Gary Reid at Copper Creek Records expressed an interest in releasing it, and he arranged studio time at Flat5 Studio in Salem, Virginia. Larry put together a fine backing band composed of himself and Asheville-area musicians Chris Sharp (guitar), George Buckner (banjo), and Kevin Sluder (bass). We called Curly's old friends Tater Tate and Herschel Sizemore to complete the group. Curly compiled a list of songs, including about a dozen of his originals, many of which had never been recorded before. On Monday, June 14, 2004, we entered the studio.

Curly planned to sing lead on many of the songs, but we wanted to feature his acclaimed tenor harmony vocals as well. One of Curly's favorite lead singers was Dudley Connell, who began his career in 1978 with the popular traditional band the Johnson Mountain Boys and went on to be a central figure in the supergroups Longview and the Seldom Scene. Dudley was thrilled to participate in the project. He recalled the magic of seeing Curly perform with Lester Flatt in the late 1970s and getting to know him in the 1980s while touring with the Johnson Mountain Boys. "We got to be pretty good friends with him, because Curly liked the fact that we were playing an older style of music," Dudley said. "He'd come around and see us [at festivals], and he'd occasionally give us some advice. He always treated us with respect and was always kind to us."[9]

Dudley arranged to spend a day in the studio and agreed to sing three songs with Curly: "Why Did You Wander?," "What a Change One Day Can Make," and "Valley of Peace." As it turned out, they were having such a good time and the music was flowing so easily that Curly started naming other songs, and they recorded two extra tracks ("Dig a Hole in the Meadow" and "We Can't Be Darlings Anymore"). "Curly had tons of ideas," Dudley recalled. "It was a great band in the studio that day, and Curly was running the show, like, 'Do you know this one? Do you know this one?' That was just as fun as it could be. It was easy work. It just felt completely natural."[10]

Curly had also wanted to record a couple of songs with Russell Moore, another singer he admired. Russell had once told Curly that the Flatt and Scruggs classic "Bouquet in Heaven" was his favorite gospel song, so that was an easy choice. Curly also decided to revive the original that he wrote with Randall Hylton, "China Grove, My Hometown." Russell was not able to attend the sessions in June, but Curly and the band laid down the tracks, with Curly singing lead, and then Russell added his tenor harmony a few weeks later at Darrin Vincent's studio in Nashville. After that session Russell wrote, "I had a BLAST singing with Curly yesterday!! Please let him know what a great time I had doing this and what an honor it was to be asked!"[11]

At Flat5 Studio Curly and the band breezed through his song list. By the third day, it became clear that we would have much more material than was needed for an album of twelve to fourteen tracks. We finished the three-day marathon with an amazing twenty-three songs, though several tracks were incomplete. Realizing that we only needed a few more songs to have enough for two albums, Larry Perkins arranged follow-up sessions in Nashville for overdubs and to record several of the "heart songs" of which Curly was so fond.

Curly recorded a new version of "A Purple Heart" with tenor vocalist Laura Weber Cash and iconic bass player Bob Moore, who played on the original Jim and Jesse recording in 1952. Laura overdubbed harmony vocals and fiddle on several tracks, and Leroy Troy, Rob Ickes, and John Carter Cash added clawhammer banjo, Dobro, and autoharp to another. Curly even wrote a brand new song called "I Miss You So Tonight" the night before one of the sessions. For another of Curly's new originals, "Bluegrass, Don't You Know," Perkins brought in Larry Cordle to sing the lead vocal.

Most of Curly's original compositions were based on personal experience. As I mentioned in the liner notes to his CD *Bluegrass, Don't You Know*, "because he writes straight from the heart, his songs sometimes take unexpected twists, contain unusual chords, and don't always follow the 'rules' of rhyme. But they are always melodic and highly evocative, and the liberties he takes are always appropriate to the feel and message of the song. These are the kinds of songs that stick in your mind, because they touch you at a gut level."[12] A perfect example is the autobiographical "The Old Man Has Retired," with its dizzying vocal range and poignant hook line: "Long, long ago the music did start / Retirement now . . . but his singing won't stop."

Curly had hoped to record a new track with Doc Watson, but scheduling issues prevented them from getting together, so Larry Perkins offered the next best thing: the lively Watson-Seckler duet "Hold the Woodpile Down," recorded several years earlier for Larry's album *A Glad Reunion Day*. We also were able to obtain permission to include a hidden track: Tony Williamson's historic recording of Curly singing tenor to Bill Monroe on "I'm Sitting on Top of the World" at Camp Springs in 1970.

The final piece of the puzzle fell into place as a result of a casual conversation I had with Larry Sparks at a festival in September. When Sparks heard about Curly's project, he remarked that he had always admired Curly and regretted never having the opportunity to sing with him. It turned out that the feeling was mutual. By this time, it had been announced that Curly would be inducted into the IBMA Hall of Fame at the awards show in Louisville in October. Since Sparks was also going to be in Louisville for the FanFest, we arranged for them to record two songs at a nearby studio on the day after Curly's induction. On October 8 they recorded "He Took Your Place" and "Brother, I'm Getting Ready to Go." Following the session Curly appeared as a special guest with Sparks on the FanFest, where they sang two other songs together.[13]

Of making the recordings with Curly, Sparks stated, "It meant a lot to me to sing with him. It was an honor. I always admired him so much, his singing, his style. He set a sound that had a big influence on people. To hear him sing, he would make people want to play this music. I think he helped shape the music as much as anybody in the business."[14]

The awards show on October 7, 2004, was a proud night for Curly. Many of his family members were present, and, at his request, Tommy Scott made the trip from Georgia to see his long-time friend honored. Eddie Stubbs, who was chairman of the Hall of Fame nominating committee, made the presentation. Eddie recalled that when he first called him to give him the news of his induction, Curly's reaction was low-key. "He didn't have a lot to say," Eddie noted. "I don't think he really understood the magnitude of it at the time. But he was very appreciative. Then, after it was done, he thanked me many times over. He wouldn't even have had to thank me at all. I did it because I loved him."[15]

The awards show was on a tight schedule, since it was being broadcast on radio. Curly's acceptance speech was long, and he had exceded his allotted time, so Eddie skillfully stepped in and guided him to center stage. There J. D. Crowe and the New South were waiting to accompany him in performing the Flatt and Scruggs classic "I'll Go Stepping Too." Playing a mandolin borrowed from Dan Tyminski, Curly took the audience back in time with his trademark mandolin chop and his distinctive tenor vocals and was rewarded with a standing ovation.

Just a few weeks later, videographer Joe Gray visited Curly to film a biographical interview conducted by Lance LeRoy for the International Bluegrass Music Museum's Video Oral History Project. The video had its debut at the museum, located in Owensboro, Kentucky, on June 23, 2005, just prior to the official unveiling of Curly's Hall of Fame plaque. That night, Curly performed on a "Legends of Bluegrass" concert in Owensboro's River Park Center as part of the museum's Second Annual ROMP (River of Music Party) Festival.

The Hall of Fame induction, together with his new recordings, marked the beginning of a new decade of music for Curly. His health was exceptional for his age (nearly eighty-five), and his voice was strong, so when I suggested arranging a few show dates for him, he readily agreed. Meanwhile, Copper Creek Records had acquired the masters for Curly's 60 Years of Bluegrass, and it was reissued in the spring of 2005 with new liner notes and graphics and a couple of additional tracks. Dave Freeman decided to reissue Curly's County album from 1971 as well. He created a new package, with several additional tracks taken from the Seckler and Spears Tribute to Lester Flatt, to make a sixteen-song set, which was retitled That Old Book of Mine.

The first album of new recordings, *Down in Caroline*, was released in September 2005, just in time for Curly's appearance at the Bass Mountain Bluegrass Festival in North Carolina. He brought his old friend Willis Spears along, and they were backed by David Parmley and Continental Divide. Larry Sparks also sang several songs with Curly on the show. Festival promoter Mike Wilson presented Curly with a plaque celebrating his seventy years in bluegrass music.

In October Curly was featured in a program moderated by WSM's Eddie Stubbs at the Country Music Hall of Fame in Nashville, at which Curly's IBMM Oral History documentary was shown. Two days later, Curly performed on the Roots and Branches Stage at the IBMA FanFest in the Nashville Convention Center. He was backed by the Chris Sharp and David Long Band, and his guest vocalists included Willis Spears, Doyle Lawson, Russell Moore, and Gerald McCormick.

In April 2006 Curly was booked at MerleFest in Wilkesboro, North Carolina, one of the largest and most prestigious music festivals on the East Coast. He needed a bluegrass band that could accompany him on the classic material as well as songs from his own repertoire. Enter the Steep Canyon Rangers, a young band from Asheville, North Carolina. Within a few years, the Rangers would rise to national prominence through their association with comedian and banjo picker Steve Martin, but in 2006 they were still essentially a regional act. They jumped at the chance to perform with a bluegrass legend. The only opportunity for rehearsal was the evening before the performance, but the Rangers did their homework. Dave Freeman, who was present at the rehearsal, wrote in the liner notes to the Rangers' next Rebel Records album, "The group amazed Curly and other onlookers with its command of and familiarity with the classic Flatt & Scruggs repertoire. After the band sailed through more than a dozen of Seckler's chosen favorites, Curly looked up and said, 'You boys can really pick.'"[16]

The MerleFest performance on April 29 was a memorable one, for the musicians as well as the audience. The Rangers' Woody Platt reflected in 2009, "People still talk about that MerleFest set. Curly can still really sing and play. [There] was just so much fresh energy between the two of us. It'll always be something that we can feel proud of."[17] Bass player Charles Humphrey added, "The crowd was really picking up on the way that we interacted with Curly. We were so thrilled to be there. It's just an honor to play with somebody from that first generation, and Curly's such an entertainer and a great person to be around."[18]

In August Curly received the news that his *Down in Caroline* CD was a finalist for IBMA's Recorded Event of the Year award. He and Larry Sparks were invited to perform the song "He Took Your Place" on the awards show on September 28 at the Grand Ole Opry House in Nashville. This was an exciting night for Curly and his family. As fate would have it, Marty Stuart happened to be the host of the awards show that year. Marty took great pride in introducing Curly to perform his song. "There he stood, like an oak tree," Marty recalled later. "His voice sounded at home going through that house. I [said], 'There it is. That's what I came to hear, right there.' It was like a piece of me was going through that house, too."[19]

When it came time to announce the winner of the Recorded Event award, Curly sat anxiously, with his fingers crossed. Many of the people he had encountered at the reception before the show had told him they had voted for him, so he began to actually believe he might win his first IBMA award. But it was not to be, and though he put on a brave face, he was clearly disappointed. He was pleased, however, to see his new friends the Steep Canyon Rangers take home the award for Emerging Artist of the Year.

On September 30 Curly took part in a Legends set as the Saturday night finale at the IBMA FanFest. Also appearing were Everett Lilly and J. D. Crowe, and the backing band included Bryan Sutton, Aubrey Haynie, Charlie Cushman, Mike Compton, Randy Kohrs, and Mike Bub. Josh Graves was scheduled to appear, but his health had been failing for some time. He had entered the hospital earlier that week, and on Saturday morning he passed away. In the hours before showtime, FanFest producer Carl Jackson contacted as many Dobro players as he could find and put together a tribute to Josh as part of the show. Everett Lilly and his sons performed first. Next came the moving Josh Graves tribute, and then Curly sang several of his favorite solos. After that, he and Everett Lilly sang together for the first time ever. They performed "He Took Your Place," a song that Everett had recorded with Flatt and Scruggs and that Curly later sang with them many times. Following J. D. Crowe's rousing rendition of "Train 45," the band romped through several Flatt and Scruggs favorites, with Carl Jackson and Bradley Walker providing the lead vocals to Curly's tenor.

Curly had a busy fall, with performances at the Poppy Mountain Festival in Kentucky, the Nashville Music Classic Festival in Ridgetop, Tennessee, the annual Lester Flatt Day in Sparta, and the Bluegrass Gospel Association Awards Show. His second new Copper Creek album, *Bluegrass, Don't You Know*, was released on October 19. In December it was chosen as one of the Top Ten Bluegrass CDs of the Year by the *Chicago Tribune*.

The chemistry between Curly and the Steep Canyon Rangers was such that both were eager to perform together again. The first opportunity came when the Rangers invited Curly to join them as a special guest at their show at the Station Inn in Nashville on November 4. Word had spread about this unique association, and the house was packed. The Rangers opened the show, and then Curly joined them to perform a handful of his signature songs and down-home storytelling, to an enthusiastic standing ovation.

Curly's next performance was at the Paramount Theater in Bristol on March 26, 2007. He and Tater Tate were honored with awards from East Tennessee State University. They performed on the program, backed by Jack Tottle and the ETSU Bluegrass Band. Tater was suffering from cancer at the time, and he passed away on October 17 of that year.

In late 2006 Curly had been contacted by one John Pharis of Roanoke, Virginia. Pharis had purchased an old Gibson F-2 mandolin at a local music store and had reason to believe that it was the instrument that once had belonged to Curly. He had sent photos to Mike Longworth and had received a letter from Longworth stating that it appeared to be the mandolin that he'd once repaired for Curly. In April 2007 Pharis visited Curly, bringing the F-2 along. Once Curly saw it, he knew it was his long-lost Gibson. The last time he had seen it was when he performed at the Camp Springs festival in 1970 with Joe Greene. Its owner had brought it to Greene's bus to show it to Curly, who was dismayed to see that it had been painted green. When Pharis acquired it the instrument was no longer green, but it had been poorly refinished and was in need of repair.

Having confirmed that it was, indeed, the instrument Curly had played for over twenty years on some of the greatest bluegrass recordings ever made, Pharis decided to sell the mandolin to help finance his child's college education. When David Grisman heard that it was for sale, he made arrangements to buy it and then sent it immediately to the Gibson Company to be restored.

Soon afterward, Grisman contacted Curly about coming to California to make a guest appearance with him at the prestigious Hardly Strictly Bluegrass Festival in San Francisco. Though it had been many years since Curly had traveled such a distance or flown on an airplane he and Eloise decided they would like to make the trip. They flew to California on Friday, October 5, and Curly performed at the festival with the David Grisman Bluegrass Experience on Sunday, October 7.

The Hardly Strictly Bluegrass Festival was a free event held at Golden Gate Park and attended by more than fifty thousand people. Grisman proudly picked the restored F-2 mandolin, and Curly played one of Grisman's guitars, as they romped through "Salty Dog Blues," "We Can't Be Darlings Anymore," and other classics. The festival summary on the Hardly Strictly web site noted, "David Grisman and the Bluegrass Experience were doling out a lesson in traditional bluegrass, with the 88-year-old Curly Seckler providing some fantastic singing and loads of quips and comical anecdotes."[20] As it turned out, the Steep Canyon Rangers were also booked to play at the festival on Sunday, so Curly made a guest appearance with them as well.

Then, on January 5, 2008, Curly reunited with the Rangers to tape the *Song of the Mountains* television program for PBS. *Song of the Mountains* first went on the air in 2005, and by 2014 it was broadcast on more than 180 PBS affiliates nationwide. The program featured a wide variety of bluegrass and Americana bands in concert at the historic Lincoln Theater in Marion, Virginia. Each edited television program usually included performances by two groups. Curly and the Rangers were given one hour-long episode, which was first shown in June 2008. Larry Sparks also performed in the concert that night, and Curly made a guest appearance with him.

The following day, *Song of the Mountains* host Tim White and the Appalachian Cultural Music Association sponsored "Curly Seckler Day" at its Mountain Music Museum in the Bristol Mall. An estimated 350 people filled the room as White unveiled a new Seckler exhibit for the museum, and Marion mayor David Helms presented Curly with a key to the city. Curly took to the stage to discuss highlights of his career, and then performed some of his trademark songs, joined by Willis Spears and the Steep Canyon Rangers. Spears had traveled 350 miles to Bristol from his home south of Nashville just to honor his hero and former partner. Likewise, Curly's old friend Tommy Scott had made the trip from Toccoa, Georgia. Also in attendance were Gary Reid of Copper Creek Records, Jim Sauceman, and Imogene Sauceman Day (siblings of the Sauceman Brothers).

At this event the audience was also treated to a few minutes of video footage from the new *Best of the Flatt & Scruggs TV Show* DVDs. Shanachie Records, in partnership with the Country Music Foundation, began releasing these DVDs in 2007, and over the course of the next three years, a total of ten volumes were released. The footage was taken from old films of the television shows that were unearthed in 1989 from the garage of Bill Graham, a representative of the advertising agency that represented Martha White Mills for many years. Soon after Graham's films were donated, the Country Music Foundation acquired additional archival footage of the Flatt and Scruggs shows from another source.[21]

The shows included on the DVDs date from the late 1950s and early 1960s. Each DVD contains two half-hour programs, including the Martha White commercials. In some cases the programs are essentially as they first appeared, and in other cases the Country Music Foundation edited parts of several episodes together to avoid repeats of the same material. These DVDs contain the only commercially available video of the Foggy Mountain Boys from their program on WSM-TV. Curly appears on all except one of the ten volumes.

The DVDs provide an opportunity for a whole new group of fans to experience the thrill of a live Foggy Mountain Boys performance. The recordings they made in the 1950s were undeniably among the greatest performances in the history of bluegrass, but they only told a part of the story. On viewing videos of this band performing live, seeing their expert choreography, their playfulness, their virtuosity, it is easy to understand why television propelled Flatt and Scruggs to the level of country music superstars. "The TV shows are what tell the story," Eddie Stubbs attested, "because you get to [see] them in action. You get to hear their personality. You get to see what these people were like, and what made them special."[22]

Several of the shows feature special guests such as Maybelle Carter, Stringbean, and Hylo Brown. Volume 3 features seven-year-old Ricky Skaggs singing and playing mandolin, while Earl's young son Randy was a guest on volume 4; both are from 1962. In October 2007 the Country Music Hall of Fame and Museum celebrated the release of those two volumes with a program featuring moderator Eddie Stubbs with Earl and Randy Scruggs and Ricky Skaggs. The videos were shown, and then the three men shared their recollections and reflections. Curly attended the event and visited with Earl backstage before joining Earl, Ricky, and Randy to sign copies of the DVDs in the gift shop.

In June 2008 Curly joined about sixty other performers at the Pioneers of Bluegrass event at the International Bluegrass Music Museum in Owensboro. On Thursday, June 26, the pioneers were honored with a dinner and concert, and on Friday morning many of them participated in a storytelling session at the River Park Center. On Saturday the museum presented the Oral History documentaries of Curly, Earl Scruggs, and the McCormick Brothers.

On August 2 Curly and Willis Spears performed at the Thirty-fourth Annual Carter Family Memorial Festival at the Carter Fold in Hiltons, Virginia. Banjo player Leroy Troy, who was also booked for the festival, joined Curly to perform one of the songs from Curly's new CD. They were backed by the Virginia-based band Big Country Bluegrass. Like the Steep Canyon Rangers, Big Country Bluegrass was thrilled to perform with a pioneer of Curly's status. Following the festival, banjo player Lynwood Lunsford wrote an Internet post that summed up the significance of the experience:

> I count this past Saturday as one of my most memorable career highlights ever! It took place at the Carter Fold, homeplace of the famous Carter Family. Booked on the show that day was, simply put, a piece of bluegrass history . . . Curly Seckler! Curly brought along his long-time singing partner, Willis Spears, and we were asked to back them up. So, with me on the banjo, Jeff Michael on fiddle, Alan Mastin on bass, Tommy Sells on mandolin, and David Nance on Dobro, we went through two sets of some of the most beloved and classic songs in bluegrass history. It was a thrill for me to try and "be" Earl Scruggs, to hear that unmistakable tenor voice of Seckler's, to listen to Willis Spears (probably the closest to Lester Flatt that's ever been) sing those old songs and make the music that I cut my teeth on. But the magnitude of what was going on didn't hit me until Willis launched into the Martha White theme song. At exactly the same moment, myself, Jeff, and David all got the biggest goosebumps that you ever saw! It was the most magical moment that I have ever experienced in music![23]

Curly made another guest appearance in October with the Steep Canyon Rangers at the Station Inn in Nashville. Just two weeks later, Curly and the Rangers were in Durham to appear on North Carolina Public Radio's *The State of Things*, an hour-long daily interview program hosted by Frank Stasio. The following day, Curly and the Rangers headed to Crewe, Virginia, for a live radio broadcast over WSVS, the station where the Foggy Mountain Boys were based in 1954 and where Jody Rainwater had been an on-air personality from 1952 through 1971. Jody joined them in the studio to reminisce with Curly before they sailed through several classic Flatt and

Scruggs tunes. That night, Curly and the Rangers performed to a capacity crowd in nearby Kenbridge, Virginia.

On November 2, 2008, the International Bluegrass Music Museum in Owensboro unveiled a new Curly Seckler exhibit that included Curly's Snyder mandolin, stage apparel, posters, photos, records, and other memorabilia. After the unveiling, Curly performed for museum staff and board members. The following day he and Eloise stopped off in Rosine to pay their respects at the graves of Bill and Charlie Monroe, Uncle Pen, and other family members. They visited the refurbished Monroe homeplace on Jerusalem Ridge and went to Beaver Dam to see the site of the hotel and café where Curly had stayed while rehearsing with Charlie Monroe in the 1940s.

Curly was honored in February 2009 with a Lifetime Achievement Award at the Thirteenth Annual Leon Kiser Memorial Awards Show at the Paramount Theater in Bristol. The event, presented by the Appalachian Cultural Music Association, helped raise funds for the Benny Sims Scholarship Fund at East Tennessee State University in Johnson City. Curly performed three songs on the program.

In Wilkesboro on May 9, Curly performed with Big Country Bluegrass at the Bluegrass in Wilkes Festival. Fiddler Jim Shumate joined them to reprise the classics "Cabin in Caroline" and "We'll Meet Again, Sweetheart," the two songs that Shumate had recorded with Flatt and Scruggs in 1948. Following that event Curly went on to Chapel Hill, where he taped the *North Carolina People* show for UNC-TV. The weekly half-hour program featured former University of North Carolina president William Friday interviewing prominent North Carolina newsmakers from all walks of life. *North Carolina People* was UNC-TV's longest-running program, having aired for more than forty years. Since Curly and Dr. Friday were contemporaries (they were born within seven months of each other and grew up in towns less than sixty miles apart), they thoroughly enjoyed chatting together, both on-screen and off.

Curly returned to Marion, Virginia, on May 16 to tape another episode of the *Song of the Mountains* television program. This time he took a young North Carolina band called Constant Change. Like Big Country Bluegrass, the members of Constant Change were enthralled by the history that Curly represented. They spent much of their time backstage listening to his stories of life with the Foggy Mountain Boys. Curly was impressed with their reverence for the music and was happy to find that there were still young musicians who could perform the classic material.

In June Curly and Willis Spears once again performed with Big Country Bluegrass, at the Song of the Mountains Festival in Groseclose, Virginia. Curly sang two songs with his old friend Jesse McReynolds as well. In July, Curly performed at Jesse's Pick Inn Festival in Gallatin, Tennessee, as Jesse celebrated his eightieth birthday. Then, in November, Jesse invited Curly to join him on the *Ernest Tubb Midnite Jamboree*, broadcast on WSM from the Texas Troubadour Theater. After the performance, Curly joined Jesse in greeting fans at Ernest Tubb Record Shop until almost 2:00 A.M.

Gerald and Martha McCormick hosted a ninetieth birthday party for Curly at their home on December 27, 2009. The McCormicks had begun hosting an annual Sunday afternoon party for Curly several years earlier, but this one was the biggest yet. Ronnie Reno of RFD-TV brought a cameraman and filmed an interview with Curly, as well as some of the non-stop celebrity jam sessions. Among the musicians attending were country singer John Conlee, Marty Stuart, Roland White, James Monroe, Eddie Stubbs, Willis Spears, Michael Cleveland, Charlie Cushman, and Haskel McCormick.

On February 4, 2010, Curly appeared at the annual McReynolds Memorial Bluegrass Music Spectacular, a benefit concert to raise funds for musicians with serious health issues. The following week Curly sang one of his favorite songs, "Mother Maybelle," at a concert honoring Maybelle Carter at David Lipscomb University in Nashville. Also on the program were Laura and John Carter Cash, Earl Scruggs, the Whites, the Del McCoury Band, Dixie and Tom T. Hall, the Gatlin Brothers, Dale Jett, and Heather Berry.

Plans were shaping up for Curly to perform at a series of events in 2010 to celebrate his seventy-fifth anniversary in music. I had booked shows in North Carolina and Virginia at the end of April, with Constant Change as his accompanying band and Dudley Connell as a special guest. But on April 3 Curly began having pain in his left arm and shoulder, and he was taken to the hospital. It turned out that he had suffered a mild heart attack and had blockages in three of his arteries. Still, the cardiologist who examined him was amazed at Curly's overall good health telling him, "Ordinarily we would not perform open heart surgery on a ninety-year-old man, but you have the body of a seventy-five-year-old. Once we do the surgery, you should be good to go for another ten years." Curly's regular mall-walking routine had paid off. On April 5 he had triple bypass surgery, and six days later he was back at home. In mid-May he resumed his morning walks at RiverGate, and on May 23 he attended Mac Wiseman's eighty-fifth birthday celebration at the Texas Troubadour Theater.

Less than three months after major heart surgery, Curly was back on stage, at the annual Pioneers of Bluegrass event in Owensboro, Kentucky. He performed on June 24, first as a special guest with Mac Martin and the Dixie Travelers in the afternoon, and then with the Whites on their evening show.

A few months later, Curly made the trip home to China Grove for his induction on October 7 into the North Carolina Music Hall of Fame in nearby Kannapolis. The ever-loyal Tommy Scott traveled from Georgia to once again witness his old friend's honor. Also among the inductees for 2010 were Andy Griffith, Doc Watson, George Hamilton IV, Arthur Smith, Don Gibson, Billy Taylor, Donna Fargo, Don Schlitz, Les Brown, Maurice Williams, Oliver (William Oliver Swofford), and Shirley Caesar. During Curly's induction, Representative Fred Steen of Rowan County presented him with a letter of congratulations from Governor Bev Perdue and a Certificate of Acknowledgment and Congratulations from the North Carolina House of Representatives. Curly performed his trademark songs "Moonlight on My Cabin" and "Mother Maybelle," accompanied by Larry Perkins and Steve Sechler (a distant cousin) on guitars.

The finale of Curly's seventy-fifth anniversary year came on December 4, when the Country Music Hall of Fame and Museum presented an event in his honor in its Ford Theater. During the first part of the program Curly discussed the highlights of his career with host Kyle Cantrell of SiriusXM Radio, accompanied by photos as well as audio and video clips. At the end of the interview, Cantrell presented Curly with a letter of congratulations from the White House, signed by both Barack and Michelle Obama. Then Curly performed along with Willis Spears, Larry Perkins, Johnny Warren, Tim Graves, Kent Blanton, Laura Cash, Jeff Hardin, and Roland White.

In January 2011 Curly taped *The Marty Stuart Show* for RFD-TV. He sang one of his favorite gospel songs, "Lord, I'm Coming Home." Announcer Eddie Stubbs wore one of the classic sash ties in Curly's honor because Curly had taught him how to tie one in 1977, and Eddie had then taught the other members of the Johnson Mountain Boys. Eddie recalled in an interview that when Curly heard that the Johnson Mountain Boys were going to disband in 1988, he asked Eddie for one of his sash ties as a memento. Eddie gave

Curly his prized red tie, and Curly told him, "If you decide to start playing again, I'll bring it back to you." As it turned out, the Johnson Mountain Boys did regroup after about a year off. At a festival in Summersville, West Virginia, Curly walked up to Eddie with the tie in hand and said, "You might need this." For Eddie, it seemed only fitting to sport that tie for Curly's performance on the *Marty Stuart Show*.

The honors spilled over into 2011. He was recognized in April with a special Senatorial Statement read in the North Carolina Legislature. It was especially meaningful for Curly because it mentioned his three brothers, with whom he had started his musical odyssey in 1935. By this time, George Sechler, who lived in Texas, was the only other surviving member of the Yodeling Rangers. Duard "Lucky" Sechler had passed away in 2001 at age seventy-six, and Marvin "Slim" Sechler died in 2009 at age ninety-four. George passed away in August 2011, just a few months after his daughter had brought him to Nashville to visit Curly.

On September 13 Curly performed at the International Bluegrass Music Museum's Bill Monroe Centennial celebration at the River Park Center in Owensboro. He was accompanied by Willis Spears, Johnny Warren, Blake Williams, Tim Graves, and Kent Blanton. A week later he was inducted into the Bill Monroe Bluegrass Hall of Fame in Bean Blossom, Indiana, at the annual Uncle Pen Days Festival. During the induction Larry Sparks joined Curly onstage to perform two songs. Curly always enjoyed singing with Sparks, and after they ran through "Dim Lights, Thick Smoke" in the dressing room, Curly grinned and exclaimed, "Wow! We ought to put that on a record!"

As it turned out, they would do just that. Sparks came to Nashville in December 2013 to begin work on his *Lonesome and Then Some* CD, a celebration of his fiftieth anniversary in music. On December 11, Curly joined him to sing "Dim Lights, Thick Smoke" and "I'm Gonna Sing, Sing, Sing." Also in the studio on that historic day were Jesse McReynolds, who sang baritone and played mandolin on "Sing, Sing, Sing," and Bobby Osborne, who played mandolin on "Dim Lights, Thick Smoke." Ron Stewart and Tim Graves were on hand to add fiddle and Dobro to the tracks. Curly made these recordings just weeks shy of his ninety-fourth birthday. He had suffered a stroke in May that had left him with significant speech problems, and initially he was hesitant about trying to record. But when he practiced the songs at home before the sessions, the words flowed out naturally, and he was able to complete the sessions like the pro he had always been. These were the last recordings Curly made, and he was pleased to be able to make them with so many of his favorite musicians. The album was released on Rebel Records in August 2014.

Curly's last public performance was on March 31, 2012, at Mule Day in Columbia, Tennessee. This huge four-day annual event included mule competitions, a parade, and entertainment. Curly performed on the final night of the festival, accompanied by Willis Spears, Johnny Warren, Charlie Cushman, John Tomlin, and Mike Bub. The band was somber that night because they had learned just days earlier of the unexpected passing of their mentor, Earl Scruggs. Curly and Eloise had attended Earl's eighty-eighth birthday party in January, and the two men had visited and reminisced about their early years together. It was the last time that Curly was to see Earl.

A crowd of mourners filled the Ryman Auditorium on Sunday, April 1, for Earl's funeral. Curly had hoped to attend, but the rigors of performing the night before had taken their toll, and he was unwell. Eloise did attend the service and was able to witness the standing ovation given in response to eulogist Eddie Stubbs's acknowledgment of Curly as the last surviving member of the iconic Foggy Mountain Boys, featured in the *Flatt & Scruggs TV Show* DVDs.

Though it was not by design, it seems fitting that Curly's final performance should have coincided with the passing of Earl Scruggs. It was the end of an era. Curly never felt as close to Scruggs as he did to Flatt, but Earl was the last living connection to the most musically creative time in Curly's life. Much of his identity as a musician was tied to his prolific years with Flatt and Scruggs. As some actors are typecast after playing a highly successful character, so Curly Seckler will forever be known and remembered for his time as a Foggy Mountain Boy. Luckily it was a role he was happy to accept and to reprise for as long as audiences demanded it and he was able.

Reflecting on that group, Marty Stuart stated, "I think that was a divinely ordered band. Even as a little boy, I knew how special Curly and Josh and Jake and Lester and Earl and Paul Warren were. And dang near forty years later, I still, more so than ever, know how special they were. God chose and selected that band. There's just something about the presence of a Foggy Mountain Boy that lifts the air in a room. Something changes. They were different men."[24]

"They had something that nobody else had," Eddie Stubbs attested. "They were what every band wanted to be, but wasn't. I think Curly will forever be linked to his days as a Foggy Mountain Boy, because he was an important link in that chain that was so successful. It's an unmistakable sound. I think he will be remembered as a stylist, and a very important ingredient in their overall sound. It seems like he's the one who was the least out-front of all of them, but without him, there's a tremendous void. There's no mistaking that voice. Curly Seckler's got a chop on the mandolin like no other. He knew how to get the most out of his instrument. It's what made them boys pick."[25]

Doyle Lawson asserted, "I really think that his input into that classic Flatt and Scruggs sound has been kind of underrated. I think Curly is as much a part of that legacy as any of them. Curly's voice was a perfect match to Lester's. Curly was the most awesome rhythm player that I ever heard. He really made himself a part of that rhythm machine that they had."[26] Mac Wiseman went a step farther, saying, "He was the glue that held it together and identified them. Curly and Flatt were just a sound that you recognized anywhere."[27]

Curly would appreciate all of this praise for his musical contributions, but he always referred to himself as an entertainer, not a musician. He liked to relate that Lester Flatt always said, "Curly, you may not be the best mandolin picker in the world, but I always liked the way you held it." That self-deprecating quip is an example of what so endeared audiences to Curly Seckler. He appreciated the fact that there is much more to entertaining than just playing music, and he loved to make people laugh. He knew his strengths, understood his limitations, and never took himself too seriously, although he was serious about conducting himself as a professional. He was able to successfully deal with the conundrum of being both an iconic figure and an approachable friend to his fans. His standards were high. He always strove to please his audience by looking his best and putting on the best performance possible.

Away from the stage, Curly was no different. His wife Eloise described him as considerate, dependable, loyal, open-minded, and a good family man. His friend Eddie Stubbs called him warm, congenial, respectful, proud, compassionate, generous, and spiritual—a gentleman and a gentle man. Though Curly suffered through many challenges and disappointments, his loved ones, his faith, his sense of humor, and his love of life kept him grounded and engaged well into his nineties.

Marty Stuart reflected, "It was so great to be in his presence. Beyond everything in the business, accomplishments and life hassles, struggles and triumphs, victories and tragedies, there's a piece of love there in my heart that has never wavered. How will he be remembered? In my opinion, the greatest tenor singer of all time, and one of the greatest men that ever walked. An honorable man. A just and good man."[28]

Looking back on his long, productive, and celebrated career, Curly himself would likely say, with a grin and a twinkle in his eye, "It's been just like a good Martha White biscuit. Goodness, gracious, it's good!"

Notes

Chapter 1. Down in Caroline: 1919–1939

1. Marty Stuart interview, April 2, 2007.

2. Patrick Hanks, Kate Hardcastle, and Flavia Hodges, *A Dictionary of First Names* (Oxford: Oxford University Press, 2006), 146.

3. See www.census.gov/population/cencounts/nc190090.txt and www.historync.org/NCCitypopulations1800s.htm.

4. Ira Lee Baker and Franklin S. Scarborough, *From Chinaberry Trees to China Grove* (Salisbury, NC: Salisbury, 1989), 2.

5. Harry T. Sifford, *Towns of Rowan County: A History of the Towns of Rowan County* (Salisbury: Heritage of Rowan County Book Committee, 1991), 5.

6. Gary N. Mock, www.textilehistory.org/CannonMills.html.

7. Tom Hanchett in *Charlotte Country Music Story* program (North Carolina Arts Council, 1985), 12.

8. See mtzionchinagrove.com/history (Mount Zion is now affiliated with the United Church of Christ).

9. *The Heritage of Rowan County, North Carolina* (Salisbury, NC: Genealogical Society of Rowan County, 1991), 1:xiv.

10. *Reformed Church Standard*, Newton, NC, vol. xviii, no. 22, February 15, 1911 (included in the Sechler family genealogy).

11. Mary Sechler Freeze and Walter Freeze interview, May 10, 2005.

12. *Heritage of Rowan County*, 58.

13. Freeze interview.

14. Marvin Sechler, "Bum Leg, Bad Breaks—Some Good Ones, Too!" *The Great Depression: How We Coped, Worked, and Played*, ed. Margaret Bigger (Charlotte: Borough, 2001), 24.

15. Freeze interview.

16. John Rumble in *Charlotte Country Music Story* program (North Carolina Arts Council, 1985), 5.

17. Ibid.

18. *Salisbury Post*, July 2, 2004.

19. Curly was referring to the song "They Gotta Quit Kickin' My Dawg Aroun'," which was popularized by various groups in the 1920s, including Gid Tanner and his Skillet Lickers.

20. *Salisbury Post*, June 9, 1940.

21. *Salisbury Post*, January 7, 1939.

22. *Salisbury Post*, May 21, 1939.

23. *Salisbury Post*, June 18, 1939.

24. Ibid.

25. *Salisbury Post*, July 7, 1939.

26. *Salisbury Post*, August 22, 1939.

Chapter 2. The Adventures of Smilin' Bill: 1939–1944

1. Richard D. Smith, *Can't You Hear Me Callin': The Life of Bill Monroe, Father of Bluegrass* (New York: Little, Brown, 2000), 43.

2. Tommy Scott interview, February 16, 2007.

3. Smith, *Can't You Hear Me Callin'*, 48.

4. Douglas B. Green, interview with Charlie Monroe, September 2, 1972, Frist Library and Archive, Country Music Hall of Fame and Museum, Nashville.

5. Dick Spottswood, liner notes to *Charlie Monroe: His Recordings, 1938–1956; I'm Old Kentucky Bound*, Bear Family BCD-16808, 48.

6. *The Robesonian*, January 30, 1939.

7. *The Robesonian*, February 3, 1939.

8. *The Robesonian*, February 6, 1939.

9. Spottswood, *Charlie Monroe: I'm Old Kentucky Bound*, 13.

10. "Doc" Tommy Scott with Shirley Noe Swiesz and Randall Franks, *Snake Oil, Super Stars, and Me: The Story of Ramblin' "Doc" Tommy Scott* (Toccoa, GA: Katona), 26.

11. Capitol Broadcasting Company, "History," http://www.capitolbroadcasting.com/history/the-people/a-j-fletcher/.

12. Scott interview, February 16, 2007.

13. Ibid.

14. *The History of WWVA*, 50th Anniversary booklet (1976), jeff560.tripod.com/wwva.html.

15. Scott, *Snake Oil*, 43.

16. Scott interview, February 16, 2007.

17. Ibid.

18. Charlie had already employed this tactic with Leon Calhoun, and he would do it a third time with Lavelle Coy.

19. Scott interview, February 16, 2007.

20. Scott, *Snake Oil*, 52.

21. Scott interview, February 16, 2007.

22. Ibid.

23. Ibid.

24. Scott, *Snake Oil*, 49.

25. Ibid., 50.

26. Ivan Tribe, *Mountaineer Jamboree: Country Music in West Virginia* (Lexington: University Press of Kentucky, 1996), 49.

27. Scott interview, February 16, 2007.

28. Douglas B. Green, interview with Tommy Scott, July 28, 1976, Frist Library and Archive, Country Music Hall of Fame and Museum, Nashville.

29. Scott interview, February 16, 2007.

30. Ibid.

31. Ibid.

32. Ibid.

33. Ibid.

34. *Anderson Independent*, January 13, 1941.

35. Scott, *Snake Oil*, 69.

36. *Salisbury Post*, March 17, 1940.

37. *Salisbury Post*, July 28, 1940.

38. *Anderson Independent*, May 28, 1941.

39. Scott, *Snake Oil*, 69.

40. *Radio Annual*, ed. Jack Alicoate (New York: Radio Daily, 1941) 394.

41. *Augusta Chronicle*, July 30, 1941.

42. *Augusta Chronicle*, August 28, 1941.

43. *Radio Annual*, 555.

44. Scott, *Snake Oil*, 80.

45. According to Reno's biographer, Jeremy Stephens, by that time Don Reno was actually working with the Crackerjacks.

46. Green, interview with Charlie Monroe, September 1, 1972.

47. Scott interview, February 16, 2007.

48. *Spartanburg Herald*, March 3, 1942.

49. Scott interview, February 18, 2011.

50. John Rice Irwin, *A People and Their Music: The Story Behind the Story of Country Music* (Atglen, PA: Schiffer, 2000), 239–241.

51. Lucile Deaderick, ed., *Heart of the Valley: A History of Knoxville, Tennessee* (Knoxville: East Tennessee Historical Society, 1976), 305.

52. *Knoxville News*, May 10, 1942.

53. Ed Hooper, *Knoxville's WNOX* (Charleston: Arcadia, 2009), 16.

54. *Knoxville News*, December 10, 1942.

55. *Knoxville News-Sentinel*, December 13, 1942.

56. Hooper, *Knoxville's WNOX*, 9.

57. Freeze interview, May 10, 2005.

58. Ibid.

Chapter 3. Don't This Road Look Rough and Rocky: 1945–1949

1. *Nashville Tennessean*, March 13, 1945.

2. *Statesville Landmark*, August 20, 1945.

3. *Charlotte Observer*, August 22, 1945.

4. Hatch Show Print order files, Charlie Monroe account, September 19, 1945, Frist Library and Archives, Country Music Hall of Fame and Museum, Nashville.

5. *Charlotte Observer*, September 28, 1945.

6. Hugh M. Morton and Edward L. Rankin, *Making a Difference in North Carolina* (Raleigh: Lightworks, 1988), 50.

7. It was listed this way in the *Charlotte Observer*, September 28, 1945.

8. *Charlotte Observer*, October 30, 1945.

9. Hatch Show Print order files, Charlie Monroe account, December 31, 1945.

10. Ibid., September 16, 1946 to November 15, 1946.

11. Mac Wiseman interview, May 27, 2010.

12. Gary Reid, interview with E. P. Williams, ca. 1981.

13. Richard Weize with Dave Sax and Dick Spottswood, *Charlie Monroe: I'm Old Kentucky Bound; The Discography,* Bear Family BCD-16808, 49.

14. Charles Wolfe, *In Close Harmony: The Story of the Louvin Brothers* (Jackson: University Press of Mississippi, 1996), 28–30.

15. *Bristol Herald-Courier*, December 13, 1946.

16. This was not the same Curly King who played fiddle with Danny Bailey. The given name of the Curly King who performed on WCYB was Cecil Crusenberry.

17. *Muleskinner News* (July 1972), 4.

18. Wiseman interview.

19. Jesse McReynolds interview, September 17, 2003.

20. Wiseman interview.

21. Monroe recorded the song as "Travelin' This Lonesome Road" on October 22, 1949, for Columbia, with himself listed as the writer.

22. Wiseman interview.

23. Ibid.

24. Jesse McReynolds interview, August 26, 2010.

25. Herb Trotman, interview with Ralph Mayo, ca.1973.

26. Ibid.

27. Ibid.

28. Mary Sechler Freeze and Walter Freeze interview, May 10, 2005.

29. Ray Seckler interview, November 4, 2006.

30. Ibid.

31. Ibid.

32. Ibid.

33. Hatch Show Print order files, Charlie Monroe account, August 25, 1948.

34. *Williamson Daily News*, September 27, 1948.

35. Hatch Show Print order files, Charlie Monroe account, October 1, 1948.

36. *Rogersville Review*, October 7, 1948.

37. Tex Willis played guitar and sang baritone in that session.

38. Tom Ewing, "Howard Watts," *Bluegrass Unlimited* (May 2002), 47.

39. Jim Shumate interview, May 1, 2009.

40. Ibid.

41. Earl Scruggs, *Earl Scruggs and the 5-String Banjo*, rev. ed. (Milwaukee: Hal Leonard, 2005), 161.

42. Wayne Erbsen, "Jim Shumate: Bluegrass Fiddler Supreme," *Bluegrass Unlimited* (April 1979), 20.

43. Scruggs, *5-String Banjo*, 162.

44. Hatch Show Print order files, Bill Monroe account, March 2, 1948.

45. Don Reno, The Musical History of *Don Reno: His Life . . . His Songs; A Pictorial and Graphic History of the Great American Country and Western Troubadour* (Hyattsville, MD: Copy-Kate, [1979]), 6.

46. Ewing, "Howard Watts," 49.

47. Jake Lambert with Curly Sechler, *Lester Flatt: The Good Things Out Weigh the Bad* (Hendersonville, TN: Jay-Lyn, 1982), 7.

48. Hatch Show Print order files, Bill Monroe account, February 6, 1948.

49. Gary Reid, "Jim Eanes," *Bluegrass Unlimited* (May 1987), 23.

50. Pete Kuykendall, "Smilin' Jim Eanes," *Bluegrass Unlimited* (February 1973), 8.

51. Erbsen, "Jim Shumate," 21.

52. *Hickory Record*, March 31, 1948.

53. *Hickory Record*, March 26, 1948.

54. In an oral history interview conducted by Eddie Stubbs for the International Bluegrass Music Museum, Scruggs maintained that Wiseman called them and said he would like to join the band.

55. *Hickory Record*, April 10, 1948.

56. Scruggs, *5-String Banjo*, 163.

57. Wiseman interview.

58. *Hickory Record*, April 28, 1948.

59. Erbsen, "Jim Shumate," 21.

60. McReynolds interview, August 26, 2010.

61. Wiseman interview.

62. Ibid.

63. Ibid.

64. Hatch Show Print order files, Charlie Monroe account, September 21, 1948 to November 17, 1948.

65. McReynolds interview, August 26, 2010.

66. Julie Knight, "Hoke Jenkins, Pioneer Banjo Man," *Bluegrass Unlimited* (September 1985), 27–28.

67. McReynolds interview, August 26, 2010.

68. Knight, "Hoke Jenkins," 29.

Chapter 4. Creating the Foggy Mountain Sound: 1949–1952

1. *Billboard*, April 9, 1949, 39.

2. Eddie Stubbs interview, February 14, 2007.

3. Tony Williamson interview, March 21, 2007.

4. *Knoxville News*, May 29, 1949.

5. *Billboard*, November 13, 1948, 38.

6. Douglas B. Green, interview with Murray Nash, May 15, 1974, Frist Library and Archive, Country Music Hall of Fame and Museum, Nashville.

7. *St. Petersburg Times*, June 17, 1949.

8. *Augusta Chronicle*, June 16, 1949.

9. *Knoxville News-Sentinel*, September 1, 1949.

10. *Billboard*, October 22, 1949, 69.

11. *Billboard*, October 15, 1949, 119.

12. *Lexington Leader*, September 4, 1949.

13. *Lexington Leader*, September 10, 1949.

14. J. D. Crowe interview, February 17, 2010.

15. *Kentucky Mountain Barn Dance Song Book* (Lexington: n.p., [1950]), n.p.

16. *Lexington Leader*, September 23, 1949.

17. *Lexington Leader*, November 5, 1949.

18. *Lexington Herald*, April 4, 1950.

19. *Lexington Leader*, November 19, 1949.

20. *Lexington Leader*, November 26, 1949.

21. Wayne Erbsen, "Wiley & Zeke: The Morris Brothers," *Bluegrass Unlimited* (August 1980), 50.

22. *Lexington Herald-Leader*, February 5, 1950.

23. Crowe interview.

24. Jesse McReynolds interview, August 26, 2010.

25. *Lexington Herald*, March 18, 1950.

26. Josh Graves interview, March 13, 2004.

27. *Bluegrass Bluesman: Josh Graves: A Memoir*, ed. Fred Bartenstein (Urbana: University of Illinois Press, 2012), 18.

28. Jody and Emma Rainwater interview, May 23, 2007.

29. *Lexington Herald*, April 4, 1950.

30. *Lexington Leader*, April 12, 1950.

31. *Lexington Herald*, April 22, 1950.

32. *Lexington Herald*, April 15, 1950.

33. *Lexington Herald*, April 21, 1950.

34. John A. Hinton, "Jody Rainwater: Bluegrass Reflections," *Bluegrass Unlimited* (January 1981), 38.

35. Rainwater interview.

36. Ibid.

37. It was cropped from a group photo the band had taken at WHKY in Hickory, and Cedric was wearing his comedy outfit.

38. *Kentucky Mountain Barn Dance Song Book*, n.p.

39. *Lexington Herald*, June 2, 1950.

40. *Kingsport News*, June 22, 1950.

41. *Kingsport News*, July 6, 1950.

42. *Bristol Herald-Courier*, August 9, 1950.

43. *Bristol Herald-Courier*, September 20, 1950.

44. See http://www.driveintheater.com/history/1950.htm.

45. *Chester Times*, September 15, 1950.

46. *Lexington Leader*, September 23, 1950.

47. Earl Scruggs interview, October 4, 2006.

48. Green, Nash interview.

49. Scruggs interview.

50. Green, Nash interview.

51. Ibid.

52. John Rumble, interview with Murray Nash, June 8, 1983, Frist Library and Archive, Country Music Hall of Fame and Museum, Nashville. Eddie Stubbs felt that Nash's memory was incorrect, because Flatt and Scruggs usually recorded with only two microphones in the early years.

53. Ibid.

54. Ibid.

55. Ibid.

56. *St. Petersburg Times*, November 6, 1950.

57. *Lexington Leader*, November 11, 1950.

58. Jewel Russell interview, March 8, 2012.

59. *Lexington Leader*, January 13, 1951.

60. Jim Sauceman interview, April 17, 2010.

61. Arvil Freeman interview, October 23, 2013.

62. Sauceman interview.

63. Freeman interview.

64. Hilary Dirlam, "Arvil Freeman," *Bluegrass Unlimited* (June 1991), 32–33.

65. *Billboard*, July 21, 1951, 77.

66. Freeman interview.

67. Ibid.

68. *Lexington Leader*, November 9, 1951.

69. Dick Spottswood, "Carl Sauceman: The Odessey of a Bluegrass Pioneer," *Bluegrass Unlimited* (August 1976), 13.

70. Neil V. Rosenberg with Edward L. Stubbs, liner notes to *The Osborne Brothers: 1956–1968*, Bear Family BCD-15598, 3.

71. Ralph Stanley with Eddie Dean, *Man of Constant Sorrow* (New York: Gotham, 2009), 157.

72. *Roanoke Times*, August 27, 1951.

73. *Lexington Leader*, November 16, 1951.

74. *Lexington Leader*, December 8, 1951.

75. Stanley, *Man of Constant Sorrow*, 158.

76. Clarence H. Greene, "George Shuffler," *Bluegrass Unlimited* (September 1991), 35.

77. George Shuffler interview, September 19, 1998.

78. *Lexington Herald*, February 28, 1952.

79. McReynolds interview, August 26, 2010.

80. *Lexington Leader*, March 1, 1952.

81. Russell interview.

82. Jesse McReynolds interview, September 17, 2003.

83. *Lexington Herald*, May 3, 1952.

84. Crowe interview.

85. McReynolds interview, September 17, 2003.

86. Ibid.

87. Ibid.

88. *Lexington Herald*, May 31, 1952.

Chapter 5. Climbing the Ladder with Flatt and Scruggs: 1952–1954

1. *Billboard*, October 20, 1951, 79.

2. *Spartanburg Herald*, December 27, 1951.

3. *Raleigh News & Observer*, January 2, 1952.

4. *Raleigh News & Observer*, January 20, 1952.

5. Jody and Emma Rainwater interview, May 23, 2007.

6. Mac Martin interview, August 27, 2008.

7. Ibid.

8. Jim Mills interview, April 13, 2012.

9. Everett Lilly interview, July 2, 2008.

10. *Raleigh News & Observer*, September 7, 1952.

11. *Country Song Roundup*, August 1952, 19.

12. Ed Hooper, *Knoxville's WNOX* (Charleston: Arcadia, 2009), 39.

13. Lance LeRoy interview, November 12, 2003.

14. Ibid.

15. Ibid.

16. Ibid.

17. Jarrett Watts interview, October 24, 2013.

18. *Billboard*, March 7, 1953, 46.

19. *Billboard*, April 25, 1953, 68.

20. Jake Lambert with Curly Sechler, *Lester Flatt; The Good Things Out Weigh the Bad* (Hendersonville, TN: Jay-Lyn, 1982), 24–26.

21. Ibid., 26.

22. *Richmond Times-Dispatch*, April 11, 1953.

23. Kent Blanton interview, April 8, 2015.

24. LeRoy interview.

25. Linda Williams Dale, "Martha White Foods," *Tennessee Encyclopedia of History and Culture*, https://tennesseeencyclopedia.net/entry.php?rec=1555.

26. According to Jim Mills, Earl Scruggs said that Cohen Williams of Martha White Mills operated a vehicle rental business on the side, and he arranged for Flatt and Scruggs to rent the Cadillac limousine for $30 per month, including replacement tires.

27. Lambert, *Lester Flatt*, 27.

28. *Lester Flatt, Earl Scruggs and the Foggy Mountain Boys Picture Album and Songbook No. 3* (Nashville: n.p., [1957]), 3.

29. Doug Green, "Red Rector Tells His Story," *Muleskinner News* (June 1972), 9.

30. Hatch Show Print order files, Martha White account, January 27, 1954, Frist Library and Archive, Country Music Hall of Fame and Museum, Nashville.

31. Hatch Show Print order files, Martha White account, February 19, 1954.

32. *Richmond Times-Dispatch*, April 4, 1954.

33. *Richmond Times-Dispatch*, April 5, 1953.

34. *Richmond Times-Dispatch*, March 28, 1954.

35. Eloise Warren Seckler interview, December 29, 2012.

36. *Richmond Times-Dispatch*, July 10, 1954.

37. *Richmond Times-Dispatch*, August 28, 1954.

38. Earl Scruggs, *Earl Scruggs and the 5-String Banjo*, rev. ed. (Milwaukee: Hal Leonard, 2005), 164.

39. *Richmond Times-Dispatch*, September 10, 1954.

40. Playbill Incorporated, *Hayride*, September 1954, http://bgcollector.net/fs-flatt-scruggs-song-books/fs-1954-hayride-playbill/.

41. John Chapman (*New York Daily News* drama critic), "'Hayride' Is a Juke Box with People," *Chicago Daily Tribune*, September 15, 1954.

42. H. L. Phillips, "The Once Over," *Hagerstown Morning Herald*, September 20, 1954.

43. Ben Eldridge interview, July 1, 2009.

44. Ibid.

45. Ibid.

46. Rainwater interview.

47. Eloise Warren Seckler interview, March 31, 2007.

48. *Richmond Times-Dispatch*, January 1, 1955.

Chapter 6. Goodness Gracious, It's Good: 1955–1962

1. *Nashville Tennessean*, January 14, 1956.

2. *Herald Dispatch* (Huntington, WV), February 2, 1955.

3. *Knoxville Journal*, February 8, 1955.

4. *Johnson City Press Chronicle*, March 8, 1955.

5. *Jackson Sun*, March 11, 1955.

6. Jake Lambert with Curly Sechler, *Lester Flatt: The Good Things Out Weigh the Bad* (Hendersonville, TN: Jay-Lyn, 1982), 28.

7. *Lester Flatt, Earl Scruggs and the Foggy Mountain Boys WSM Grand Ole Opry Song and Picture Album No. 1* (Nashville: n.p., 1955), 4.

8. Graves was also known as "Buck."

9. Dobro is a registered trademark of the Gibson Guitar Company.

10. Josh Graves interview, March 13, 2004.

11. *Bluegrass Bluesman; Josh Graves; A Memoir*, ed. Fred Bartenstein (Urbana: University of Illinois Press, 2012), 23.

12. Earl Scruggs interview, October 4, 2006.

13. Neil Rosenberg, liner notes to *Country & Western Classics: Flatt & Scruggs*, Time-Life Records TLCW-04, 1982, 23.

14. Graves interview.

15. Josh can be seen playing this instrument on the *Flatt & Scruggs TV Show,* with a recording date given as July 30, 1956, and released on Shanachie DVD-617. Curly felt that the actual date of the show might have been earlier, since Josh was still playing the old guitar.

16. This was the instrument that Josh always referred to as "Julie."

17. Graves interview.

18. *Nashville Tennessean*, June 4, 1955.

19. Hatch Show Print order files, Martha White account, July 1, 1955, Frist Library and Archive, Country Music Hall of Fame and Museum, Nashville.

20. *Nashville Banner*, September 10, 1955.

21. Lambert, *Lester Flatt*, 32.

22. *Billboard*, June 25, 1955, 1.

23. *Nashville Banner*, October 3, 1955.

24. *Lester Flatt, Earl Scruggs and the Foggy Mountain Boys Picture Album and Songbook No. 3* (Nashville: n.p., [1957]), 3.

25. Melvin Goins interview, May 23, 2008.

26. Graves interview.

27. Gary Tullock interview, April 2, 2014.

28. *Billboard*, October 8, 1955, 50.

29. Graves interview.

30. Sircy may have been driving for them as early as 1956. He was pictured in two photos of the band with their first bus in *Lester Flatt, Earl Scruggs and the Foggy Mountain Boys Radio and TV Album and Songbook No. 2* (Nashville: n.p., [1956]), n.p.

31. Tullock interview.

32. Longworth's expertise was such that in 1968 he was hired by Martin Guitars, where he worked for the next twenty-seven years.

33. *Kentucky New Era*, Saturday television listings, July 16, 1955 to October 1, 1955.

34. *Radio and TV Album and Songbook No. 2*, n.p.

35. Scruggs interview.

36. Graves interview.

37. Paul Warren date book, 1957 (personal collection of Eloise Warren Seckler). On this program, Curly appears to be playing the mandolin he borrowed while his Gibson F-2 was being repaired.

38. Hatch Show Print order files, Martha White account, April 23, 1958.

39. According to Paul Warren's date book, they played at West Side High School in Rocky Face, Georgia, on Monday, May 19, 1958.

40. Graves interview.

41. Ibid.

42. Haskel and Gerald McCormick interview, October 2, 2006.

43. Ibid.

44. Lilly interview.

45. Hatch Show Print order files, Martha White account, February 20 to April 8, 1959; September 14, 1959.

46. Paul Warren date book, 1959.

47. Earl can be seen playing this instrument on the *Flatt & Scruggs TV Show* dated July 30, 1956, and released on Shanachie DVD-617.

48. Lambert, *Lester Flatt*, 38–39.

49. *Sky King* was the name of a popular television program at that time.

50. Lester made such a reference in volume 5, show 2 (July 1961) of the *Flatt & Scruggs TV Show* DVDs (Shanachie DVD-615).

51. Neil V. Rosenberg, liner notes to *Flatt & Scruggs: 1959–1963*, Bear Family BCD-15559, 3.

52. Paul Warren date books, 1960, 1961.

53. Ibid.

54. Linda Sowards Kuhn interview, January 25, 2008.

55. Ray Seckler interview, November 4, 2006.

56. Scruggs interview.

57. Lance LeRoy interview, November 12, 2003.

58. Graves interview.

Chapter 7. Traveling Down This Lonesome Road: 1962–1972

1. The last Flatt-Seckler duet they recorded was "I Don't Care Anymore" in January 1958.

2. Josh Graves interview, March 13, 2004.

3. Lance LeRoy interview, November 12, 2003.

4. Graves interview.

5. Paul Warren date book, 1969 (personal collection of Eloise Warren Seckler).

6. Monroe had performed the song on his Saturday night set in the key of C.

7. Tony Williamson tapes, 1970.

8. Herschel Sizemore interview, April 7, 2004.

9. Tony Williamson interview, March 21, 2007.

10. Ibid.

11. Ibid.

12. Dave Freeman interview, July 23, 2004.

13. Sizemore interview.

14. Vernon would also write liner notes for Curly's album.

15. Freeman interview.

16. Ibid.

17. Sizemore interview.

18. "Record Reviews," *Bluegrass Unlimited* (February 1972), 10.

Chapter 8. The Nashville Grass: 1973–1994

1. Marty Stuart interview, April 2, 2007.

2. Ibid.

3. Ibid.

4. Ibid.

5. Roland White interview, September 26, 2012.

6. Stuart interview.

7. Ibid.

8. Ibid.

9. Ibid.

10. Mac Wiseman interview, May 27, 2010.

11. Stuart interview.

12. Paul Warren date book, 1973 (personal collection of Eloise Warren Seckler).

13. This recording was reissued on CD in 2003 by CMH as *The Essential Lester Flatt and the Nashville Grass* (CMH-8414).

14. Jake Lambert with Curly Sechler, *Lester Flatt: The Good Things Out Weigh the Bad* (Hendersonville: Jay-Lyn, 1982), 71.

15. Eddie Stubbs interview, November 3, 2006.

16. Ibid.

17. Stuart interview.

18. Ibid.

19. *Chattanooga News–Free Press*, March 9, 1979.

20. Stuart interview.

21. Ibid.

22. Bassham stated that this occurred in 1978, but Curly maintained that it was in 1979, shortly before Flatt died.

23. Lambert, *Lester Flatt*, 106.

24. Lance LeRoy interview, November 12, 2003.

25. Lambert, *Lester Flatt*, 77.

26. LeRoy interview.

27. Olan Bassham, *Lester Flatt: Baron of Bluegrass (Cragrock to Carnegie Hall)* (Manchester, TN: Browning Printing Services, 1980), 8.

28. Lambert, *Lester Flatt*, 80.

29. Bill Vernon, liner notes to *No Doubt About It*, Revonah-933, 1979.

30. *In Memory of the Man: Dedicated to Lester Flatt*, FTS-31073, released in 1980.

31. Johnny Warren interview, March 9, 2009.

32. Stubbs interview, November 3, 2006.

33. Willis Spears interview, November 4, 2007.

34. Ibid.

35. Curly made two albums with Nix: *Songs That Never Grow Old* (with Josh Graves and Tater Tate) (Flying Squirrel Records FS-101, 1991) and *Real Bluegrass* (with Tater Tate, Charlie Cushman, Gene Wooten, Pat Enright, and Terry Smith) (Walking Tree Productions WT-101, 1983). Both are out of print.

36. "Dawg" was Grisman's nickname (derived from his initials).

37. Frank Godbey, "Thanks, Earl," *Bluegrass Unlimited* (August 1988), 7.

38. Stuart interview.

39. Ray Seckler interview, November 4, 2006.

40. Mary Sechler Freeze and Walter Freeze interview, May 10, 2005.

41. LeRoy interview.

42. Freeze interview.

43. Ibid.

44. Ray Seckler interview.

45. Ibid.

Chapter 9. The Old Man Has (Not) Retired: 1995–2014

1. Eloise Warren Seckler interview, March 31, 2007.

2. Ibid.

3. Ibid.

4. Marty Stuart interview, April 2, 2007.

5. Ibid.

6. Ibid.

7. Eddie Stubbs interview, November 3, 2006.

8. Penny Parsons, "Curly Seckler: Bluegrass Pioneer," *Bluegrass Unlimited* (June 2004), 38–45.

9. Dudley Connell interview, April 22, 2014.

10. Ibid.

11. Russell Moore, email message to author, July 1, 2004.

12. Penny Parsons, liner notes to *Bluegrass, Don't You Know*, CC-0243, 2006.

13. The songs were "Some Old Day" and "Dim Lights, Thick Smoke."

14. Larry Sparks interview, August 11, 2010.

15. Stubbs interview, November 3, 2006.

16. Dave Freeman, liner notes to *Lovin' Pretty Women*, REB-1824-CD, 2007.

17. Woody Platt interview, May 23, 2009.

18. Charles Humphrey interview, April 22, 2009.

19. Stuart interview.

20. Jon Pruett, Jim Welte, and Chris Streng, "Hardly Strictly Bluegrass 2007 (Sunday)," www.hardlystrictlybluegrass.com/2007/editorial/Sunday.

21. Jay Orr, liner notes to *Best of the Flatt & Scruggs TV Show*, Shanachie Entertainment, 2007, 7–8.

22. Stubbs interview, November 3, 2006.

23. Lynwood Lunsford, on BGRASS-L (online bluegrass music discussion forum), August 5, 2008. http://lsv.uky.edu/scripts/wa.exe?A2=ind0808a&L=bgrass -l&F=&S=&P=22285.

24. Stuart interview.

25. Stubbs interview, November 3, 2006.

26. Doyle Lawson interview, December 10, 2007.

27. Mac Wiseman interview, May 27, 2010.

28. Stuart interview.

Selected Listening

Many of the recordings mentioned in this book are now out of print. For more detailed information about them, please see Charley Pennell's excellent online Bluegrass Discography, www.ibiblio.org/hillwilliam/BGdiscography/.

The following is a list of selected recordings that are currently available on CD, DVD, or by special order and represent Curly Seckler's work through the years.

CDs and Boxed Sets

With Charlie Monroe

Charlie Monroe, *I'm Old Kentucky Bound: His Recordings, 1938–1956*, Bear Family BCD-16808 DK (four-CD boxed set, 2007)

> Seckler appears on four tracks (including "Mother's Not Dead, She's Only Sleeping"), recorded on September 30, 1946; also appearing on these tracks are Larry "Tex" Isley, Paul Prince, and Robert "Pickles" Lambert.

With Tommy Scott

Now and Then, Folkways-31078 (1980)

> With Marty Stuart, Tater Tate, Gaines Blevins, Gordon Reid, Scotty Lee Blevins. Available by special order from Smithsonian-Folkways Recordings.

Bluegrass, Old and New, Katona Records, no number (2011)

> Includes several tracks from 1941 radio transcriptions by "Ramblin' Scotty and Smilin' Bill," along with recordings from later years. With Scotty Lee Blevins, Cleo Scott Cheek, Sam Baxter, Sandra Scott Whitworth, Larry Perkins, and others. Available by special order from sales@curlyseckler.net or Katona Productions, Inc.

With Flatt and Scruggs

Flatt & Scruggs, 1948–1959, Bear Family BCD-15472 (four-CD boxed set, 1991)

> Contains the complete recordings from their formative years on Mercury and Columbia Records. Fourteen-page booklet with photos, session notes, and liner notes by Neil Rosenberg. Seckler appears on 86 of the 112 tracks.

Flatt & Scruggs, 1959–1963, Bear Family BCD-15559 EI (five-CD boxed set, 1992)

> Contains their recordings with Mother Maybelle Carter and Gordon Terry, plus their complete Carnegie Hall concert from December 1962 (after Seckler had left the band) and songs from their Vanderbilt University concert in May 1963. Eighteen-page booklet with photos, session notes, and liner notes by Neil Rosenberg. Seckler appears on 52 of the 129 tracks.

With the Sauceman Brothers

On WCYB–Bristol, Copper Creek-0124 (1994)

> Radio transcriptions from WCYB in the spring of 1951. With Carl and J. P. Sauceman, Joe Stuart, Arvil Freeman, and Carmon Freeman (these transcriptions were made before Larry Richardson joined the band).

With Jim and Jesse

Jim & Jesse, 1952–1955, Bear Family BCD-15635 (1992)

> Compilation of Capitol recordings; 20 tracks, with 16-page booklet. Seckler appears on eight tracks recorded on June 13, 1952. Also appearing on these tracks are Hoke Jenkins, Bob Moore, and Sonny James.

With Lester Flatt and the Nashville Grass

Lester Raymond Flatt, Flying Fish-015 (LP released in 1976; CD released in 1992)

> With Flatt, Seckler, Paul Warren, Kenny Ingram, Charlie Nixon, Marty Stuart, Jack Hicks, and guest Buddy Spicher. Includes several spoken remarks by Flatt.

Flatt on Victor Plus More, Bear Family BCD-15975 FI (five-CD boxed set, 1999)

> Seckler appears on twenty-six tracks, eighteen of which came from the albums *Before You Go*, APL1-0470 (1973) and *Lester Flatt Live! Bluegrass Festival*, APL1-0588 (1974), and eight of which were previously unreleased.

The Essential Lester Flatt and the Nashville Grass, CMH-8414 (2003)

> Reissue of *A Living Legend*, CMH-9002 (1976). Nice collection of material mostly from the Flatt and Scruggs repertoire, with Flatt, Seckler, Paul Warren, Kenny Ingram, Charlie Nixon, Marty Stuart, and Jack Hicks.

Essential Bluegrass Gospel, CMH-6298 (2004)

> Reissue compilation of Nashville Grass material released between 1976 and 1981. Includes tracks from *Heaven's Bluegrass Band* (CMH-6207) and *There's Gonna Be a Singing* with guest Betty Jean Robinson (CMH-6257).

Flatt Gospel, Music Mill Entertainment-70051 (2005)

> Reissue of Canaan-LP-9775 (1975). With Flatt, Seckler, Paul Warren, Kenny Ingram, Charlie Nixon, Marty Stuart, and Jack Hicks.

Curly Seckler

The Nashville Grass with Curly Seckler: *China Grove, My Hometown*, Folkways-31095 (1983)

> With Willis Spears, Kenny Ingram, Johnny Warren, Gene Wooten, and J. T. Gray. Available by special order from Smithsonian-Folkways Recordings.

60 Years of Bluegrass with My Friends, Copper Creek-0227 (2005)

> Reissue of Vine Street-107 (1995). Guests include Jimmy Martin, Mac Wiseman, Benny Sims, Josh Graves, Benny Martin, Ralph Stanley, Jim and Jesse McReynolds, Doyle Lawson, Alan O'Bryant, Willis Spears, Grant Turner, Tater Tate, and Larry Perkins.

Down in Caroline, Copper Creek-0236 (2005)

> Recorded in 2004. Guests include Dudley Connell, Russell Moore, Larry Sparks, Tater Tate, Herschel Sizemore, Laura Weber Cash, John Carter Cash, Leroy Troy, and Larry Perkins.

That Old Book of Mine, County-2740 (2005)

> Compilation of tracks from *Curly Seckler Sings Again* (County-732), recorded in 1971 with the Shenandoah Cutups, and *Tribute to Lester Flatt* (Rebel-C-4301), recorded in 1989 with Willis Spears, Ron Stewart, Larry Perkins, Philip Staff, and Harold Jones (the latter appears on one track).

Bluegrass, Don't You Know, Copper Creek-0243 (2006)

> Recorded in 2004. Guests include Dudley Connell, Russell Moore, Larry Sparks, Larry Cordle, Tater Tate, Herschel Sizemore, Laura Weber Cash, Rob Ickes, Bob Moore, and Larry Perkins.

Miscellaneous Guest Appearances

With Red Allen

In Memory of the Man: Dedicated to Lester Flatt, FTS-31073 (1980)

> Seckler appears on eleven of the twelve tracks. With Marty Stuart, Harley Allen Jr., Tater Tate, Kenny Ingram, Gene Wooten, Blake Williams, and Pete Corum. Available by special order from Smithsonian-Folkways Recordings.

With David Grisman

Home Is Where the Heart Is, Rounder 0251 (1988)

> Two-CD set. Seckler appears on three tracks, along with Doc Watson, Tony Rice, J. D. Crowe, Jim Buchanan, Sam Bush, and Roy Huskey Jr.

With Jim and Jesse

Music Among Friends, Rounder 0279 (1991)

> Seckler appears on one track: "We'll Meet Again, Sweetheart." Also appearing on this track are Carl Jackson, Tony Rice, and Jerry Douglas.

With Johnny Warren and Charlie Cushman

Tribute to Fiddlin' Paul Warren, no label (2009)

> Seckler appears on one track, along with Earl Scruggs, Marty Stuart, and others.

With Larry Sparks

Lonesome and Then Some, Rebel-1846 (2014)

> Seckler appears on two tracks along with Jesse McReynolds, Bobby Osborne, Tim Graves, Ron Stewart, and others.

DVDs

A set of DVDs titled *Best of the Flatt & Scruggs TV Show: Classic Bluegrass From 1956 to 1962*, released by Shanachie Entertainment in collaboration with the Country Music Foundation, shows the Foggy Mountain Boys in their prime, as they appeared on WSM-TV in the late 1950s and early 1960s. Band members were Lester Flatt, Earl Scruggs, Curly Seckler, Paul Warren, Josh Graves, and Jake Tullock. Each DVD contains two half-hour programs, complete with Martha White commercials. Occasional guests include Kentucky Slim, Hylo Brown, Mother Maybelle Carter, Ricky Skaggs, and Randy Scruggs.

Vol. 1, Shanachie DVD-611 (2007)

> Includes shows from August 1961 and February 1962.

Vol. 2, Shanachie DVD-612 (2007)

> Includes shows from July 1961 and August 1961, with guest Mother Maybelle Carter.

Vol. 3, Shanachie DVD-613 (2007)

> Includes shows from November or December 1961 and January 1962, with guest Ricky Skaggs (age seven). Curly sings "You Took My Sunshine."

Vol. 4, Shanachie DVD-614 (2007)

> Includes one undated show and a show from March 1962, with guest Randy Lynn Scruggs.

Vol. 5, Shanachie DVD-615 (2008)

> Includes shows from July 1961 and March 1962, with guest Hylo Brown. Curly sings "Please Help Me, I'm Falling."

Vol. 7, Shanachie DVD-617 (2009)

> Includes shows from 1956 (with Kentucky Slim) and 1960–1961 combined.

Vol. 8, Shanachie DVD-618 (2009)

> Includes shows from 1960 and 1961 combined. Curly sings "What's the Matter Now."

Vol. 9, Shanachie DVD-619 (2010)

> Includes shows from 1961 and 1962 combined. Curly sings "You Won't Be Satisfied That Way."

Vol. 10, Shanachie DVD-620 (2010)

> Includes shows from 1961 and 1962 combined.

Curly does not appear on volume 6, Shanachie DVD-616.

Except where otherwise noted, all of these DVDs and Curly Seckler's solo projects are available at curlyseckler.net/store.htm.

Interviews

Quotations from Curly Seckler were taken from multiple interviews conducted by the author, either in person or by telephone, between April 2003 and July 2014. Except where otherwise noted, all other interviews were conducted by the author as listed below.

Blanton, Kent. Telephone interview, April 8, 2015.

Connell, Dudley. Telephone interview, April 22, 2014.

Crowe, J. D. Telephone interview, February 17, 2010.

Day, Imogene Sauceman. Telephone interview, August 20, 2010.

Eldridge, Ben. Telephone interview, July 1, 2009.

Freeman, Arvil. Telephone interview, October 23, 2013.

Freeman, Dave. Charlottesville, Virginia, July 23, 2004.

Freeze, Mary Sechler, and Walter. China Grove, North Carolina, May 10, 2005.

Goins, Melvin. Snow Camp, North Carolina, May 23, 2008.

Graves, Josh. Smithfield, North Carolina, March 13, 2004.

Humphrey, Charles. Telephone interview, April 22, 2009.

Kuhn, Linda Sowards. Telephone interview, January 25, 2008.

Lawson, Doyle. Telephone interview, December 10, 2007.

LeRoy, Lance. Hendersonville, Tennessee, November 12, 2003.

Lewis, Little Roy. Louisburg, North Carolina, March 5, 2011.

Lilly, Everett. Beckley, West Virginia, July 2, 2008.

Martin, Mac. Telephone interview, August 27, 2008.

Mathis, Larry. Telephone interview, February 14, 2013.

Mayo, Ralph. Interview conducted by Herb Trotman, circa 1973. Courtesy Gary Reid.

McCormick, Gerald, and Haskel McCormick. Goodlettsville, Tennessee, October 2, 2006.

McReynolds, Jesse. Telephone interviews, September 17, 2003, and August 26, 2010.

Mills, Jim. Telephone interview, April 13, 2012; Durham, North Carolina, March 31, 2015.

Mitchell, Harold. Telephone interview, March 7, 2013.

Moore, Russell. Email correspondence, July 1, 2004.

Platt, Woody. Snow Camp, North Carolina, May 23, 2009.

Rainwater, Jody, and Emma Rainwater. Crewe, Virginia, May 23, 2007.

Russell, Jewel. Telephone interview, March 8, 2012.

Sauceman, Jim. Telephone interview, April 7, 2010.

Scott, Tommy. Telephone interviews, February 16, 2007, and February 18, 2011.

Scruggs, Earl. Nashville, Tennessee, October 4, 2006.

Seckler, Eloise Warren. Hendersonville, Tennessee, March 31, 2007 and December 29, 2012.

Seckler, Ray. Nashville, Tennessee, November 4, 2006.

Shuffler, George. Valdese, North Carolina, September 19, 1998.

Shumate, Jim. Telephone interview, May 1, 2009.

Sizemore, Herschel. Telephone interview, April 7, 2004.

Sparks, Larry. Telephone interview, August 11, 2010.

Spears, Willis. Hendersonville, Tennessee, November 4, 2007.

Stuart, Marty. Hendersonville, Tennessee, April 2, 2007.

Stubbs, Eddie. Nashville, Tennessee, November 3, 2006; telephone interview, February 14, 2007.

Tullock, Gary. Telephone interview, April 2, 2014.

Warren, Johnny. Hendersonville, Tennessee, November 4, 2007; telephone interview, March 9, 2009.

Watts, Jarrett. Telephone interview, October 24, 2013.

White, Roland. Nashville, Tennessee, September 26, 2012.

Williams, Blake. Telephone interview, July 28, 2014.

Williams, E. P. Telephone interview conducted by Gary Reid, circa 1981. Courtesy Gary Reid.

Williamson, Tony. Chapel Hill, North Carolina, March 21, 2007.

Wiseman, Mac. Telephone interview, May 27, 2010.

General Index

Song Index

Music journalist Penny Parsons was
Curly Seckler's manager and is a regular
contributor to bluegrass publications.

Music in American Life

Heartbeat of the People: Music and Dance of the Northern Pow-wow
  Tara Browner

My Lord, What a Morning: An Autobiography   *Marian Anderson*

Marian Anderson: A Singer's Journey   *Allan Keiler*

Charles Ives Remembered: An Oral History   *Vivian Perlis*

Henry Cowell, Bohemian   *Michael Hicks*

Rap Music and Street Consciousness   *Cheryl L. Keyes*

Louis Prima   *Garry Boulard*

Marian McPartland's Jazz World: All in Good Time   *Marian McPartland*

Robert Johnson: Lost and Found   *Barry Lee Pearson and Bill McCulloch*

Bound for America: Three British Composers   *Nicholas Temperley*

Lost Sounds: Blacks and the Birth of the Recording Industry, 1890–1919
  Tim Brooks

Burn, Baby! BURN! The Autobiography of Magnificent Montague
  Magnificent Montague with Bob Baker

Way Up North in Dixie: A Black Family's Claim to the Confederate
  Anthem   *Howard L. Sacks and Judith Rose Sacks*

The Bluegrass Reader   *Edited by Thomas Goldsmith*

Colin McPhee: Composer in Two Worlds   *Carol J. Oja*

Robert Johnson, Mythmaking, and Contemporary American Culture
  Patricia R. Schroeder

Composing a World: Lou Harrison, Musical Wayfarer   *Leta E. Miller and
  Fredric Lieberman*

Fritz Reiner, Maestro and Martinet   *Kenneth Morgan*

That Toddlin' Town: Chicago's White Dance Bands and Orchestras, 1900–1950
  Charles A. Sengstock Jr.

Dewey and Elvis: The Life and Times of a Rock 'n' Roll Deejay   *Louis Cantor*

Come Hither to Go Yonder: Playing Bluegrass with Bill Monroe   *Bob Black*

Chicago Blues: Portraits and Stories   *David Whiteis*

The Incredible Band of John Philip Sousa   *Paul E. Bierley*

"Maximum Clarity" and Other Writings on Music   *Ben Johnston,
  edited by Bob Gilmore*

Staging Tradition: John Lair and Sarah Gertrude Knott   *Michael Ann Williams*

Homegrown Music: Discovering Bluegrass   *Stephanie P. Ledgin*

Tales of a Theatrical Guru   *Danny Newman*

The Music of Bill Monroe   *Neil V. Rosenberg and Charles K. Wolfe*

Pressing On: The Roni Stoneman Story   *Roni Stoneman, as told to Ellen Wright*

The University of Illinois Press
is a founding member of the
Association of American University Presses.

University of Illinois Press
1325 South Oak Street
Champaign, IL 61820-6903
www.press.uillinois.edu